ANNA YELISTRATOVA

NIKOLAI GOGOL

AND THE
WEST EUROPEAN
NOVEL

RADUGA **PUBLISHERS**

MOSCOW

Translated from the Russian
by *Christopher English*

Designed
by *Vladislav Losev*

А. ЕЛИСТРАТОВА

НИКОЛАЙ ГОГОЛЬ И ПРОБЛЕМЫ
ЗАПАДНОЕВРОПЕЙСКОГО РОМАНА

$$E \frac{4603000000-424}{031(01)-84} \, 046-84$$

Printed in the Union of Soviet Socialist Republics

CONTENTS

CONTENTS

INTRODUCTION

The theme of this book is broad and multifaceted and can be approached from a number of different angles. As it has been comparatively little explored the author has not undertaken to treat it comprehensively, but has merely attempted a typological analysis of Nikolai Gogol's *Dead Souls* in the context of a number of similar narrative works written at the same time or shortly before. (Gogol's other works will of course be brought into this discussion where relevant). The main works with which Gogol's *poema* * will be compared are the picaresque novel, Fielding's "comic epic-poem", Smollett's satirical novel of manners, certain works by Rousseau and other Enlightenment writers, Goethe's *Wilhelm Meisters Lehrjahre, Wilhelm Meisters Wunderjahre* and the novels of Scott, Thackeray, Dickens and Balzac. When necessary the author has allowed herself to range beyond the bounds of narrative prose, since certain essential features of Gogol's prose poem can be better highlighted by typological comparison to examples of the dramatic and lyrical-epic poetry of the late eighteenth and early nineteenth centuries.

---

* *Poema*—long, narrative poem—is the genre description which Gogol himself selected for his *Dead Souls*. As there is no exact English equivalent for the term the Russian word has been retained in this translation.

Although the primary concern of this study is to compare *Dead Souls* with contemporaneous and near-contemporaneous works, and not to trace the influence of Gogol on the subsequent development of West European literature, the author has still taken into account attitudes to *Dead Souls* expressed by modern critics in the West.

For those critics who endeavour to prove Gogol a direct precursor and confrère of the surrealists, Kafka school and stream of consciousness writers—best exemplified by Joyce—the most suitable material to be found not in *Dead Souls* but in Gogol's more grotesque *St. Petersburg Stories*, with their tragic tension, such as *The Nose, Diary of a Madman, Nevsky Prospekt*, and others. But even *Dead Souls* is often subjected to this sort of treatment.

We cannot justifiably ignore, however, the interpretations of *Dead Souls* advanced by such modern critics as Vladimir Nabokov, Victor Erlich, and Janko Lavrin. However misguided we may think these views, which stem from a desire to exclude Gogol from the realist school and to proclaim him as a master of the irrational world view, as an inspired madman and visionary who gives concrete form in his writings to the fruits of his delirious imagination, nonetheless these views merit our own attention and polemic refutation, since they enjoy wide currency in the West.

The above-named authors take as the point of departure for their arguments the categorical assertion that Gogol had no real acquaintance with Russian life and that the supposedly mistaken view of Gogol as a realist can only be attributed to the "naïveté" of many generations of "civic-minded" Russian readers. Nabokov, who develops this line of argument most extensively, [1] goes so far as to claim that Gogol ruined himself at the moment he began (in *Dead Souls*, Vol. 2) to study the "facts" of Russian life rather than merely making them up. The milieu and social conditions in which Gogol's heroes exist are, according to Nabokov, of no consequence whatever. Chichikov is a kind of infernal image, an "ill-paid representative of the Devil" of the 19th century, born of Gogol's imagination, a "travelling salesman" of "the Satan & Co. firm". [2] As for the style of the book, Nabokov claims to detect, as he puts it, a "curious anachronistic" coincidence of intonation and narrative devices in Gogol's *Dead Souls* and Joyce's *Ulysses*. This coincidence supposedly consists in the two writers' shared predilection for interminable lists (in Nabokov's metaphor, the hordes of characters who enter *Dead Souls* without any connection to the book's action "straddling Gogol's pen like a witch riding a broomstick"). [3]

The comparison with Joyce strikes us as forced. For all Joyce's undeniable artistic talent, his endless lists, which reflect the chaos of modern life and the chaotic minds of the individuals groping helplessly through this world, lead to the inevitable and increasingly severe collapse both of his overall picture of reality, a picture that disintegrates into tiny fragments like a shattered mirror, and of the characters, whose spiritual world dissolves in the author's incoherent and deliberately alogical stream of consciousness. Quite a different purpose is served by the complex stylistic constructions in Gogol's work to which Nabokov alludes. Their function in *Dead Souls* is a directly opposite, artistic one—not the destruction of a coherent picture of life, as with Joyce, but, on the contrary, the restoration of this picture in all its paradox and complexity. Gogol's fantastical humor, which Nabokov and many other Western critics endeavour to raise to an absolute, divorcing it from the author's realism, is in actual fact an integral part of this realism and serves the same goals. To Gogol Chichikov is only an "unreal" person in the sense that true human nature with all its commendable qualities has been fatally and deplorably perverted in him. In Nabokov's view Chichikov is no more than a "soap bubble, blown by the Devil", and he even invests particular symbolic significance in the arrangement of Chichikov's travelling box, which has in the centre a special round soap-container—i.e. something directly cognate with the very essence of its proprietor! [4]

It would be naïve to dismiss this interpretation of Gogol's work as an absurd fancy of the critic's perverse imagination. It is significant that Nabokov's study of Gogol was published in 1944, at the end of the Second World War and when the role of the Soviet Union in the victory over Nazi Germany was obvious to all. His book contains a strong political subtext, which at times is allowed to come to the surface.

Quoting the celebrated final passage of *Dead Souls*, Vol. 1, in which Russia is compared to a "swift *troika*", Nabokov continues: "Beautiful as all this final crescendo sounds, it is from the stylistic point of view merely a conjuror's patter enabling an object to disappear, the particular object being—Chichikov." [5]

A comparison of Gogol to Kafka is surely as forced and improbable as that to Joyce. It is true that Kafka was familiar with Gogol's work, which had long been popular amongst the Czech intelligentsia. Kafka's diaries contain entries in which he refers directly to Gogol. From one of these, for March 14, 1915, we know that Kafka had read Gogol's article on lyricism [6]; another, more detailed entry, dated February 14, 1915, contains impressions gathered from Kafka's reading of *Dead Souls*. Kafka writes of the "infinite gravitational force of Russia". But in searching for an image which will best express this force he opposes to Gogol's *troika* his own characteristically sombre image of an immense river, "whose yellowish waters flow in low waves. Along its banks stretches a desolate steppe, covered with withered and down-trodden grass". "Everything here is dying out" [7], concludes Kafka. There is an obvious contrast between this symbolically cheerless landscape and the lyrical elation of Gogol's concluding image in Volume 1.

The arguments advanced by Victor Erlich in his article "Gogol and Kafka" are mainly founded on the "irrational motives" which he attempts to unearth in *The Nose* and other stories by Gogol. To some extent he is referring to the *Dead Souls* as well. Comparing these works primarily with Kafka's *Die Verwandlung*, Erlich sees the kinship of the two writers in the notion of the degradation of man, a view to which, he alleges, both authors subscribe in equal measure, and in man's constant willingness to squander his human nature, and metamorphose into an animal or insect. [8] Even Gogol's comparison of Sobakevich to a bear is construed as analogous to the symbolic idea behind Kafka's sinister story about the metamorphosis of a nondescript commercial traveller into a monstrous insect. This argument, however, loses sight of the essential difference between the attitudes of the two writers towards man and his place in life. It is a fact that Gogol frequently employs animal metaphors—his characters become "bestial" and "bear-like". But these images express not only his keen anxiety about his fellow man who loses his human aspect, but also something that is not found in Kafka's world: a firm conviction that man can and must remain human and that there is no decline so hopeless that he cannot once more restore his lost humanity.

Janko Lavrin also detects in Gogol's work "*a surrealist* anticipation of the psycho-analytical symbolism". [9] With reference to *Dead Souls*, the unusual genre qualities of this work, which lend it its inimitable nature, only arouse Lavrin's disapproval. This applies in particular to Gogol's "frequent digressions, personal comments, lyrical and moralizing passages, many of which," the critic maintains, "seem to have been squeezed in when the 'epic' had already been finished". [10]

What in point of fact constitutes the very unity of Gogol's conception, of his endeavour to divine the past and future of his people in their present, Lavrin rejects as an absurd incongruity: it seems to him as though the lyrical digressions of *Dead Souls* "have been written by another person".

Closely echoing Nabokov in this, Lavrin takes a sceptical view of the concluding symbolic comparison of Russia to a swift *troika*. He is not only struck by Gogol's "inconsistency" in concluding his series of gloomy pictures and his succession of knaves with such a "paean" of Russia, but also regards this "paean" as "almost suggestive of a Russian equivalent to 'Deutschland über alles'!" [11]

It is thus hardly surprising that Lavrin should dismiss as "something of misunderstanding" Belinsky's proclamation of Gogol as the founder of Russian realism. He accordingly regards as the direct continuation of *Dead Souls* in the twentieth century, its "modernist counterpart", Fyodor Sologub's novel *Petty Demon*. [12]

Similarly misleading views of Gogol, who is portrayed as the precursor of modernism in its various manifestations, abound in the West. It is thus all the more urgent that we should attempt in this comparative typological analysis of *Dead Souls* to identify the similarities between Gogol's *poema* and works forming the mainstream development of realism in the West European novel of the eighteenth and nineteenth centuries, and also to show the national essence of this masterpiece of Russian literature.

It is essential that we should counterpose to the above-quoted interpretations of *Dead Souls* by Nabokov, Erlich, Lavrin and others the splendid analysis of Gogol's work given in the speech delivered by the French poet Paul Éluard at the ceremonial assembly held in Gogol's memory at the Bolshoi Theatre in Moscow in March 1952.

Éluard's analysis is based on a profound penetration of the national essence of Gogol's work, of writing which was born of the author's deep patriotism, and fortified by the "spiritual wealth" of the people. It is precisely this spiritual wealth, which has retained its moral force to this day that Éluard sees in Gogol's *poema* with its all-pervading belief in the people.

Éluard argues that the true historical significance of Gogol's prophetic lyrical digressions in *Dead Souls* only became manifest after the Great October Socialist Revolution. For it was then that the mighty word "forwards!" was at last proclaimed, a proclamation so yearned for by the author of *Dead Souls*.

From the very first steps in his literary career Gogol's remarkable, inimitable work provoked comparisons with various aspects of the Western literature. These comparisons themselves varied widely, reflecting at that early date not only the special features of Gogol's work, but also the divergent attitudes to him taken by the critics.

In his "Letter to A. F. Voyeikov, the Publisher of *The Russian Invalid Literary Supplement*", Pushkin waxes enthusiastic about Gogol's *Village Evenings Near Dikanka* and places the young author's name on a level with Molière and Fielding. [13] Later, in a critical note on Gogol's stories, Pushkin also compares him with Sir Walter Scott.

This comparison with Walter Scott was also made by Belinsky—this time with reference to *Dead Souls*. [14] Meanwhile the reactionary Russian critics of the day derided the lowliness and "filth" which they found in Gogol's realism, and could find no more distinguished comparison for him than with the French writer of entertaining but trivial novels of manners Paul de Kock. Gogol's letters testify to the injury this comparison caused him.

In his diary for 1848-1852 Chernyshevsky compares Gogol with Fielding and with Dickens. In his later writings we find many more comparisons between Gogol and Dickens.

Literary historians in pre-revolutionary Russia were primarily concerned not with typological and comparative studies of Gogol's work, but with the analysis of West European literary phenomena which might have influenced his writing. It is in this light that Alexei Veselovsky discusses Gogol, somewhat cursorily, in his book *Zapadnoye vliyaniye v novoi russkoi literature* (Western Influence in New Russian Literature). The scholar Georgi Chudakov treats him in a similar vein in his book *Otnosheniye tvorchestva*

Gogolya k zapadno-evropeiskoi literature (Gogol's Work and West European Literature).

Soviet literary scholars have produced a number of comparative analyses of Gogol's work and the West European novel. Prominent in this field in the 1920s was Viktor Vinogradov, who was concerned particularly with Gogol's Sterneian tendencies and his relation to Scott. Viktor Shklovsky also made a number of interesting observations on this question. [15]

The authors of Soviet monographs on Gogol's work have frequently touched in passing on the typological relation between *Dead Souls* and various aspects of the West European novel. Thus, Valeri Gippius focusses on the possible affinity between Gogol, on the one hand, and Fielding and Sterne, on the other. [16] Mikhail Khrapchenko makes a special comparison between Gogol and Dickens, showing both their similarities and points of difference. [17] Nikolai Stepanov devoted an entire article to the national essence of *Dead Souls*, in which he compares the work to Balzac's novels and other works of Western realism. [18] In her interesting article E. A. Smirnova discusses Gogol's attitude to the ideas of Enlightenment humanism, and, in particular, to the writings of Rousseau. [19]

Vassily Kuleshov's substantial book on literary relations between Russia and the West in the last century contains valuable observations about the "typological affinites" between Russian and West European narrative prose in Gogol's time. [20]

Gogol's place in the general development of realism in the European novel has been discussed by A. Chicherin. [21]

A particularly large contribution to the typological study of the problem of Gogol's international significance has been made by Mikhail Alexeyev. [22]

In the course of this book the author shall frequently have recourse to the works of these Soviet scholars, and the list given above is not of course intended to be exhaustive.

NOTES

[1] Vladimir Nabokov, *Nikolai Gogol,* Norfolk (Conn.), 1944, pp. 35, 85, 115-116 et passim.

[2] Ibid., p. 73.

[3] Ibid., p. 84.

[4] Ibid., pp. 90-91.

[5] Ibid., p. 113.

[6] Franz Kafka, *Tagebücher,* 1910-1923, N.Y., 1954, p. 334.

[7] Ibid., p. 332.

[8] Victor Erlich, "Gogol and Kafka: a Note on 'Realism' and 'Surrealism'", In: *For Roman Jakobson. Essays on the Occasion of his Sixtieth Birthday,* The Hague, 1956.

[9] Janko Lavrin, *Nikolai Gogol,* N.Y., 1962, p. 69.

[10] Ibid., pp. 106-107.

[11] Ibid., p. 107.

[12] Ibid., p. 146.

[13] "Molière and Fielding would doubtless have been glad to make their type-setters laugh," wrote Pushkin, relating how the printers laughed as they set up the pages of *Village Evenings.*— A. S. Pushkin, *Collected Works,* Vol. 5, Moscow, 1954, p. 151 (in Russian).

[14] Belinsky's general view, connected with his idea that Russia's historical backwardness prevented Russian literature from playing a worthy part in the world literary processes of the time, is also reflected in his underestimation of the world significance of Gogol's work, and, in particular, of *Dead Souls.* It is this that gives rise to the rather biassed nature of his comparison between the latter novel and the works of Scott. Scott's novels, in Belinsky's view, reflect "universal life", something which is lacking in *Dead Souls* since this work is entirely concerned with Russian reality, and thus has great significance, but only for Russian readers—Vissarion Belinsky, *Collected Works,* Vol. VI, Moscow, 1955, pp. 417 et al. (in Russian).

[15] V. B. Shklovsky, *Povesti o proze.* Razmyshleniya i razbory {Tales about Prose. Reflections and Analyses), Vol. 2, Moscow, 1966.

[16] V. V. Gippius, *Gogol,* Leningrad, 1924.

[17] M. B. Khrapchenko, *Tvorchestvo Gogolya* (Gogol's Work), Moscow, 1961.

[18] N. L. Stepanov, "Natsionalnoye svoyeobrazie *Mertvych Dush*" (The National Essence of *Dead Souls*), *Izvestiya OLYa AN SSSR,* Proceedings of the USSR Academy of Sciences' Department of Literature and Language, Vol. XI, issue 1, 1952.

[19] E. A. Smirnova, "Gogol i ideya 'yestestvennogo' tcheloveka v literature XVIII veka" (Gogol and the Idea of "Natural" Man in

Eighteenth Century Literature). In *Russkaya literatura XVIII veka. Epokha klassitsizma* (Eighteenth Century Russian Literature. Epoch of Classicism), Moscow-Leningrad, 1964.

[20] V. I. Kuleshov, *Literaturnye svyazi Rossii i Zapadnoy Yevropy v XIX veke (pervaya polovina)* (Literary Relations between Russia and Western Europe in the Nineteenth Century, First Half), Moscow, 1965.

[21] A. V. Chicherin, "Sootvetstviya v istorii raznych literatur" (Correspondences in the History of Different Literatures), *Voprosy literatury*, 1965, No. 10.

[22] M. P. Alexeyev, "Mirovoye znacheniye Gogolya" (The Universal Significance of Gogol), in *Gogol v shkole. Sbornik statei* (Gogol in the School. Collection of Articles), Moscow, 1959. See also his commentaries to the Russian translation of Barbey d'Aurevilly's article on Gogol—in *N. V. Gogol. Materialy i issledovaniya* (Nikolai Gogol: Materials and Analyses), ed. by V. V. Gippius, Vol. 1, Moscow-Leningrad, 1936 and his article "Drama Gogolya iz anglo-saksonskoi istorii" (Gogol's Drama from Anglo-Saxon History), ibid., Vol. 2.

CHAPTER ONE

DEAD SOULS AND THE EPIC NOVEL

Je commence l'analyse du roman de N. Gogol. Il l'intitule poème; ce titre est une
espèce d'énigme, le roman en est une
autre...

Mérimée, Nicolai Gogol

Why should I be to blame if the public
is stupid and if in its eyes I am the
same as Paul de Kock: Paul de Kock
writes a novel a year, so why should I not
write one too, for this is also a novel, apparently, and only called a poem for a
joke.

Gogol to Prokopovich, May 1843

1

Nigh on one hundred and fifty years have passed since
the publication of *Dead Souls*, Volume 1. Nevertheless, the
misunderstandings created by the author with his definition
of the genre of *Dead Souls* have still not been altogether
dispelled. The "enigmatic" quality which Mérimée detects
in *Dead Souls* [1] frequently confounds modern Western
scholars of Gogol too. [2]

There is no general consensus of agreement on the question of the genre of *Dead Souls* amongst Soviet literary
critics either.

Those passages of *Dead Souls* devoted to the Russian
land and people have become the common property of all
Russians; the idea behind the book, partially expressed in
Volume 1, and in the author's letters and in his *Author's
Confession*, has also become familiar to all. Right from his
first confessions to Zhukovsky in 1836 Gogol harps on the
same note in his interpretation of the design of *Dead Souls*:
"If I accomplish this work as it should be accomplished,
then ... what an enormous, what an original plot! What
a great variety of characters! All of Russia will appear in

it!"[3] Much later, after the catastrophic fiasco of *Selected Passages from Correspondence with My Friends*, Gogol returned to this same task in a letter to Zhukovsky of January 1848, this time with reference to the continuation of *Dead Souls*, but also with hindsight to Volume 1. And once again, but this time more distinctly expressed, he gives prominence to the idea of the Russian people as the main theme of the work. As if to explain his tendency towards an *epic* treatment of Russian life he writes: "I have seen and embraced many of the parts separately, but I just could not determine clearly the scheme of the whole... At every step I felt that there was some deficiency in me, that I was still unable either to tie together or to unloose events and that I had to study the arrangement of the major works of great masters. I set about this task, commencing with our beloved Homer" (XIV, 35).

Despite this such a critic as Alexei Chicherin in his book on the rise of the epic novel[4] categorically denies *Dead Souls* the right to lay claim to the epic genre.

On the other hand the critic Vadim Kozhinov in an article on realism in the 1830s does not for a moment express any doubt as to the epic principle of *Dead Souls*. But he interprets Gogol's *poema* as a work which is more comparable with "Renaissance realism" than with literary phenomena of the modern age. *Dead Souls*, the author maintains, belongs in a direct line of descendance with Rabelais's *Gargantua and Pantagruel* and Cervantes's *Don Quixote*, and only in this context can we hope to understand its real artistic nature.

This conception is in general extremely controversial, as are the specific arguments adduced in its favour by the author. In Kozhinov's view a recognition of the epic wholeness of Gogol's work presupposes a rejection of its satirical tendency, which, he claims, has been ascribed to *Dead Souls* since Belinsky's day through some unaccountable misunderstanding. Kozhinov argues that the characters of *Dead Souls* are not so much "monstrous" as merely "odd and eccentric",[5] and that "Gogol's heroes cannot and should not arouse the unprejudiced reader's distaste and irritation in the way that, for instance, some of Shchedrin's characters do".[6]

There is no need to reiterate the many substantial objections raised to this conception during the polemic which followed the publication of Kozhinov's article. Suffice it to mention one or two essential points which have so far escaped serious consideration.

First of all, it is doubtful whether Kozhinov is justified in "excluding" all direct satirical ridicule from the great works of "Renaissance realism". Mikhail Bakhtin's brilliant study of Rabelais, to which Kozhinov refers, does not, as Bakhtin explicitly states, claim to be an exhaustive interpretation of *all* aspects of Rabelais's work. The element of folk "carnivalization", which Bakhtin subjects to such a profound and original analysis, is not the sole merit of Rabelais's achievement. Another such, for example, is the philosophical content of his writing, such as the Utopian constructs of his humanist vision (e.g., the ideals of true pedagogy achieved by Ponocrat, or the utopia of the Abbey of Thélème). The same holds true for the direct and biting political and religious satire which spills from almost every page in *Gargantua and Pantagruel*, and which manifestly cannot be reduced to a form of universal "carnival" debunking and spontaneous removal of "masks". There is far too much here that is anything but spontaneous, that is, on the contrary, carefully weighed deliberate satire, based on extensive knowledge and sincere conviction. It is thus questionable whether we can appeal to Rabelais's realism in order by analogy to demonstrate the absence of satire in Gogol's work. On the other hand, it is surely obvious that these two writers are separated by a great historical distance. Their work is in both cases dominated by the grotesque, but with Rabelais this is grotesque on a grand, fantastic scale, in which the author's narration itself sometimes erupts into immense fountains of words and his story about the good and wise giants embraces the entire speculative and natural science of his age. Panurge alone embodies both the sensual nature of man "in general", with all its desires and temptations, egoism and cowardice, and the human aspect of the Renaissance age seen in a historical light, liberated from all feudal bonds, from religious humility and class prejudice... Panurge is at once amusing and awesome with his infinite cynicism and rapacity; an image of such historical plenitude and archetypal breadth could indeed only have been created by the realism of the Renaissance. But it is precisely here that we see the decisive and most essential difference between Rabelais's fantastic and universal archetypes and the images of Gogol, far more concrete both in their historical content and principles of their delineation.

In certain respects the comparison with Cervantes would seem more justifiable, if we think of the panoramic breadth of his portrayal of life and the spirit of ironic dialectic with which it is permeated. But is this how Gogol himself understood Cervantes?

If we turn to Gogol's *Primer of Literature for Russian Youth* we read, after a general description of "lesser varieties of the epic": "Thus did Ariosto depict the almost fabulous passion for adventure and the marvellous with which for a time the entire age was seized, while *Cervantes derided the thirst for adventure which abided in some people after the rococo period, at a time when the world itself had changed around them*, and both writers grew accustomed to their chosen view. It irresistibly filled their minds and thus acquired a strict and deliberate significance; it penetrates throughout and lends their works the minor aspect of an epic, despite the jocular tone, the levity and even the fact that one of them is written in prose" (VIII, 735; my italics. — *A. Y.*).

The italicized lines above show that Gogol held a fairly superficial and traditional view of the content and philosophical significance of Cervantes's masterpiece. The concluding remarks in the quotation return us to the ideas which are of great importance for an understanding of *Dead Souls* and which had already been expressed in the introductory section of the chapter "Lesser Varieties of the Epic". But Gogol did not only base these ideas on the example of Cervantes. It is significant that in a variant of this passage he also refers to "the novels of Fielding and finally of many others" (VIII, 735). We might suppose that the tradition of *Don Quixote* was perceived by Gogol in precisely its Enlightenment interpretation, through the mediation in particular of Fielding's "Cervantesque" "comic epic-poem". We find evidence of this in his somewhat didactic interpretation of *Don Quixote*, reminiscent of eighteenth century rationalism. In any event, the above-quoted treatment of *Don Quixote* brings into sharper focus the historical distance between the realism of the Renaissance and that of *Dead Souls* and itself refutes the hypothesis that Gogol's *poema* belongs to the same school of literary phenomena as the works of Cervantes and Rabelais.

The question of the unique nature of *Dead Souls* and the presence or absence of social satire in it can only be answered if we first establish the degree of historicism

Gogol brings to bear on his interpretation of the age he lived in. At the time the author was working on *Dead Souls* he was familiar not only with Pushkin's *Boris Godunov* and *The Captain's Daughter*, both set in the past, but also with his *Dubrovsky* and *Eugene Onegin*—the "encyclopedia of Russian life" in Belinsky's phrase—in which not only the mores but also the social ills of the age are depicted with an unprecedented liberty and poetic flair, as well as with keen satirical scrutiny. It is hardly coincidental that in his remarkable article "Several Words on Pushkin" (1832), in a discussion of the national character of Pushkin's work (and it is here that we read: "true national quality consists not in the description of a sarafan, * but in the very soul of the people"—VIII, 51), Gogol should single out for defence what we would describe as the realism of the mature Pushkin. He rejects the view of the "mass of the public", who prefer the early, Romantic poems of Pushkin, inspired by the Crimea and Caucasus, to his later works in which he "immerses himself in the heart of Russia", devoting himself to a deeper study of the manners and life of his fellow-countrymen in his new desire to be a truly national poet (VIII, 52). This account is most striking, for it was precisely thus that Gogol was subsequently to see his own mission. Equally noteworthy is the example quoted by Gogol further down of what he considers a truly significant object of portrayal. "No one will dispute the fact," he writes, "that a savage mountaineer in his martial garb, a man as free as the wind, and his own lord and master, is far more vivid a character than some government official, and though he has just ambushed a foe, or rased a whole village to the ground, he is more attractive and likable, than *our average judge in his threadbare, tobacco-stained tailcoat, who with most righteous of miens through pettyfogging has reduced to begging any number of peasants, both serfs and freemen.* But they are both people out of our world; they should both have a right to our attention, although for natural reasons our imagination is always more forcibly struck by that which we see more rarely and to prefer the commonplace to the extraordinary is no more than the miscalculation of the poet—a miscalculation before his large public, and not before himself. He does not in any way injure his merit, even, perhaps, increases it, but only in the

---

* *Sarajan*—a folk Russian dress worn by women—*Tr.*

eyes of a few truly discerning people" (VIII, 53; my italics.—A.Y.). Surely here we already see the stirrings, long
before Gogol conceived the idea of *Dead Souls,* of his theme
of the typical evils and malpractice, so inconspicuous
for the very reason that they are so commonplace, for they
are ingrained in the feudal and bureaucratic structure of
Russia. At the same time we can also see here, in embryo,
Gogol's future definition of his own onerous but exalted
mission as a writer who would disregard the cheap success
to be gained by describing imaginary and fantastical characters and devote himself instead to the depiction of the
"poverty and imperfection" of Russia as it actually was.

In the draft of the concluding chapter of *Dead Souls,*
Volume 2 the theme of the social injustices of a system of
serfdom resounds more clearly and with more general application: "Chichikov did not so much steal as make use of
things. After all each of us has occasion to make use of
things: one man of government timber, another of treasury
funds, a third will deprive his children for the sake of some
visiting actress, a fourth his peasants for the sake of a suite
of Hambs furniture or a carriage" (VII, 97).

In a letter to his sisters (of April 3rd 1849) Gogol returns to this question, which disturbed him so deeply, of the
unnatural relations between landowners and their serfs.
Here there is no more place for the conciliatory ideas of
the "divine right" of the landed gentry over the peasantry.
Perhaps, that was a period of sobriety after the disaster of
Selected Passages from Correspondence With My Friends,
when all traces of the writer's old illusions had been removed by Belinsky's impassioned letter, by Gogol's own information about the terrible reprisals exacted by the rioting
peasants over their masters.

If we turn to the preliminary notes to the *Dead Souls,*
Volume 1 we can at once identify as the central theme of
the entire volume the angry satirical denunciation of the indolence, futility and emptiness of the existence of the officials and landowners who are to play a prominent role in
the subsequent narrative. It would be appropriate at this
juncture to quote these remarkably succinct notes, which
illuminate so clearly the idea behind Gogol's epic.

"The concept of the town. The epitome of hollow thought.
Idle chatter. Gossip transcending all bounds—all this
is the offspring of idleness grown ridiculous to the highest
degree...

"Thus the hollowness and senselessness of life yields place to the grisly nothingness of death, a frightful happening rounded off so meaninglessly. Yet no hearts are moved... All the more should the reader be made aware of the deadening inertness of life.

"Life sinks into the Stygian murk with the mystery of death unrevealed. How horrendous a phenomenon! Riotous,* and purposeless—how awesome a spectacle is life..." (VI, 692).

We are struck here not only by the repetition of the life of "the town"—in other words, of its officials, but also by the dramatic, almost tragic tone of these notes. "Ridiculous to the highest degree" is not merely juxtaposed, it is fused together with "deadening", "horrendous", "awesome". Thus even at this early stage the social significance of Gogol's theme and the special role in it of the tragi-comic and grotesque are beginning to be defined. The phenomena whose "mystery" the writer wishes to plumb, are at once comic and frightful, and such do they appear in the images and situations of *Dead Souls*.

The lyrical digressions and image of the author that emerges from them are inseparable from his desire to divine this "mystery", which, in Gogol's view, has a significance both national and universal.

Dead Souls is in many respects also comparable with the lyric epic poem of the early nineteenth century. Some of his contemporaries quite justifiably likened the author of *Dead Souls* to Byron, although they intended this comparison to be degrading and even offensive. Let us recall, for instance, the article by Barbey d'Aurevilly which strikes a direct comparison between *Dead Souls* and *Don Juan*. "What in essence was this literary Spartacus," asks d'Aurevilly, referring to Gogol, "if not a Russian writer who has read Byron and become infected with the irony of the English poet, who in *Don Juan* and his political verse dons the mask of a Jacobite and Carbonaro? Imitator of Byron, imitator of Rousseau, combining the misanthropy of the one with the misanthropy of the other, a comedian, liar, a man who has lost his footing, a *bousingot*—this is who Gogol was! His crazy passion for irony, his desire to ridicule and

---

* This word is evidently being used here with the meaning "chaotic", "meaningless".

debase his own country were similarly no more than imitation; to an even greater extent these were no more than the pursuit of an effect, which had the result that the author himself was horrified at it and suffered from it!" [7]

In his commentary to this escapade Mikhail Alexeyev explains the subjective reasons for the animosity with which d'Aurevilly endeavoured to denounce *Dead Souls* and ridicule its French translator Charrière. But although d'Aurevilly advances the comparison with Byron's *Don Juan* as an argument intended to "disgrace" Gogol's *poema* in the eyes of French readers, it is in itself not without foundation. However different the political convictions of Byron and Gogol, however far apart their philosophical and religious beliefs, there is much that is similar in the actual poetic structure of their works: they both present a panoramic view of life in all its breadth, with abrupt shifts from the satirical portrayal of the basest and most prosaic aspects of life to an elated lyricism, and vice versa: they both select fairly traditional modes of presenting their material (the "adventures" or "voyages" of a none-too-scrupulous hero), enabling them to interpolate any events and phenomena into their respective works, which are related in a similarly ironic tone.

Gogol was keenly interested by Byron and Byronism. Even when taking issue with the English writer he readily expresses his profound admiration of his poetry and, which is particularly noteworthy, of the breadth of his portrayal of life. In his article "On the Poetry of Kozlov" he writes of the "amazement" with which his contemporaries beheld Byron, "who so marvellously embraced with his immense, sombre soul the whole of life and so audaciously scoffed at it, perhaps from his inability to convey its individual radiance and greatness" (VIII, 153). Even Byron's "delusions" strike Gogol as "brilliant" (VIII, 381), and the imitation of Byron, the "epidemic" "when the entire world tuned their instruments to Byron's lyre" in his opinion "was not ridiculous: there was even something consoling in this aspiration" (VIII, 181-182). At the same time we might suppose that in *Dead Souls*—and particularly in his work on Volume 2—Gogol was engaged in an inner polemic with Byron. This polemic was most clearly manifest in a letter to Sergei Aksakov of May 16th 1844, in which, metaphorically declaring dejection to be the work of the devil ("to frighten, to swindle, to make us despondent—this is his work"), he declares that he is determined to overcome these moods: "...I will call the devil simply a devil and I will not give him a magnificent costume à la Byron—and that is my last word!" (XII, 300-301).

However, for all the significance of its lyrical element his prose *poema* is also perfectly comparable from a typological point of view with the West European epic novel— a genre which had its origins in the literature of the new age, beginning with Fielding's "comic epic-poem", gaining substantial enrichment from the pen of Sir Walter Scott and reaching its prime in the works of Balzac, Thackeray and Dickens.

In a letter to Zhukovsky of January 10th 1848, which has the character of an artistic *confession*, Gogol writes with reference to his work on *Dead Souls*, as we can gather from the context: "Art must portray to us the people of our world in such a way that each of us should feel that these are *live people*, created and drawn from the very same body as we ourselves. Art must exhibit to our view all our valorous *popular* qualities and properties, not even excluding those which, lacking the scope for free development, are not apprehended by us all, so that each of us should feel them within us and should be fired with the desire to develop and nurture within us that which we have cast aside and forgotten... Only then and only by acting thus will art fulfil its purpose and bring order and harmony into society!" (XIV, 37-38).

These judgements partially are (in their emphasis on the self-improvement and self-education of each of us and the proclamation of reconciliation, order and harmony as that primary social goal of art) survivals of attitudes espoused by Gogol during the period of *Selected Passages*.

But even here he retains, as the main idea behind the creation of *Dead Souls*, the ambition he had declared at an earlier date to learn and portray the Russian people from every side, with all the special features of their national character, including, which is of singular importance to Gogol, those features which remain latent within them, biding their time before emerging to the surface. Gogol is concerned with this task both in the first part of his work, and, insofar as we can judge from the surviving fragments and reports of witnesses, in its continuation. Such an undertaking cannot but be defined as "epic". The doubts and confusion that have bedevilled so many scholars when defining the genre of *Dead Souls* (as we have seen in the isolated examples given above) and considering the possibility of classing this work with the epic novels of the nineteenth century, appear to arise from two main sources.

The first of these is to be found in the exceptional originality of *Dead Souls,* which presents a unique fusion of the most minute description of mores and satirical generalizations of immense breadth and power, of a plot which appears trivial to the point of vulgarity, and exalted flights of the lyrical fancy of an author who looks prophetically into the future and foretells what it will bring. *Dead Souls* is not a novel, and Gogol was right to insist on this. But as a lyrical epic poem in prose this work is typologically comparable both with the lyrical epic, so prominent in the work of the early nineteenth century Romantics, and—to an even greater extent—with the social epic novel, which reached its zenith in the work of Gogol's contemporaries in Western Europe. This unique quality of *Dead Souls* is a manifestation not only of the originality of its author's artistic gift, but also of the exceptional path followed by the Russian nineteenth century classical literature, in which the critical realism of the thirties and forties assimilated—not in the form of a "concession" to the past, but in an entirely organic manner—many elements of Romanticism and even of Enlightenment literature.

The second reason for the confusion surrounding the definition of *Dead Souls* as an epic work has to do with the manner in which the book was written. Gogol's masterpiece was created amidst great agonies and torment, and it has not come down to us in its original form, which it retained until the fateful day of February 11th 1852. Immediately after Volume 1 was published Gogol, who had never sought to identify himself with the Slavophiles, found himself, much against his wishes, in the middle of a great critical furore stirred up by the efforts of Slavophile critics to claim *Dead Souls* as an example of Slavophilism. By an ironic twist Konstantin Aksakov's pamphlet on *Dead Souls*, a youthfully naïve and ecstatic eulogy (whose publication distressed Gogol himself), was fated to play a far more significant role in the critical history of *Dead Souls* than it would have in different circumstances. The two sharp critical ripostes delivered by Belinsky to this pamphlet were, as can be seen from the entire context of the quarrel, in fact directed not so much against the comparison of Gogol to

Homer, advanced by Aksakov and others, as against the desire implicit in this to "liberate" *Dead Souls* from its satirical, denunciatory import and to ascribe to Gogol a serene, Olympian perception of Russia in its patriarchal, primordial innocence. Belinsky takes up arms against this interpretation and in his polemic ardour he even goes so far as to revoke certain vital aspects of his original assessment of the work; in particular, in his second pronouncement on Aksakov's pamphlet he prefers to regard Gogol's definition of the genre of *Dead Souls* as either a mere joke, or a "grave mistake". [8] He had written in quite a different vein in his first long article on *Dead Souls* (*Otechestvennye zapiski*, 1842, XXIII, No. 6, section VI). Here he describes it as a "pure Russian work, a national creation, drawn from the inmost recesses of Russian life, as true to life as it is patriotic, mercilessly unmasking the facts of life and breathing an impassioned love for the fruitful kernel of Russian life; a work which is infinitely artistic in conception and execution, in the characters of its protagonists and the details of Russian mores—and at the same time profound in thought, social, civic and historical..." [9]

Here, in this first, deeply considered and felt article, Belinsky can see nothing strange in the definition of *Dead Souls* as a *poema*. Furthermore, quoting the two magnificent digressions from Chapter 11 ("...Russia! Russia! I see thee, from my wondrous, beautiful afar..." and the celebrated closing passage), Belinsky writes: "It is sad to think that this exalted flight of lyrical sentiment, these ringing, plangent dithyrambs of a lofty national self-awareness, worthy of a great Russian poet, will be far from accessible to all, that people in their genial ignorance will laugh uproariously at that which will make another's hair to stand on end in trepidation... Yet this is how it is, and it cannot be otherwise. The exalted, inspired *poema* will be regarded by the majority as a 'killingly funny joke'..." [10]

Later, alarmed by the Slavophiles' misinterpretation of *Dead Souls*, Belinsky was inclined to see Gogol's mistake in his appeal to the future, which was the basis for the poem's "majestic flow" and its lyrical onward message. "The essence of the people," Belinsky wrote, "can be a subject for a poem only if understood rationally, when it represents something concrete and actual, and not something hypothetical or conjectural, and when it already has a past and a present, not only a future... That is why already it is most mistaken for an author to write a poem which is possible only in the future."

In re-examining his initial opinion of *Dead Souls* as a *poema*, Belinsky was motivated by fears raised by the Slavophiles' attempts to influence Gogol. At the same time in the passage quoted above, one can see a certain underestimation of what can be referred to as the *romantic* tendencies in Gogol's realism, which Belinsky, at other times, not only accepted but considered a natural and fruitful beginning for art.

The concrete social forms in which Gogol tried to realize his ideal of the future in the second volume, turned out to be an untenable Utopia. But his lyrical appeal to the future, based on a deep faith in the potential of the Russian people, has proved its worth and shown its vitality.

It is precisely as a "work ... profound in thought, social, civic and historical", permeated at the same time with an "all-embracing and humane subjectivity", that we, following Belinsky, prefer to regard *Dead Souls* as we compare the work to other typologically similar examples of the West European epic novel.

2

The close parallels between Gogol and Fielding (and to some extent Sterne) were observed long ago by Valeri Gippius. "The relationship between the English novelist and Gogol still requires investigation," he wrote, with reference to Fielding. Gippius noted in particular that "the manner in which the author controls the action, the continuous commentary, consisting of comic lyrical interruptions, might have been adopted by Gogol under the influence not only of Sterne, but also of Fielding, particularly at those times when he decided to juxtapose comic and moving situations". [11]

Leaving aside for the moment the question of Gogol's relation to Sterne (who occupies a special place in the history of the English Enlightenment novel), it would appear possible to establish a typological affinity between *Dead Souls* and Fielding's "comic epic-poem", and to some extent the satirical novels of Smollett.

Fielding is mentioned by Gogol on a number of occasions and in contexts which demonstrate that the author of *Dead Souls* had studied the work of the English writer with close attention.

26

In the early manuscripts of *Dead Souls* Fielding is named as one of Gogol's like-minded mentors and sources of inspiration. The author, writes Gogol about himself, "is not in the habit of looking about himself when he writes, and it is only by their own volition that his eyes occasionally light on the portraits hanging on the wall before him, of Shakespeare, Ariosto, Fielding, Cervantes and Pushkin, men who reflected nature as it was, and not as it suited someone or other that it should be" (VI, 553; cf. also VI, 554, 664 and 645).

The polemic tone of this extract (which was originally intended for the passage in Volume 1, chapter 11 where Gogol explains why he chose Chichikov as the hero of his *poema*) is at once manifest. In its spirit this reference to his great predecessors, "who reflected nature as it was", is cognate with Gogol's characteristic defence of realism, of a bold and accurate portrayal of life, with all its dirt and baseness, as a counter to hypocritical and biased idealisation. This same idea can be encountered in embryonic form on several occasions in the theoretical introductory chapters to *The History of Tom Jones a Foundling*. We might recall, for example, the chapter, "containing instructions very necessary to be perused by modern critics", in which Fielding warns the reader that he does not intend to introduce into his narrative either characters of "angelic perfection" or embodiments of "diabolical depravity"... "If thou dost delight in these models of perfection, there are books now written to gratify thy taste; but, as we have, not in the course of our conversation, ever happened to meet with any such person, we have not chosen to introduce any such here". [12]

There is another extremely interesting mention of Fielding in the rough version of Gogol's *Primer of Literature for Russian Youth*, which the commentators to the Academy edition of Gogol's works presume to have been composed in 1844-1845.

This *Primer* contains a special section on "Lesser Varieties of the Epic", the first paragraph of which we shall quote in toto.

"The new age," writes Gogol, "has seen the emergence of a type of narrative work which as it were constitutes the mid-point between the novel and the epic, with a hero who may tend to be a private and inconspicuous character, but who is nonetheless significant in many respects for the

27

observer of the human soul. The author guides his life through a chain of adventures and times in order thereby to present in vivid reality a true picture of all significant features and mores of the time he has chosen, to show a mundane, almost statistically comprehended picture of the shortcomings, abuses, vices and everything else he has observed in this epoch which is worthy of the attention of any observant contemporary, if he should seek in the past vital lessons for the present. From time to time such phenomena have occurred with many nations. Many of them may be written in prose, but they may nonetheless be regarded as creations of poetry" (VIII, 478-479).

In the rough version this was immediately followed by: "As for example Cervantes's Don Quixote, to some extent Fielding's novels, * and finally, many others... He takes either an almost topographical portrayal of life..." (VIII, 735). With this phrase the passage abruptly stops: but even in this state it demonstrates the direction of Gogol's thought. This description is equally applicable both to *Dead Souls* and to the realistic novel of manners which was taking shape in the work of Fielding, to a lesser extent Smollett, and other English Enlightenment authors. But it defines only one aspect of these works. "Topography" and "statistics" are inwardly interpreted and animated by the artist's aesthetic feeling: the life of a "private and inconspicuous character" provided material for the exploration of universal problems of human nature. For both *Tom Jones* and *The Adventures of Roderick Random* (and the list could be extended to include many other English Enlightenment novels) can be regarded as more than mere entertaining narratives, as a sort of experiment in the field of moral philosophy and at the same time an attempt at a practical exposition of the "science of life" (to use an expression favoured by Gogol, but dating to the eighteenth century).

The picaresque novel had already presented its readers with a vivid picture of the life of an age, with a kaleidoscopic succession of colourful episodes. Born in the tempestuous age of the decline of feudalism and emergence of new,

---

* We should also note the list of authors and books compiled by Gogol in all probability in the late 1840s and intended as a recommended guide. Fielding's name is accorded prominence: he follows Shakespeare at the head of the list of the most important representatives of "English" literature; in addition to them the list includes only Scott, Byron and Richardson.

bourgeois relations, the picaresque novel reflected all the colour and variety of the "Falstaffian backcloth" of life of the time. Its pages featured those "remarkably characteristis images" which, in Engels's words, "were provided by this age of the decline of feudal bonds in the person of vagrant kings, beggar noblemen and every manner of adventurer". [13]

But although the roots of the picaresque novel reach deep into the Renaissance, it lacks the harmonious, generalizing majesty and wholeness of Renaissance art. Its element is disharmony and fragmentation, abrupt contrasts, strident and grotesque dissonance, in which the coarsest naturalist situation comedy alternates with the tragedy of the eternal loneliness of that wretched predatory biped, homo sapiens. The whim of Fortune, on whose wheel a hero may in one moment be lifted to the peak of prosperity only the next to be dashed to the depths of misery, constitutes the only basis for the advancement of the plot of these novels. The tragic aspect of the picaresque novel is most powerfully reflected in Quevedo's *El Buscón* (1626): the prologue to this book recounts with bitter irony the vain attempt of the gods of Olympus to restore on earth the justice destroyed by the caprice of Fortune.

In the Enlightenment age the picaresque novel underwent substantial changes. The Enlightenment writers valued the infinite opportunities afforded them by this genre for the satirical observation of social and private moeurs. But in their hands the picaresque novel becomes somehow "regulated", losing its quaint excesses and chaotic structure. The disjointed and fragmented views of man and the world, so typical of Baroque art, to which the seventeenth-century picaresque novel gravitated, gave way to the rationalist logic of Enlightenment humanism. The transformation of the picaresque novel into that of the Enlightenment can be already noted—albeit at an early stage—in *Gil Blas de Santillane* (1715-1735) by Lesage.

The plot structure of the novel, which has a largely Spanish provenance, retains the traditional *vicissitudes* of fate as the primary motive force behind the action. But the actual attitude of the author to his hero is markedly different. Where the moral range of the classical picaresque hero was, as a rule, confined to the small distance between naïve cynicism and cynicism elevated to the status of a philosophy, Gil Blas is shown to have a somewhat different character. Gil Blas is neither good nor evil, he consists entirely of instincts, he is *l'homme même*. His behaviour, like the behaviour of his predecessors, depends entirely on circumstances: not only reduced to extreme need, but even simply conducted by his author "into temptation" he proves to be no less a rogue than any of his mentors in this universal métier. But Lesage is interested not only in the "falls" of his hero, but also in his ability to return to good, an ability he never loses despite the many trials and temptations in his path. Ascending the entire ladder of society, from a robber's den to the regal palace, growing convinced of the vanity of court glitter and the futility of noble favour, Gil Blas sagely resolves to renounce further pursuit of Fortune and to content himself with the joys of that "middle state" which it has granted him. In this sense Lesage's novel already contains in embryo the basic element of the Enlightenment novel, in which satire is also combined with a study of the way "human nature" changes—for better or for worse—under the influence of circumstances and education in the broadest meaning of the word. But by the time the Enlightenment novel had reached its zenith *Gil Blas* no longer fully satisfied the requirements of the aesthetics of that movement.

It is interesting in this connection to recall the polemic with Lesage with which Smollett prefaced his first novel *The Adventure of Roderick Random* (1748). Paying tribute to the "infinite humour and perspicacity" of Lesage, declaring him to be his mentor in the portrayal of "ordinary life", Smollett hastens to qualify this with his fundamental differences of opinion with the author of *Gil Blas*. Many situations in Lesage's novel strike the English writer as excessively "unusual, extravagant", and the moral which should have resulted from them is insufficiently clear. It is precisely such reproaches that appear to be implicit in the following remarks with which Smollett cautions his readers about the innovations which he intends to introduce into his novel in departure from the tradition of *Gil Blas*. "The disgraces of Gil Blas," he writes in the preface to *Roderick Random*, "are, for the most part, such as rather excite mirth than compassion; he himself laughs at them; and his transitions from distress to happiness, or at least ease, are so sudden, that neither the reader has time to pity him, nor himself to be acquainted with affliction. This conduct, in my opinion, not only deviates from probability, but prevents that generous indignation which ought to animate the reader, against the sordid and vicious disposition of the world." [14]

In these remarks, which are consistent with the aesthetic programme of the mature Enlightenment novel, we should note in particular both the principle of "verisimilitude", which Smollett opposes to the Baroque "extravagance" of Lesage, and the endeavour to show life in its real, and not conventional, dramatism (the hero must experience grief, or else his experience of life will be incomplete and inaccurate). Finally, one essential point of this Enlightenment polemic with Lesage expresses the requirement for the direct emotional and philosophical effect of the work: it must not only entertain the reader but also arouse his "generous indignation" at social vices.

It is worth keeping this polemic in mind, reflecting as it does, in microcosm, the development of narrative genres in European literature from the picaresque novel of the seventeenth and eighteenth centuries to the Enlightenment novel of the eighteenth century, when we return to our discussion of Gogol.

Ever since the mid-nineteenth century Western critics have assiduously pursued the analogy between *Dead Souls* and Lesage's *Gil Blas*. One of the most notable chapters in this critical history was written in France at the end of the 1850s, after the publication of Charrière's translation of *Dead Souls*. Thus, Barbey d'Aurevilly was prepared to accept the comparison between Gogol and Lesage, but only because it struck him as far from flattering to Gogol. "M. Charrière," he wrote, "does not hesitate to place *Dead Souls* on a level with *Gil Blas*; if this gives M. Charrière pleasure we will not object to the translator's opinion, because the fame of *Gil Blas* is not such as to withstand the passing of time. It has passed, withered like the 'hortensias' coloured bands with which our grandfathers tied their nightcaps". [15]

The English critic Stephen Graham also compared *Dead Souls* with *Gil Blas,* but in a more neutral context.

In France Henri Mongault, author of an introductory article to Mérimée's *Études de littérature russe*, defends Mérimée from the accusation of Russian critics that he had underestimated the universal importance of *Dead Souls*, arguing that Gogol "originally intended quite simply to write a picaresque novel". Mongault even laments Gogol's deviation from this traditional design. "Only afterwards does the happy gigue (*le joyeux branle*) give way to the dance of death, and this change of tone adversely affected the unity of the work and prevented the author bringing it to a successful conclusion". [16]

The American scholar Donald Fanger, who even doubts whether *Dead Souls* can rightfully be called a realistic work at all, unhesitatingly calls Gogol's *poema* a "picaresque novel". [17] This approach to the problem in fact completely side-steps the question of the unusual genre of *Dead Souls* and ignores the author's express intentions. For it was only with the utmost unwillingness, under the pressure of the censors, that Gogol was forced, in order to save his book, to enlarge his original, well-worn title, chosen so carefully and so long before, and so full of meaning: *Dead Souls*. A *poema*, with the traditional, typically picaresque heading: "The Adventures of Chichikov".

Such analogies between *Dead Souls* and the picaresque novel in general, and *Gil Blas* in particular, are not confined to these direct derivations. The influence of the picaresque novel also made itself felt on Gogol indirectly, through the mediation of Fielding's "comic epic-poem" or Smollett's satire, with their reinterpretation and re-working of the picaresque themes, and even on nineteenth century writers, as attentive analysis will show, sometimes in the sub-text and sometimes more explicitly in the prose of Balzac, Thackeray and Dickens.

The student of picaresque influences in Russian literature would do best to guide his search for direct correspondences to the novel *Ivan Vyzhigin* by Bulgarin, the final wretched epigone of a once glorious tradition.

Fanger makes another, more interesting and constructive observation, that *Dead Souls* belongs "in point of technique as much to the European eighteenth century as to the Russian nineteenth". [18] But this idea remains undeveloped and the author unjustifiably divorces "technique" from the essence of Gogol's work, ignoring actual historical and literary correspondences, and separates *Dead Souls* from its proper age and "re-locates" it too far back in the past, in the 18th century.

There is an undoubted typological similarity between *Dead Souls* and a certain direction taken by the development of West European narrative prose in the eighteenth century, but this similarity is by no means confined to "technique". On the contrary, it is to be seen most clearly in the congruence of many of Gogol's fundamental views and those of his predecessors, the West European Enlightenment writers, on both "human nature" and the goals of art.

The unusual syncretic development of realism in nineteenth century Russian literature with its intense and rapid growth meant that the various stages of this development, which in most Western literatures succeeded or opposed one another, became contracted and converged in time, or were at least less marked and less clearly articulated. The social and historical conditions in which the Enlightenment flourished as a political and philosophical movement survived in Russia until the 1860s. Such men as Belinsky, Herzen, Dobrolyubov and Chernyshevsky were all Enlightenment thinkers of a revolutionary, democratic mould, although, of course, the new historical conditions prevailing in their world meant that their enlightenment was in many respects markedly different from that of Western Europe which had led the way to the French Revolution. The significant advantages of Russian democratic Enlightenment thinking included freedom from the many idealistic illusions of its Western parent, a better understanding of the laws of history, a new, far more profound appreciation of the role of the people in history, based on the rich experience of the Russian peasant movements, on the lessons of the Napoleonic war of 1812, on the tragic outcome of Decembrism and at the same time on the entire course of West European history since the French Revolution. However, this is the subject of a special study. For our present purposes it is only necessary to recall these circumstances in order to understand how the right preconditions might have existed in Russian social thought to bring about a rapprochement between Gogol and the Enlightenment.

This rapprochement had a variety of manifestations. As many scholars have shown, Gogol was nurtured on the ideas of the Enlightenment since his early youth, in his years at the Nezhin Lyceum. His Nezhin teachers inculcated in him the seditious ideas of "natural right" and service of one's country as the supreme duty of every citizen. Rousseau and other Enlightenment writers, whose works he devoured at an early age, reinforced his faith in human nature, in the passions of man, so often directed to evil by a bad upbringing, by social prejudice or by unpropitious circumstances, but which can be turned towards good by the might of conviction and by changing the environment in which people have been placed. The great humanist principle of Enlightenment ethics—the principle of man's infinite potential for improvement—was applauded by Gogol and became one of the fundamental driving forces in the general design of *Dead Souls*. Gogol also inherited from the Enlightenment—and from its Russian as well as Western schools—his profound conviction of the high civic mission of art as a mighty vehicle for the study and improvement of life.

Thus were the necessary preconditions established for the similarity between Gogol's *poema* and certain outstanding examples of Western Enlightenment prose of the eighteenth century, most particularly the "comic epic-poems" of Fielding, a similarity that is far-reaching and essentially typological, and by no means confined to technique.

Above all we should note the *deliberate breadth* of their portrayal of life, so fundamentally different from the chaotic succession of episodes which characterizes the picaresque novel.

The epigraph to *The History of Tom Jones a Foundling,* taken from Horace: *"Mores hominum multorum vidit"* ("He has seen the ways of many men") has an indubitably programmatic significance.

At the same time Fielding insisted that his imaginary "histories" * were true-to-life not only in their detail but also because they grasped and imprinted the most significant—or typical, as we would say today—phenomena. He accords immense importance to the principle of the *selection* of facts, and with tongue in cheek demonstrates the superiority of his works over learned compositions which he calls the "History of England". For it is insufficient, argues Fielding, for the creator of such a "history" or "comic epic-pome in prose", as Tom Jones, to possess talent and a good heart and to be well-read. "Again, there is another sort of knowledge, beyond the power of learning to bestow, and this is to be had by conversation," [19] he writes.

---

* We cannot help feeling the profoundly considered design in the insistence with which Fielding includes this word in his titles: *The History of the Late Jonathan Wild the Great, The History of the Adventures of Joseph Andrews and His Friend Mr. Abraham Adams, The History of Tom Jones a Foundling.*

In the same manner the more immersed Gogol became in his work on *Dead Souls* the more eagerly and impatiently he sought ever new sources for his study of the "headlong life" of his country, pumping his friends and readers for information about the customs and manners of Russia, studying works of statistics, geography, natural science and cramming his notebooks with a mass of hasty notes about farm work, popular customs, rites and turns of phrase. "I cannot publish the last volumes of my work until I have gained some knowledge of Russian life from all its aspects, at least to the extent to which I need to know it for my work," (VI, 589) he exclaims in the foreword to the second edition of Volume 1 of *Dead Souls*.

This conscious orientation towards the immense scope of his narrative and its profound cognitive tendency provide further manifestation of the closeness between Gogol's *poema* and Fielding's books. Defining the goals and possibilities of his new narrative genre Fielding varied its name from the general concept "comic-epic", sometimes calling it a "prosaicomic-epic writing", sometimes "heroic-historic-prosaic poem", but he consistently maintained that his epic composition had nothing in common with the "novel" in the sense the word was understood at that time.

The reference to Homer as his model, which Fielding makes at the beginning of his foreword to *Joseph Andrews,* is not made in jest. Fielding insisted on precisely the *epic* features of his narrative genre, which, in his words, differed from comedy "as the serious epic from tragedy: its action being more extended and comprehensive; containing a much larger circle of incidents and introducing a greater variety of characters". [20] Some critics even in our time have regarded Fielding's arguments as premature and reduce the role of the epic principle in his "comic epics" to trivial details. But the great writers of the nineteenth century who rested in their various ways on Fielding's tradition took a different view of his claims. Byron, who read and re-read Fielding with great enthusiasm whilst working on *Don Juan,* described the novelist as a Homer of prose. Stendhal declared that *The History of Tom Jones a Foundling* occupied a position amongst the world's novels as exceptional as that of the *Iliad* amongst epics.

The key to Fielding's innovatory creation of the "comic epic-poem" can be sought in the Enlightenment view of real, terrestrial, sensual man—and, furthermore, man of simple or middling means—as the measure of all things. This man must be understood and portrayed in his real environment, with all his needs, whims and passions, habits and foibles. Anticipating the accusations of "baseness" and impropriety, which were heaped on him by English critics as ferociously as they were applied a century later to Gogol by Bulgarin, Senkovsky and company, Fielding exclaims: "To say the truth, as no known inhabitant of this globe is really more than man, so none need to be ashamed of submitting to what the necessities of man demand..." [21]

Fielding's close attention to all the "base" details of the daily routine of his countrymen is fundamentally justified in his "comic epic-poems" by his endeavour to achieve the aesthetic "rehabilitation" of the real life of Englishmen of his day by raising it to the level of something worthy of artistic depiction. Shortly before his death Fielding makes an interesting confession in his *Journal of a Voyage to Lisbon* (1754): "and for my part I must confess I should have honoured and loved Homer more had he written a true history of his own times in humble prose, than those noble poems that have so justly collected the praise of all ages". [22] Surely it is precisely this that both Fielding and Gogol are endeavouring to do, by turning to "humble prose", Fielding in his "comic epic-poems" and Gogol in his *poema*?

When he describes his works as *histories,* and thereby equates himself with a historian, much as Gogol is to do when he describes himself in *Dead Souls* as the "historian of the events presented herewith" (VI, 36), Fielding is in fact emphasizing above all the inner regularity of narrative as one of the most important features of the new genre whose creator he proudly considered himself. The apparent "trifles" of everyday life often provide the reader of Fielding's works with a clue to the character of the hero or decisively influence the latter's fate. Taken in their totality they constitute a vivid image of mid-eighteenth century England, which to this day has attracted historians for its authenticity.

If the concept of a "comic epic-poem in prose" meant for Fielding above all the artist's right to introduce into his narrative the "base" material of ordinary life, the role of "historian" signified, as it did for Gogol, the necessity to *generalize* this world of ordinariness.

He does not want his work to be "a newspaper". The "epic" exposition of events entails, in his mind, not only being loyal to the facts but generalizing them and revealing the dramatic inner contradictions of their development.

Thus, departing from the usual structure of the picaresque novel along the biographical principle (a system Fielding openly scorned) he brings onto the scene an elderly curate Adams and his two young friends—Joseph Andrews and his betrothed, leaving it up to the reader to reconstruct their past histories from the few cursory items of essential information he is granted, and in *Tom Jones* he boldly skips years at a time in his account of the childhood and youth of his hero, in order to precipitate his reader into the thick of things. Thus too does Gogol devote practically the entire first volume of *Dead Souls* to the events of a few days spent by his hero in the town of N., relegating Chichikov's prehistory, once again contrary to all the rules of the picaresque novel, to the eleventh and last chapter of the volume.

It is well known that Gogol firmly insisted on the significance of even the most seemingly trivial events in his *poema*, on that hidden inner meaning which the reader is supposed to discern through the "apparent uninterrupted trivia of life" (XII, 91). Such declarations were also frequently made by Fielding.

The deliberate inner harmony and regularity of the narration, which constitutes the essential feature of Fielding's "comic epic-poem", is equally removed from the chaotic variety of the picaresque novel and the subjective fragmentation of Sterne's *Tristram Shandy,* in which the action is dominated by the author's reflexes. In this respect, too, there is a close similarity between the author of *Joseph Andrews* and *Tom Jones* and Gogol.

The range of typological analogies noted above between Gogol's poema and Fielding's "comic-epic poem" as well as cognate phenomena in the English Enlightenment novel would be incomplete without mention of the more highly important feature of the works being compared, viz. the role played in them by humour and satire and the form that these take in the narrative.

As is apparent from the very definition of his "comic epic-poem", Fielding had decreed that humour was to set the tone of his work. It is indicative that in the list of his inspirers and mentors the author of *Tom Jones* should include such masters of satire and humour as Aristophanes and Lucian, Rabelais, Shakespeare and Cervantes, Ben Jonson, Molière and Swift. Fielding's interpretation of the role of comedy in literature in many respects anticipates the views of Gogol. The idea of the great power of laughter in the fight against social and individual vice runs throughout Fielding's work. Affectation (arising either from vanity or from hypocrisy) is proclaimed in the foreword to *Joseph Andrews* as "the only source of the true ridiculous". The tongue-in-cheek irony of his "comic epic-poems in prose" is permeated with philosophical reflections about man and society.

This attitude to comedy is remarkably close to that espoused by Gogol, who considered laughter to be the only honest character in his *Government Inspector* and wrote with great feeling in *Dead Souls* of "high, enthusiastic laughter", which is divided "by an entire chasm" from the "grimacing of a fairground jester" (VI, 134).

Situation comedy, which plays a large part both with Fielding and Gogol, is still of secondary importance for both writers, especially Gogol. A much more important role is accorded, both in Fielding's "comic epic-poem" and in *Dead Souls,* by a comedy of relativity, based on the contrasting appearance and reality of characters and their activities. In Fielding's case this is most apparent in *Tom Jones,* his most mature and accomplished work. In this process the effect achieved both by Gogol and Fielding, through a constant interplay of the images of the two worlds of reality and appearance, would be incomplete if it were not intensified and supported by the author's constant presence in the person of an *ironic* observer, chronicler and commentator of all the proceedings. This question will be explored more fully below, when we consider the characters of *Dead Souls* in comparison to those of a number of West European novelists of varying typological closeness to Gogol. But even here, in discussing the special genre of Gogol's work, it is essential that we note the caustic irony of the narrative, an inherent feature of Fielding's work too, manifested in the dead-pan way the author records the basest and most vulgar details, in the apparent deference, even unction, displayed in the depiction of patently futile and worthless occupations, conversations and interests pursued by the heroes, in the cunning way the author has his characters from time to time play the most decorous roles until their masks are reft from them to reveal their true faces. The devious Blifil and deferential Chichikov, as we shall see below, have numerous affinities not only in their manners and desires, but also in the way they are described by their creators and in the ironic atmosphere that surrounds them in the narrative.

The problem of the corruption of human nature by the passions which steadily erode it had already been confronted by Fielding. Alongside the petty tyranny, cruelty and wilfulness of his landed gentry and aristocrats, an equally menacing role is played in his "histories" by vices which are more the product of bourgeois greed than a relic of the feudal order. Through his books files an entire procession of "masters" and "acquirers", to use Gogol's terminology, led by the supremely decorous figure of Mr. Blifil, who for the sake of his uncle's fortune is ready to send his own brother to the gallows, and the "Great" swindler Jonathan Wild. Almost as if anticipating Gogol's generalizing, "transforming" realism, Fielding aimed with his Jonathan Wild to show "roguery, and not a rogue", proceeding from the isolated fact to a type of social and political evil.

Enlightened thinkers in Russia even in the eighteenth century applauded this archetypal breadth of Fielding's satirical images, which enabled the reader to see in his "histories", or "comic epic-poems", the reflection of important social processes traced by the author.

"...Everywhere there is profit, vainglory, hypocrisy or frivolity; everywhere there are Blifils..."[23] wrote Andrian Gribovsky, author of an essay "Expression of Gratitude to Mr Fielding for Tom Jones".

The History of Jonathan Wild the Great presents an even fuller, "transforming" and ironically allegorical account of the nefarious doings of an *isolated* swindler and rogue.

The very principle of such a generalizing, allegorical approach to his theme and plot in Fielding's story of a criminal has an obvious similarity with the design of *Dead Souls*, with its allegorical, "hidden" meaning, to which Gogol repeatedly alluded. For all the difference in content and structure of these works their respective authors are guided by a single desire: namely, to describe significant and disturbing social phenomena through isolated and trivial facts.

Feelding's unique position in English Enlightenment literature is due to the fact that, in contrast to the majority of his contemporaries, he was beginning to realise that freeing man from the scourge of ignorance, barbarism and tyranny might as yet be insufficient for the true emancipation of the individual and that the soul-destroying pursuit of material gain was no less disastrous for human dignity than class inequality or religious fanaticism.

In his "comic epic-poems" it is already possible to make out—with a retrospective knowledge of the subsequent development of English literature—certain new social tendencies connected with economic shifts in the English provinces and the transference of property from one owner to another.

With Smollett's *The Expedition of Humphry Clinker* (1771), written shortly before the author's death and after the industrial revolution had started, the English Enlightenment novel extended its limits still further and furnished its readers with varied pictures of social changes taking place all over the country. The old landed estates were going to ruin. Some of them were even housing the newly appeared factories, and the din of machinery, reverberating all the way to the local graveyard, disturbed the slumbers of the noble ancestors of the now impoverished and degenerate families. The novel's hero, the englightened but jaundiced Matthew Bramble, is amazed and alarmed by the destruction of the old class distinctions and by the rapid acquisition of wealth by traders and businessmen.

This fearful premonition of the ominous, even "demonic" changes distorting the former aspect and life of the country out of all recognition imparts to Smollett's novel features of historicism which were as yet lacking in Fielding's "comic epic-poems". We can observe a certain similarity here between the views manifested here of one of the last English Enlightenment writers and the standpoint of Gogol. The later Smollett, like the Gogol of *Dead Souls,* Volume 2, was exasperated by the ubiquitous greed, vanity, parasitism and decay of the good old moral foundations, and at the same time the English writer admired the magnanimity of a certain Mr Brown, who resolved to employ the fortune he had amassed in the East Indies, by setting up "a manufacture ... to give employment and bread to the industrious". [24] In a similar vein Gogol inveighs against factories and the false needs they propagate amongst the people to the detriment of their natural industry and morality, yet makes an exception of Kostanzhoglo, who "derives profit from any rubbish" (VII, 68), and for Murazov, whose millions have been amassed in an allegedly blameless manner. This similarity can hardly be dismissed as a coincidence, but is more probably the product in both cases of a collision between the Enlightenment ideals of a simple, "natural" life of positive activity and harsh reality, which left no place for such ideals.

As we can see, both the "comic epic-poem" of Fielding and its close cousin Smollett's satirical novel of manners, are by no means confined to a mere depiction of private mores, but represented these against a broad social background which was also fairly differentiated for its time. Furthermore, as we have already noted above, the author retains the apparent objective nature of the narrative only to reserve his absolute right to make satirical judgements, sly, derogatory insinuations and ironic "plaudits" which are more lethal than the most direct denunciation. Smollett achieves the same effect by usually having his argumentative characters persuade and dissuade one another in word and deed, deriving the lessons of life's wisdom from their own experience. Fielding takes this mission on himself.

Heinrich Heine, a great master of satire and irony, recognized in Fielding a kindred spirit. In his *Die Romantische Schule,* when he discusses Fielding, Heine singles out the scornful and denunciatory spirit of his work. The author "at once leads us into the wings, he shows us the deceptive rouge concealing all feelings, the coarse springs activating the most gentle deeds, he reveals the colophony which will at some later stage flash with the lightning of animated fervour, the kettledrums with their drumsticks peacefully resting on them, which later will pound out the mighty thunders of passion; in other words, he *shows* us the entire inner mechanism, all that *great lie which makes people appear to us other than they are in reality*". [25] This description, whose intensity of feeling is to some extent itself a product of that Romantic fervour at once disputed and shared by Heine, is in fact applicable both to the Enlightenment "comic epic-poems" of Fielding and, to an even greater extent, to Gogol's *Dead Souls*.

The role of the author in the works we have been comparing has another similarity, too. Both Fielding and Gogol are not merely "present" throughout the action alongside their characters, reminding the reader of their presence with the ironic touches in the descriptions, and with what we might call their authorial comments, which constitute an inherent part of the narrative. In addition, they both arrogate to themselves, in bold violation of the apparent "objectivity" of the exposition, the right to engage the reader in direct conversation—conversation that is by no means confined to the described events, but ranges over everything that strikes them as of vital importance. In *The History of Tom Jones* Fielding contrives, through the structure of the work, to motivate these digressions. To each of the eighteen books of his "comic epic-poem" he prefaces a special introductory chapter, usually with a deliberately comic title and discussing with light-hearted irony but often great inner seriousness questions of morality and aesthetics which particularly concern him. In these introductory chapters Fielding finds a means of vesting his Enlightenment didactics in the form of a witty and invariably natural (irrespective of the grave subject matter) "essay", which is interpolated into his "epic" narrative, partially elucidating the narrative and partially assisting a deliberate and well-calculated retardation of the action, which is sometimes interrupted at the most dramatic moment for the hero or heroine.

Gogol's authorial digressions are only partially comparable with those in Fielding's "comic epic-poems". The Enlightenment view of the exalted cognitive and "edifying" significance of art, a view which Gogol himself espoused and maintained to the end of his life, brings his position close to that of Fielding. Both writers recognize and exercise their right to converse aloud with the reader, to take issue with their more unscrupulous critics and to defend their ideal of truthful and honest art.

Fielding's digressions are written with a predominantly didactic and humorous intonation. As far as the author's feelings are concerned, these are usually manifested in the parodistic form of "travesty", turned "upside down", as for example, in Fielding's well-known appeal to the "buxom dame", from whom the author seeks his inspiration (in place of the traditional ethereal and idealized Muse of Antiquity) or in the absurdly high-flown passage, bursting with mythological allusions, which anticipates the reader's acquaintance with the heroine of this "comic epic-poem",

Sophia Western. As an Enlightenment writer and humanist Fielding was not disposed to despise deep and serious feelings; he has his own sacred convictions, which he steadfastly defends. But given the existing disposition of literary forces in his time he was inclined to treat starry-eyed tirades and lachrymose sentiment with the utmost suspicion, believing that they hindered a truthful and natural portrayal of life.

It must be remembered that an entire literary age—the Romantic age—lay between the "comic epic-poem" and Gogol's *Dead Souls*. The profound and fundamental differences between Gogol's *poema* and its distant prototypes in English Enlightenment literature are perhaps nowhere so pronounced and graphically evident as in the variety and flexibility of his emotional shades, in the immense range of intonation, reaching from the sternly prophetic, full of profound drama, to the mundane, undemanding tone of friendly confidences, which, however, carries an explosive charge of derision concealed in its subtext. From "sacred horror" (to employ a phrase of Pushkin's), inspired intuition, lyrical elation we are suddenly precipitated in abrupt changes of mood and imagery to an imperturbably ironic depiction of the vulgar daily existence of worthless drifters and idlers. It is this that most significantly divides *Dead Souls* from the age of the Enlightenment and sets strictly defined limits to any typological similarity between Gogol's *poema* and the "comic epic-poems" or satirical novels of mores created by the English Enlihtenment writers of the eighteenth century. Another, no less essential distinction can be seen in the *historicism of Gogol's writing*.

In both respects *Dead Souls* demands comparison with the aesthetic theories of the Romantics, and, accordingly, with the literature of the Romantic age.

3

The name of Sir Walter Scott is of course one of the first to come to mind in this connection.

Gogol (who in his correspondence and conversations with friends was in general very reticent—by comparison to Byron or Pushkin, for example—about his own reading and views on other writers) mentioned no other Western writer of his own era so frequently or with such invariable admiration as he did the "Scottish enchanter". *

In his article "Schlözer, Miller and Herder", published in the 1835 collection *Arabesques,* but dated as early as 1832, Gogol concludes a comparative analysis of the works of these "great architects of universal history" (VIII, 85) with his reflections on the qualities that their successor would need to possess, if, combining the merits of the three listed historians and even surpassing them, he were to be able to answer all 'that world history required". Characterically Gogol's mind turns to three great names from literature. His ideal historian would command the "dramatic interest" of Schiller, possess the "Shakespearian art of developing the strong lines of character in narrow limits" and combine these with "some of the diverting power of Scott's narrative and his ability to observe the very finest nuances" (VIII, 89).

In an outspoken article "On the Movement of Journal Literature in 1834 and 1835", printed in Pushkin's journal *Sovremennik* (Contemporary) (1836) and intended as a contribution to the polemic with the journal *Biblioteka dlya chteniya* (Library for Reading) and its main contributor and editor Senkovsky (Brambeus)—subsequently one of the most hostile critics of *Dead Souls*—the young Gogol refers several times to Scott, fiercely defending him against unjust and unscrupulous attacks.

To demonstrate Senkovsky's unprincipled behaviour ("...for him a review is not a matter of conviction and feeling, it is merely the consequence of mood and circumstances") Gogol adduces as one of the first and most eloquent examples Senkovsky's review article on Scott. "Walter Scott," writes Gogol with indignation, "this great genius, *whose immortal creations* embrace life with such fullness, Walter Scott is called a charlatan. And this has been read by Russia, this has been said to people of education, people who have already read Walter Scott" (VIII, 160; my italics.—*A.Y.*).

Scott's name appears again in the concluding section of the article and here too in a most important context. Ac-

---

* As an eighteen-year-old at the Nezhin Lyceum Gogol sent his sister a Russian translation of Scott's *Lord of the Isles* (October 1827) regarding the publication of this translation as a major literary event.

cusing this time not only *Biblioteka dlya chteniya* but also other journals such as *Moskovsky telegraf* and *Moskovsky nablyudatel* (Moscow Observer) of lacking "guide-lines", of an interest in "shallow matters", he supports this accusation with an entire list of significant subjects and events which, in his opinion, should have been commented on by their critics but which were ignored.

The first item in this list of complaints voiced by the young Gogol against the entire Russian periodical press, is directly concerned with Scott. "An illustrious Scotsman has died, a *great chronicler of the heart, nature and life;* the most complete, extensive genius of the nineteenth century" (VIII, 171; my italics.—*A.Y.*). "But," continues Gogol, "were we told by our journals, guided as they are by such strict deliberation, who Walter Scott was, in what his influence consisted, what contemporary French literature is, whence and how it came about, what occasioned the false deviation in taste and of what nature it was? Why poetry has given way to prose compositions?.. All we have done is to abuse Walter Scott" (VIII, 172).

Gogol's letters from abroad written at the time he was planning and working on *Dead Souls,* Volume 1 also demonstrate that Scott was indeed his constant companion in his daily life and work in this period.

"I am undertaking to re-read all Walter Scott, and then perhaps, I shall take up the pen" (XI, 60), he writes to Pogodin from Geneva on the 23rd of August 1836. In a letter to Zhukovsky of the 12th of November of that year two new names appear alongside that of Scott. Gogol recalls how in his Swiss seclusion he has "set about re-reading... Molière, Shakespeare, and Walter Scott... Lovely autumn weather has at last come to Vevey, practically like summer. It has become quite warm in my room and I have set to work on *Dead Souls,* which I began in St. Petersburg. I have redone everything, thought out the entire plan more thoroughly and I am now calmly writing it out, like a chronicle" (XI, 73).

The quotations given above might at first appear superfluous, but it is worth examining them more closely. For a start they establish beyond any doubt that Gogol was both profoundly interested in, and sympathetic to, Scott. But in addition, we can observe in them—and sometimes also in their context, which we shall be looking at later—the *special,* even selective nature of this interest, which makes it possible to determine more exactly wherein the typological similarity between Gogol's *poema* and the novels of the "author of 'Waverley'" (as for many years Scott introduced himself to his public) consists.

We might note right away the strange fact that Gogol never once, in his mentions of Scott (not even when placing him on equal footing with professional *historians* like Schlözer, Miller and Herder) deems it necessary to dwell on the genre of Scott's works as historical novels, or, roughly speaking, *novels about the past*. From the late 1830s onwards, i.e. from the time of Gogol's most substantial comments about Scott, the literary experience accumulated in the latter's novels is most closely related in Gogol's thinking to those of his own projects which are concerned with the present day of Russia, and not with the past, or with foreign ways.

Ah yes, someone might object, but what about *Taras Bulba*, what about *Rome*? A detailed study of these works lies beyond the bounds of the present work, but we should at least point out that in both these works Gogol displays as many points of difference—moreover, of a substantial degree—from Scott as he does similarities with him. *Rome* is the fragment of an unfinished novel that was published (on Pogodin's insistence and against Gogol's wishes) in the journal *Moskovityanin* (The Muscovite) (1842, No. 3), and although its date of publication almost coincides with that of *Dead Souls* it actually belongs in spirit and style to a much earlier—Romantic—period of Gogol's work. From a typological point of view it is more comparable with novels popular at that time with educated Russian readers such as Mme de Staël's *Corinne ou l'Italie* (1807), in which, as in the introductory section of *Rome*, pride of place is accorded to the study of the comparative and historically conditioned features of the national cultures, national characters, and the roads of national development of the different West European countries.

Rome remained unfinished, displaced by Gogol's absorption in *Dead Souls*. However, in a letter to Shevyryov (1st of September 1843) in which Gogol answers critical remarks by Belinsky about the anti-democratic, tendentious quality of *Rome*, Gogol offers an explanation of the idea behind his unfinished novel. What is particularly interesting here is his anxiety to distinguish between himself and his hero. "He (Belinsky.—*A.Y.*) would have a prince in

Rome hold the same view of Paris and the French as he does himself. I would be at fault if I were to ascribe even to the prince of Rome the same view that I hold of Paris, because I, although I may share artistic tastes with my hero, cannot share his opinion. I belong to a living modern nation, and he to one extinct. The idea of the novel was not at all bad. The aim was to show the significance of a nation that had had its day, and that had lived splendidly by contrast to present nations. Although initially, of course, it is impossible to conclude anything definitely, it is still evident that what counts is the impression made by the growing maelstrom of a new society on one for whom the modern age practically does not exist" (XII, 211). These remarks made in explanation of an already abandoned project, are also more reminiscent of the principles of Mme de Staël's novel (an attempt at a generalized description of the national spirit of a nation through a Romantic narrative) than of the far more analytic and measured method of Scott the novelist, with its constant weighing of social and historical pros and cons.

In his historical novels Scott almost invariably proceeds from a dialectical analysis of conflicting social forces. At the same time, whilst observing the past (particularly when concerned with the history of Scotland and England) in the light of the present, Scott was inclined to interpret the entire historical process, the various stages of which feature in his novels, as a constant process, albeit achieved through bloody and agonizing struggle, of the *resolution* of conflicts through compromise. Thus in *Ivanhoe* the conflicts between the Norman "Conquerors" and the conquered, but not subdued, Saxons are "resolved". In *Woodstock* the restoration of the Stuarts proves to be a natural consequence of the tyrannical excesses of Cromwell's dictatorship. And in *Old Mortality* the fierce struggle of the Royalists under Claverhouse against the insurgent Puritans led by the frenzied tyrant-hater Balfour of Burley plays, from the historical point of view, the role of a prologue to the state revolution, which found a political compromise by ousting the last Stuart king and putting William of Orange in his place, leaving all the power in the hands of the leading financiers and landowners. This ironic dialectic twist of history, in which—as related in Scott's novels—neither side really wins, true victory going to the middle path of compromise, is not given great emphasis by the author himself. Scott, who is generous both in description and in the psychological motivation of his characters' actions, does not permit himself the luxury of extended authorial excursuses of a philosophical or historical nature (as, for example, we find in the works of Hugo). But this idea emerges from the majority of his novels with sufficient clarity and consistency.

The disposition of his characters and their role in the plot is determined accordingly. Scott himself poked fun at the insipid figures of his "cavaliers" and their sweethearts. But—with very few exceptions, notable amongst these being such remarkable novels as *The Bride of Lammermoor* and *St. Ronan's Well*—it is the flimsy craft of precisely these characters that remains afloat on the turbulent waters of life and reaches harbour in the "happy" endings of Scott's novels. Robin Hood with his band of merry men, Rob Roy and his rebellious clan of McGregors, the gypsy girl Meg Merrilies who in the name of her persecuted kinsmen curses the entire breed of hostile landowners, Balfour of Burley, fanatically irreconcilable enemy of the Stuarts and the episcopalian church, who leads the Scottish peasantry in a rebellion against them—all these vivid and picturesque characters who embody the rebellious passions seething within the *people,* perform an important but nonetheless strictly limited function in the plot of Scott's novels. They appear when necessary, in order to tighten the knot of conflicts which determines the fate of the protagonists, and they withdraw into the wings or die when they have completed their allotted mission.

What could be more different from this portrayal of the stormy, freedom-loving and proud passions of the people than the manner in which they are represented in Gogol's *Taras Bulba*!

The terrible judgement passed by the father on his traitor son would hardly have found a place amongst the pictures painted by Scott. The *Setch* with its panache and daring, its wild revelry and daredevil bravery, would have receded into the background, although it would still have featured amongst the colourful scenes that Scott describes so well. The end of the story might have been given a note of reconciliation: it would suffice to shift the action to one of the periods in Ukrainian history when the *Setch* (as Gogol himself recalls) concluded a temporary peace with Poland, in order that the union between Andriy and his beloved should not seem too impossible. But this hypothetical, "Waverley" version of *Taras Bulba* would forfeit one of Gogol's important principles, namely everything connected with the sacred notion of "comradeship" and patriotic beliefs which go hand-in-hand with this notion.

However tempting it may be to draw direct analogies between Gogol as a master of *historical* narrative and Scott as precisely a *historical* novelist in the proper sense of the word, as far as *Taras Bulba* is concerned these analogies seem highly doubtful. Gogol's story surely owes more to the traditional ballads (*dumas*) and legends of the Ukraine, and not in its motifs but also in the spirit of their artistic interpretation.

As for *Dead Souls,* paradoxical though it may seem, I believe Gogol shows more similarity with Scott in this *poema,* designed to capture *contemporary* Russian life, especially if Scott's legacy is not viewed in the narrow aspect of evolving the *genre of the historical* novel, but far more broadly, as did both Belinsky and Balzac in their day.

"Walter Scott is also to be taken seriously: this man gave a historical and social direction to recent European art,"[26] wrote Belinsky. He also proclaimed, on two separate occasions, the direct connection between the Scottish novelist and Gogol. "We believe that Gogol was not descended from Homer at all, nor is he distantly related to him; we believe he is descended from Walter Scott, from that Walter Scott who was able to happen entirely on his own, without Gogol, but without whom Gogol could not have happened,"[27] he wrote in a polemic answer to Konstantin Aksakov's pamphlet, repeating this same idea almost verbatim when replying to Aksakov's objections several months later: "There would have been no Gogol without Walter Scott; and ... if we can compare Gogol with anyone at all, then it is of course with Walter Scott, to whom he, like all modern novelists, owes so much ..."[28]

Making allowances for the polemic ardour of these lines, we should single out in them not so much the idea of Scott's direct influence on Gogol as the indication, so much more fruitful from the point of view of our topic, of Gogol's closeness to Scott. The key to the character of this closeness, of the common ground shared by the two writers, is to be found in a number of observations made by Belinsky during the same polemic. These include the most general definition, according to which "the novel ... is the epic of the modern world, historically produced and developed by life itself and now acting as its mirror"[29] and a direct comparison between Gogol's epic and Scott's epic, once again made polemically after a quotation from Aksakov's pamphlet. "'Gogol's *poema*'", quotes Belinsky, "'offers us an entire form of life ... a world, which appears to us as a profound whole, the profound, inner content of *universal life,* connecting with a single spirit all its phenomena.'" After quoting this observation Belinsky once again rejects the parallel with Homer on which Aksakov insists and continues: "But, in the first place, this is as much a description of Gogol's epic as of the epic of Walter Scott, with the mere difference that it is precisely Walter Scott's epic which has this content of *universal life,* while with Gogol this 'universal life' only appears as a suggestion, as a conjecture provoked by the *total absence* of anything universal in the life he portrays. There can be no objection to this: it is self-evident. Just consider: what *universal life* is there in the Chichikovs, Selifans, Manilovs, Plyushkins, Sobakeviches and all that fine coterie who engage the reader's attention with their vulgarity in *Dead Souls*?"[30]

The concluding part of this last quotation returns us to those doubts and reservations which were dimly aroused, as a "conjecture", in Belinsky by Gogol's avowed intention, expressed in Volume 1, to extend the horizons of *Dead Souls* and introduce into it new—"ideal"—characters. Belinsky was afraid that Gogol would follow the Slavophiles by depicting an idealized and imaginary patriarchal Russia, primordial and united. Hence the excessive imbalance of his concluding opposition of Gogol to Scott—as if the "universal life" in the society depicted by Scott, the relatively recent Scotland of the eighteenth century, or mediaeval England and France, were not also woven from a conflicting mesh of social, class and private interests, whether recognized as such, or still only stirring and as yet unexpressed... And as if, as they approached the nineteenth century—in *The Surgeon's Daughter* and *St. Ronan's Well*—Scott's novels did not also show with increasing clarity that same egoistic "fragmentation" of character, the same power exercised by acquisitive lusts, that so disturbed Gogol. *

---

* It is noteworthy that Belinsky, when reflecting on Scott's

But elsewhere Belinsky correctly assesses the close relation between Gogol and Scott, particularly in the endeavour of both writers to capture "universal life" in all its breadth. It is not the reconstruction of the past, but above all the *fullness* of his portrayal of life that so impressed the future author of *Dead Souls* in Sir Walter Scott: for it was to just such a full portrayal of contemporary Russian life that he was to aspire himself.

When assessing Scott's achievement as an innovatory novelist his most perceptive western readers (including the historians of his day, who had so much to thank him for) felt that he had returned to literature concepts and images of the people, nation and country which had not been featured with such vividness since the time of Shakespeare. As a Russian writer Gogol did not need the stimulating example of the author of "Waverley": he could draw from the great patriotic tradition of Russian poetry and prose which extended back from Pushkin deep into the eighteenth century—to Radishchev, Derzhavin, Lomonosov. His debt to these writers is clearly acknowledged in his articles on Russian literature. We should however note that Gogol, following in Pushkin's footsteps, concurs with Scott in many respects whilst continuing this intrinsically Russian tradition.

It is of interest that one of the very first oblique references to Scott in Gogol's letters is concerned precisely with Scott's interpretation of the role of the people in history.

---

novels in another connection, should point out features in them which are also particularly characteristic of Dead Souls, Volume 1: "His novels," he writes of Scott, "were a mirror of reality in which reality was more like itself than if it had remained mere reality. In his novels you sometimes encounter villains, but you understand why they are villains and you sometimes take an interest in their fate. For the most part in his novels you come across petty scoundrels, who are the source of all the misfortune in the novels, which is also the case in life itself. Heroes of good and evil are extremely rare in real life, and the masters in life are people in the middle, not one thing nor the other" (Op. cit., Vol. VI, p. 35). This aspect of Scott's work, so neatly described by Belinsky, at once recalls to us the selection of characters in Gogol's *poema* as well as the reasons the author himself gives for his reluctance to take the hackneyed "virtuous man" as his hero, and for his contrary preference for people who are "not one thing nor the other" and "petty rogues", like Chichikov himself, who, moreover, to judge from the fragments of Volume 2, might have grown into a true "villain"...

When Scott's *Life of Napoleon,* in which the Scottish writer correctly identifies the great swell of patriotism as the primary reason for Napoleon's defeat in Russia, was translated into Russian, the journal *Moskovsky telegraf* (1833, No. 9) published a review by Ksenofont Polevoi, who took issue with Scott and rejected the popular nature of the Patriotic war of 1812. Gogol ridiculed this article by Polevoi in a letter to Pogodin on the 20th of February 1835. Berating the mismanagement of the editors of the journal *Moskovsky nablyudatel* he sarcastically exclaims: "I doubt whether there was ever unanimity and self-sacrifice in Moscow, and I am beginning to believe that Polevoi might be right when he says that the 1812 war was not a national event at all and that Moscow was innocent of it" (X, 353). Subsequently, in *Dead Souls,* Volume 2, the 1812 war was to play an important role as precisely a "national event" in the conversations of the heroes and in revealing the characters of Tentetnikov, Betrishchev and Ulenka.

Balzac's foreword to *La Comédie humaine,* dated July 1842, after the publication of *Dead Souls,* Volume 1, contains a memorable eulogy of Scott as the writer who raised the novel to the level of a philosophy of history, and Balzac justifies his own ambitious attempt to reconstruct contemporary French society in all its social variety by citing the great achievement of Scott. Balzac and Gogol had much in common in their attitude to the legacy of Scott, resolving not to imitate him by "Walter-Scottizing" history (as Balzac ridicules this tendency in one of his articles) but by availing themselves of his experience of social and historical analysis of the past in their portrayal of the present.

It is surely this that Gogol had in mind when he undertook to re-read "all of Walter Scott" in Geneva, before returning to his work on *Dead Souls.* His later remark that, having carefully thought out the plan of *Dead Souls* he was now "calmly writing it out, like a chronicle" is entirely consistent with our hypothesis that the epic principle inherent in the novels of Scott could well have porvided the stimulus for the creation of *Dead Souls.*

Scott's novels, like Gogol's *poema,* reveal a certain typological similarity with the Enlightenment novel of manners and the satirical novel which had such a heyday in eighteenth century English literature. Scott's fascinating articles on Fielding and Smollett eloquently demonstrate how close these writers were to him in many ways. There is, in particular, a remarkable comparison of the "histories" of Fielding to a river, which as it meanders smoothly along reflects everything on its banks: this image in itself shows how profoundly aware Scott was of the significance of Fielding's work as realism. It is interesting—particularly in the context of Gogol's above-quoted remarks not only on Scott, but also on the creators of "lesser varieties of the epic" —that Byron, a great admirer of Scott, bestowed on him two expressive epithets which together encapsulate the two tendencies intertwined in the work of the great Scotsman. In his verse he hails him as the "Ariosto of the North", and in his prose "the Scottish Fielding".

As a writer Scott stood on the threshold between Romanticism and realism. His realistic, rationally comprehensible perception and reconstruction of historical events and of the motives of the "makers of history", blithely unaware that the results of their actions would suddenly conflict violently with their own private incentives and goals, was one of the great achievements of Scott the novelist. But this "rational kernel" can only be artificially "husked" from the picturesque, poetic, and sometimes even fantastic context in which Scott places it, and at the total expense of the over-all, integral aesthetic effect of the novels. Scott's Romanticism is more than the mere window-dressing provided by the tourneys and donjons, beautiful maidens, improbable disguises and masquerades or bold anachronisms such as, for example, in *Ivanhoe* where Ulrica, who as a young girl falls into the power of the Norman conquerors at the time of the 1066 invasion, survives into the reign of William's great-great-grandson, Richard the Lionheart (1189-1199). It is something much more serious and significant: a deep empathy with the poetry of the people, of their life and spirit as it is captured in their folklore, their customs, beliefs, superstitions, proverbs and songs.

Augustin Thierry, whose historical method was formed under the direct influence of Scott, once wrote that he regarded the author of *Ivanhoe* "the greatest master of historical *divination* who has ever lived." We should remark this word "divination" and recall the concept of *ugadyvanie,* which translates as divination, that Gogol considered so essential in his poetics.

Another concept which is equally vital to an understanding of the poetic charm of Scott's novels is the awareness —once again derived from Romanticism—of the fusion of nature and history, an awareness that informs all his novels. Fielding recalls both in *Joseph Andrews* and, in greater detail, in the early chapters of *Tom Jones*, the beautiful landscapes of his native Somerset. But even the most attentive reader would have difficulty forming a visual picture of these landscapes, so general and conventional are the descriptions and so unrelated to the action of these books. Smollett in *The Expedition of Humphrey Clinker*, the first book to anticipate Scott by showing signs of historicism in the depiction of the social and national movements and conflicts of his age, makes far more use of landscape in his narrative. But even here landscape plays a predominantly auxiliary, decorative role.

Landscape acquired immense significance in the narrative prose, as it did in the poetry of sentimentalism. With its emotional colouring and dramatism it ceases to be a mere backcloth for the action in, for example, *The Sorrows of Young Werther* or *Julie, ou la nouvelle Héloïse,* but actively participates in it, either soothing the heroes' spiritual storms or responding ominously to them and hastening the fateful denouement... But with Scott nature does not enter the characters' spiritual world as a mere lyrical principle: it actually constitutes an inalienable part of the *epic* narrative. In Scott's novels we encounter a form of "historical geography". The landscape and buildings inform us about the past and the present of the people, about memorable acts of heroism or treachery, about battles fought long ago and the seething passions of the present day about to explode into action.

In this respect Scott's novels can be seen to have much in common with the principles of representation adopted by Gogol in *Dead Souls*. The two writers have a shared desire to apprehend the true character of the people and special nature of its destiny in its moeurs and in its actions, in its historical traditions and in the very land on which it lives. It was with good reason that the young Gogol, repeating his insistence on the special "fullness" of Scott's genius, should have listed together the three most important aspects of his work: to him Scott was "a great chronicler of the heart, of nature and of life". Indeed, was it not towards this kind of synthetic and single-minded depiction of Russia, in which the poetry and prose of the nation's life would be presented to the reader in their contradictory interfusion that Gogol himself also strove in *Dead Souls,*

We must note yet another vital similarity between Scott's novels and Gogol's *poema,* and, more broadly, between the two writers' aesthetic views. This is their profound and passionate love for folk poetry, and above all folk song. They were both keen collectors and students of folklore. For both of them folk song was a living monument of the people's history. "A stone with an eloquent bas-relief, with a historical inscription, is nothing against this living, talking chronicle which informs us about the past," wrote Gogol. "In this respect the songs of Malorossia* are everything: they are poetry, and history, and the graves of our fathers." In them we find reflected "the true way of life, elements of the character, all the variations and shades of feeling, of the excitement, suffering and merry-making of the people they portray..." (VIII, 91). Very similar remarks about folk-song can be found in the writings of Walter Scott.

Accordingly, both Gogol and Scott make extensive use of genuine folk songs and variations or arrangements of folkloric art in their own writings. Scott's cycle of Scottish novels is punctuated throughout by snatches of ballad and folk song, sometimes forming part of the dialogue and hepling to characterize the protagonists, sometimes included in the form of an epigraph, as it were from the author himself, anticipating the coming events and reconstructing their atmosphere. We hardly need dwell here on the role of folk song in Gogol's cycle *Village Evenings near Dikanka.* In the context of our theme it is perhaps more important to recall the way elements of music and song, a lyrical motif, are preserved even in Gogol's later works. Scholars have already pointed out the harsh dissonance created in the "prosaic", or rather, grotesque, context of *Diary of a Madman* by the unexpected system of tragic musical allusions in its closing passages: the jingling bells of a troika, a string resounding in the mist—and all this deep in the moonlit forest, and, next to that the sea, and Italy, on the one hand, and plain Russian huts, on the other... Thus does not all this usher in, as it were, the lyrical digressions in *Dead Souls,* in which Russian folk song rings out time and again, and in the most varied emotional contexts?

At the same time we are struck by an essential point

---

* The Ukraine.—*Ed.*

of difference. With Scott, as with the young Gogol of *Sorochintsy Fair, A Night in May, The Terrible Revenge,* song is either ethnographically authentic, or has at least an air of authenticity. The situation is quite different in *Dead Souls.* Here the words are hardly ever given (with the exception of those round songs performed by the "vociferous lasses" on Tentetnikov's estate). On the other hand, everything is determined by the context and the mood of author and reader, and is invested not only with literal meaning but also with—to employ a favourite word of Gogol's—"transforming", symbolic significance, which is often infinitely more capacious and expressive than those few, superficial words to which the author restricts himself.

At the one pole we find vulgarity, * which also raises its voice to sing its own glory. At the other: the people. This is the people not as embodied by the drunkard Selifan and the scarecrow Petrushka, or the stupid, muddleheaded Mityai and Minyai, but the people of all the Russian land, which Gogol can still see in the hinterground of his *poema,* with its vigour and daring, its thirst for "a life of freedom" or "the revelry of expansive living" (VI, 139). Here too—but in quite a different key—we hear a song, without which his figurative description of the turbulent festivities of the people and their onerous toil would be incomplete. A gang of boatmen make merry: they are singing and dancing, "the whole village square seethes with life" (VI, 139).

The association of the "endless" song with the infinite expanses of the Russian plain, prophesying the great destiny to the people—"Is this not the place for a legendary giant, here where there is the room for him to launch out and stride about?" (VI, 221)—this association has a vital role in the figurative system of *Dead Souls.* We encounter it later too, in Volume 2, when landowner Petukh arranges a sail on the lake for his guests and twelve oarsmen give voice to a song, "and it flowed as boundless as Russia herself" (VII, 55).

---

* "Poshlost"—a crucial concept in Gogol's work, combining the notions of affectation, vulgarity and banality. An extensive, if somewhat idiosyncratic, discussion of this word and its importance in Gogol's world can be found in Nabokov's *Gogol,* pp. 65-66. In this translation the inadequate but nearest English equivalent "vulgarity" has been used throughout. See also the note on p. 58—*Tr.*

The leitmotif of folk song as a kind of two-pronged symbol—of the artist's own deep bond with his native land, whose call he can hear in this refrain, and at the same time of the prophetic significance of this allusion to the hidden power latent in the bosom of the land—rings out most insistently and expressively in the eleventh chapter of Volume 1.

In this impassioned authorial digression we hear not just the doleful song of the coachman, but the voice of Russia herself, calling to the artist in his mighty flight of inspiration. "Why does there incessantly echo and re-echo in my ears the mournful song which drifts across your entire length and breadth, from sea to sea? What is the burden of that song? Why does it call, and sob, and catch at my heart?" Then all at once, a few lines on, he switches to a different tone, more down-to-earth, even humorous: "...and in your half-sleep you hear the coachman's song ... and the snorting of the horses, and the rattle of the wheels, and then you, too, are already snoring, squashing your fellow-passenger against the corner" (VI, 220-221). Finally, the strains of Russian folk-song enter the narrative again, complementing the superb symbolic description, in the closing passage of this same chapter, of the author's native land as a "swift troika, which no one can overtake" as it careers along the path of history. The coachman "stands up, cracks his whip, and bursts into a song"... And horses "catching the sound of the familiar song from above" with one accord strain their mighty chests... (VI, 246-247).

We are struck here, as earlier in the authorial digression from the same passage, by the bold modulation so typical of this work, by means of which an image veers from the exalted and sublime to the mundane and near-ridiculous and vice versa, without forfeiting any of its cogency or spontaneity.

The freedom with which Gogol expresses his lyrical rapture or lyrical indignation sharply distinguishes him from the far more tranquil, objective narrative manner of Scott. This freedom is far more typical of the meditative prose and essays of the Romantics (broadly speaking, from Wackenroder to Heine), or, if we turn to poetry, of the lyrical epic poem, particularly as exemplified in the work of the Romantics. Similarly, the sense of two worlds existing side by side which we find in Gogol's *poema*—the exalted world of the writer, with his prophetic vision, his visible laughter and invisible tears, with his sorrowful, ascetic solitude, his high creative "mysteries" and as yet unknown goals, on the one hand, and the world of base vulgarity, on the other —this same sense is surely also a legacy of Romanticism.

The very concept of vulgarity in its literary aspect has its own history, and the way it is treated by Gogol does much to explain the similarities between the author of *Dead Souls* and Romanticism, as well as the differences between them. *

Confining ourselves to the literature of the modern age it is perhaps possible to say that even the "Cervantesque", Enlightenment novels of Fielding, Smollett and others had lost to a great extent, if not entirely, that keen awareness, almost tragic in its intensity, of the contradiction between the vulgarity which reigns supreme in life, and the high, chivalrous and humanistic ideals at which it scoffs, so characteristic of Cervantes's epic novel. We are not even referring here so much to Sancho Panza, who, for all his practical grasp of affairs, displays a truly noble spirit. Vulgarity in *Don Quixote* is many-faced, and in the figures of the resplendent duke and duchess and their attendants it is no less—perhaps even more—repulsive than in all the sensible philistines, from the barber, priest and housemaid to the horde of inn-keepers, muleteers and alguazils who take up arms against the Knight of the Sorrowful Figure sustained by his great dream.

Real vulgarity can also be found in Fielding's "comic epic-poems", and in Smollett's satirical novels. But it is not as "vulgarity" that it is so interesting and disturbing

---

* Certain Western scholars working on Gogol regard the word *poshlost* as a quintessentially Russian concept, with no direct equivalent in other languages, and transliterate it rather than attempt a translation, Nabokov as "poshlust", Fanger (who defines the word as "complacent vulgarity") as "poshlost". This exotic "making strange" of the Russian word appears slightly forced. In any event, the philistinism derided by both Hoffman and Heine, the snobbery attacked by Thackeray and the bourgeois attitudes so repugnant to Flaubert are all variants of the same thing—or at least of closely related phenomena.

Vulgarity is also encountered in Shakespeare's plays as a clearly identified and tragically perceived category. We need only turn to *Hamlet*: Polonius, Rosenkrantz and Guildenstern, Osric—they all show various faces of vulgarity, all the more terrible because they embody the "norm", the "order" of a "time out of joint".

to these Enlightenment writers. From their point of view, a far more serious threat to the happiness of mankind is posed by tyrants and despots of all sizes—from Fielding's gallows-bird Jonathan Wild the Great (an archetype of all the celebrated invaders and aggressors, reaching right back to Alexander of Macedon and Julius Caesar) to the meanest tyrant of a landowner, bullying police captain or the judge with an itching palm. Alongside them there is an entire procession of people who pose no less a threat to mankind, who consciously hide behind a mask of virtue in order to cover up their mercenary aims. They are the hypocritical money grabbers like Fielding's Pounce, Blifil and others (in Smollett there is no counting them).

As for vanity, pettiness, complacent emptiness, querulousness, and foolishness—the true definitions of the word "vulgar"—they are all present in many forms in the realistic novels of the Enlightenment, but only as a comic background of everyday life which remains essentially unchanged throughout the development of the plot, and to which the denouement, no matter how it changes the lives of the main characters, does not introduce any particular alterations.

Only towards the end of the Enlightenment, when its conflicts deepened and new problems arose "like shadows of future events", to quote an English saying, vulgarity begins to take on a more generalized, definite form, appearing not simply as an accessory to a motley, multi-faceted life, but as a specific, aesthetic, psychological and, in part, social category.

In that sense, particularly noteworthy interpretations can be found in the works of two great writers of the 18th century, Laurence Sterne's *Tristram Shandy* and *Sentimental Journey*, and Denis Diderot's *Le Neveu de Rameau*.

Sterne purposely gave his first novel the polemic sounding title *The Life and Opinions of Tristram Shandy Gentleman*. The title itself indicates that the author's (and reader's) attention will not be centred around adventures or even specific events. A novel of "opinions" was an innovation, and by no means simply a formal one. It allowed man to apprehend the relativity of opinions of himself and those around him, and to look into the depths of his conscious mind, an area where, before Sterne, the novel of the eighteenth century Enlightenment hardly tred. This was the first appearance of discoveries which later generations of readers, particularly those during the period of Romanticism, were to interpret even tragically. Everyone remembers the poetic testimonial to Sterne in *The Romantic School* by Heine, who, using his cherished image of a broken heart, ascribed a bleeding heart which has experienced all the injuries of the world to the creator of Tristram and Yorick. That seems to be a romantic hyperbole, but it is indisputable that Sterne was the first writer of the Enlightenment to discern the various shades of vulgarity. Heine speaks of that in passing: "And while the author of *Tristram Shandy* sometimes lapses into the crudest of trivialities, he is also capable of reminding us of his regal dignity with sudden, majestic transitions." Meanwhile, those "crudest of trivialities", which are present not only in the actions of his characters, but in their thoughts as well, including those of the narrator, are the source of great aesthetic enjoyment for Sterne. This does not mean that he gets particular pleasure out of digging in filth—a stereotypic accusation of which generations of orthodox critics ascribed to Fielding, Byron and Gogol. In describing vulgarity in all its forms and aspects he realized that he created a new field of literature, and in his own way broadened the sphere of knowledge of human nature and human intelligence, according to classical terms of the Enlightenment. The owner of Shandy Hall, the cantankerous and stubborn old pedant Walter Shandy, reveling in his senseless oratory and riduculous schemes, and his laconic wife, who possesses the rare talent of blurting out her foolishness at the most inopportune moment, like most of their household, can take their places beside the Manilovs and Korobochka. Their lives are no less vulgar and empty. Even death, that great mystery, doesn't soften, but only serves to grotesquely increase that inevitable vulgarity. The scene when the family receives the news of the death of the old squire's eldest son and heir, Bobby Shandy, is one of the best in the novel.

In Gogol such an episode would have been frightening, as the terrifying old age of Plyushkin, despite its comic features. There are not yet tragic tears in Sterne's ironic presentations of such scenes. As a writer, he is even happy that "human nature" is so far from the ideal to which the philosophers of the Enlightenment wanted to raise it. If they had succeeded, so much that is absurd and ridiculous would have disappeared from the clever observer's field of vision. "It is a singular blessing," he exclaims, "that nature has formed the mind of man with the same happy backwardness and renitency against conviction, which is observed in old dogs—'of not learning new tricks'."

Vulgarity, as a phenomenon of life, is noted by Sterne, but although it plays a certain role in his peculiar dialectics of feelings, where sentimental affection is so easily transformed into sneers, and vice versa, that vulgarity is still not perceived as a dangerous or sinister social trend. Its individual carriers, for example the satirical portrayals of the characters in *Tristram Shandy* who go by the names of Somnolentus, Gastripheres and Phutatorius, the pillars of the church and the oppressors of Pastor Yorick, could be interpreted as being repulsive as well as ridiculous.

However, on the whole the humorous digressions which play such an important role in Sterne's narrative style do not possess the range or the sharp condemnation of the vulgarity of ordinary life, as later appears in West European and Russian literature. Accordingly, in Sterne, the image of the narrator in all his masks—whether he is the good-humoured though cunning Tristram or the sarcastic Yorick of *A Sentimental Journey,* who even ridicules his own sensitivity—lacks those tragic features which are so often acquired by the image Gogol projects of himself in *Dead Souls.*

Vulgarity is given a somewhat different treatment in Diderot's *Le Neveau de Rameau.* In this remarkable dialogue the European Enlightenment, then at the zenith of its development, subjects itself to a form of remorseless critical inspection, comparing its own ideals and system of thought to the new social tendencies whose development and consolidation it, by an irony of history, was supposed to assist. In *Le Neveu de Rameau* Diderot brilliantly "divines" that new type of person who has freed himself from all the bonds of feudalism, as well as from all sentimental, religious, group, and other prejudice, and was to come to the surface of history after Thermidor as the free, egoistic individual of bourgeois society. Rameau's nephew is of course the very embodiment of the vulgarity of bourgeois egoistic consciousness. His vanity at once suppresses and accentuates—depending on the circumstances—all his other qualities and instincts. He is prepared to sell anything, from his talent to his wife (whose beauty he praises like a horse-dealer a pedigree horse: point by point—"and what a crupper! What a splendid crupper!"). He firmly believes that everything has its price, and only that which you can sell has any value. This form of vulgarity is all the more terrible because it acts fully armed with cynical philosophy, a great experience of life and an unbounded self-confidence.

Appropriately, it was in the literature that arose from the ashes of the old world, destroyed by the French Revolution, that the theme of vulgarity was first treated in an ominous, tragic light. It was precisely in Romanticism, a literary movement that was a response to the French Revolution and the Enlightenment philosophy that went together with it, that vulgarity features predominantly in a grotesque form, in which the comic and the repulsive are also frightening. At the same time we can observe in Romanticism a heightened opposition between the world of vulgarity and the world of beauty.

The highly fragmented nature of so much Romantic narrative is itself a direct reflection of this opposition of two worlds, which are interconnected, but negate one another. This is particularly evident in Hoffman's *Kreislerbuch* and *Lebensansichten des Katers Murr*. With Heine, a poet who was closely connected with Romanticism, and who never really sundered this bond, we see it in his "lyrical-epic" prose, with its constant digressions—from a satirical portrayal of the world of vulgarity to poetic flights of fancy into the world of nature, fantasy, dream and heroic valour.

With Gogol the realisation of this fragmentary nature is most prominent in *Arabesques*. It comes across most forcefully in *Nevsky Prospekt,* with its opposition between triumphant vulgarity in all its various guises, embodied by Lieutenant Pirogov, and the ideal world of beauty and nobility which exists only in the imagination of the hapless artist Piskaryov. Art itself here appears impotent against the onset of life's vulgar prose. The more splendid the visions which appear before Piskaryov—who knows only too well with his reason that his beloved is nothing but a strumpet—the more terrible his torments and the quicker he approaches his end.

But certain of the articles in this collection, particularly the early (dated 1831) "Sculpture, Painting and Music", profess a more optimistic view of the potential of art in overcoming the tragic dislocation of the modern world. In this article Gogol regards these three varieties of artistic activity as three successive stages of man's development, corresponding to the pagan past, Christian Middle Ages and, finally, the present day (an idea probably suggested indirectly by Schelling) and he especially singles out music. It is precisely this creative métier, "more rapturous, ... more energetic than both its sisters" (VIII, 11), that is able, in the author's opinion, to offer more to the soul of nineteenth century man. This ardently Romantic paean to music (which in its tone and content is at once reminiscent of many passages by Hoffmann) contains a perceptive description of the nineteenth century itself, which in many respects anticipates those vital issues that Gogol was to tackle not only in his Petersburg stories, which are included in *Arabesques,* but later too, in *Dead Souls,* and to the end of his life.

An image of vulgarity, of this antithesis of all high and noble art, emerges here from the definitions which are remarkable for their social and historical precision. Gogol writes not only of all the "trivial whims and delights dreamed up with such great effort by our nineteenth century", he also employs the highly significant epithet "*mercantile* souls", and sets the "robber" and "speculator" side by side as the "heroes" of the new age (VIII, 12; my italics.—*A.Y.*). The theme of *salvation* of those souls poisoned by "a cold and terrible egoism, which endeavours to take possession of our world"—a theme which was destined to become a live nerve in *Dead Souls*—dominates the impassioned conclusion of the article. Gogol's hymn in praise of music is a perhaps naïve, but sincere appeal by an artist, convinced that he is right, to this art *not to abandon* mankind, not to let us sink further into the mire of vulgarity. "May the mighty stroke of your bow cause the troubled soul of the robber to feel, if only for a moment, the pangs of conscience, the speculator to abandon his calculations, and the impudent and brazen to shed an involuntary tear before the creation of talent. No, goddess, do not abandon us!" (VIII, 12). When we re-read these Romantic sentiments after *Dead Souls* we see that they contain ideas that were overcome and rejected by Gogol, and at the same time retained in a reconsidered and transformed apsect in his *poema.*

Any Romantic trust in the sudden miraculous moral transformation which art might bring about in the soul of such "robbers" and "speculators" had already been rejected, or rather, overcome in the bitter disillusionment experienced by the characters of *Arabesques,* notably in *Nevsky Prospekt* and *The Portrait.* As for *Dead Souls,* Chichikov's communion with the arts is confined to an unfinished, odd volume of *La Duchesse de Lavalière.*

However, Gogol retains the vital awareness of the urgent necessity to create the world anew, to counter the fatal "mercantile" and egoistic tendencies which crush and destroy human characters. He retains his anxiety for the human soul—a concept which he understands not just in its religious context, but in the broadest, humanistic sense—indeed, in *Dead Souls,* Volume 1 there is no mention anywhere either of church or of religion. And, finally, he retains his belief in the profound responsibility of the artist, of those whose duty it is to create—a conviction which both inspired Gogol in his work on *Dead Souls,* and became for him the source of tragic torment, the kind unknown to writers of lesser stature and with less sensitive consciences.

It can be said that the lyrical digressions in *Dead Souls* are directly related to romantic poetry and in many respects, to the aesthetics of Romanticism. In this work, Gogol did not proclaim the superiority of art over the world of reality and did not cut himself off from that world. On the contrary, he wants to examine that world in all its vulgarity and unattractiveness. But he speaks of his mission as a writer and realist (here we are referring to Gogol with a term that he himself never used) in the language of a romantic, beginning with unexpected, grand, symbolic images and allegories and ending with sharp contrasts, sudden and abrupt interruptions or changes in speech and bold, pathetic inversions. The understanding of artistic perception as divining the mysteries of life, important for the aesthetics of Romanticism, is preserved. While Gogol—the realist in Dead Souls did not exclude other forms of studying and probing reality, he made a major contribution to the perception of the still hidden potentials of the Russian character and national history.

4

When comparing Gogol to his close contemporaries, Balzac, Thackeray, Dickens, and representatives of critical realism in the West European novel of the middle of the nineteenth century it is necessary to keep in mind one important peculiarity of *Dead Souls*—being fundamentally a realistic epic it preserved many Romantic methods and ways of perceiving and interpreting the world. The romantic principle played a definite role in the preparation of the works of all of these writers, but not in the same form and with different artistic results. As a writer, Thackeray developed in direct polemics with Romanticism, and not only with its imitators such as Bulwer-Lytton, and Disraeli, but with Scott himself, whose works he magnificently parodied in many satiric burlesques and ironic stories (although it is well known that Scott and even Shelley were favourite authors of the young Thackeray). Balzac, in destroying romantic illusions of the social and political structure of the France of his day and mercilessly dissecting the dishonest and self-seeking interests and passions of its rulers, allowed himself not only sentimental expressions of his personal sympathies towards the remnants of the old aristocracy being swept away by the course of history, but used bold exaggerations, fantastic symbolism and even mysticism to widen the range of an artistic assimilation of the world. In Dickens, the Romantic principle appears in symbolic images and, most graphically of all, in fairy-tale elements which play such an important role in his realistic novels and stories, sometimes appearing in separate figures and motifs, and sometimes even overriding the logic of action.

Using the most general working formula, it is possible to make the assumption that Gogol, Balzac and Dickens, although far from employing identical methods, all tried to go beyond the limits of a critical, realistic representation of life. In this they differ from Thackeray who, despite the satirical irony with which he looked upon the surrounding Vanity Fair, did not try to oppose it with anything but bitter stoicism. His tales (he, like Dickens, wrote Christmas stories and, as his "The Rose and the Ring" shows, just as brilliantly) do not contain anything moving and even their happy endings are more derisive than consoling. As far as breaking through to the range of social utopias, which talked about the transformation of the characters and lives of many people as opposed to separate individuals, of our chosen writers only Gogol and Balzac did this. (See Chapter Three: "*Dead Souls* and the Utopian Novel.")

In Soviet literary criticism, the idea of the possibility of a typological comparison of the above-mentioned writers was expressed in a more defined and well-reasoned form by A. Chicherin in the article "Correspondences in the History of Different Literatures" (1965). It would be appropriate to mention the basic proposition of that interesting article. Chicherin writes: "The Gogolian (or Dickensian) period did not only exist in Russian literature. It was a natural stage of critical realism and included writers who did not know the works of Gogol and who may have been unknown to Gogol.

"This was a time when realism was most strongly opposed to Romanticism, when great significance was attached to humour: the author saw something comic in clothing, in appearances, observed things which degraded the image of man and destroyed Romantic illusions. At the same time details of ordinary life acquired a form of monumental significance and were highly particularized, almost supplanting any other description of the characters (witness Sobakevich's house, the home of Mr. Dombey, Gobseck's residence). All these writers: Dickens with his hyperbole and grotesque, and his eternal opponent Thackeray with his determination never to exaggerate, but always to portray people in an entirely natural way, and Gogol, Božena Nemcová, and Mickiewicz of *Pan Tadeusz*, surely belong to one and the same stage in the history of critical realism.

"...It would seem more appropriate to describe this stage in the history of critical realism in accordance with its essence, rather than after any particular author: the stage of monumental realism, tinged with humour." [31]

We can accept this conception with certain amplifications. One of these has to do with the ambivalent attitude, discussed above, which the great majority of these writers (with the sole exception, perhaps, of Thackeray) held towards Romanticism: whilst "overcoming" Romanticism they adopted many of its precepts, retaining them in a new, dominant and realistic context. Surely even Thackeray's irony, with its jesting undertones mellowing the author's bitter diatribe against "the vanity of vanities" also contains echoes of the Romantic irony of Byron?

Another amplification concerns Balzac, whom Chicherin is inclined to compare with the early Pisemsky (despite the immense disparity in their respective talents!), arguing that these two writers are only akin to Gogol and Thackeray "to a certain, although not insignificant extent". In the critic's opinion, the difference between Balzac and Pisemsky on the one hand, and Gogol and Thackeray on the other consists in the fact that "the first two are the most consistent and eager realists, who both impart with apparent nonchalance something quite mundane to their very style. The monumental quality of images and detail therefore begins to diminish in their works." [32]

Let us leave aside Pisemsky, with reference to whom this comment would appear quite justified, and take issue with certain of the writer's remarks about Balzac. It would appear above all that Chicherin is not making sufficient allowance for something we have already touched on above: the role of the Romantic principle in Balzac's realism, a principle which does not contradict his "apparent nonchalance" with its "mundane" style, but even illuminates this mundane element in an ominous and tragic light. Compare the pension run by Mme Vauquer with Mrs. Todgers's boarding house in *Martin Chuzzlewit*. We see the same stinginess, misery, vulgarity and avarice. But in Balzac's interpretation this is the stage on which the immense figures of Vautrin and Rastignac act out their parts. Dickens makes a sentimental and conciliatory "Romantic" adjustment to the harshly realistic initial description of the scene where the two despicable nonentities are to meet—the hypocrite Pecksniff and the murderer Jonas Chuzzlewit. Much later, at the end of the novel, Mrs. Todgers, who appears to be totally obsessed by her household calculations and oppressed by her lodgers' appetites and the cost of foodstuffs, proves to be the perfect reincarnation of the good Samaritan, a metamorphosis which would be quite unthinkable with Mme Vauquer. As for the monumental quality of image and details, this is surely retained even in Balzac's late works: there is something unmistakably monumental about the images of Cousine Bette (who, according to Balzac, is a combination of Iago and Richard III), of Hulot, so repulsive in his debauchery and moral degeneration, and, finally, of so many of the heroes of *Les Paysans*, with their terrible rapacity and avarice.

Gogol has frequently been compared with Balzac. Mérimée regarded *Dead Souls* as an imitation of Balzac—on the mere grounds that Gogol, like Balzac (about whom this allegation is strictly not true) primarily depicts provincial life. On the other hand, Barbey d'Aurevilly, in the article quoted above, rounds angrily on Charrière for daring to place *Dead Souls* on a level with the works of Balzac.

Leonid Grossman in his classic work *Balzac v Rossii*

(Balzac in Russia), in which he demonstrates the immense popularity of Balzac's works in Russia during the author's own lifetime, suggests that the "encounter" between Gogol and Balzac "was not entirely without consequence". However, the author does not develop this line of argument. Quoting the example of similar situations in "The Greatcoat" and "Père Goriot" (the mocking of Akaki Akakievich and of Balzac's senile hero) Grossman declares: "On the whole the question of Gogol's attitude to Balzac, which presents a mass of interesting material (e. g., the bureaucratic world in Balzac's *Les Employés* and in *Dead Souls*) has not been studied in our literature". [33]

Gogol was able to poke fun at his own future researchers: the only one of his reviews which is directly concerned with Balzac (dealing, furthermore, with the novel *La Peau de chagrin*, of particular interest to the author of *Arabesques*), is written in such a way that Balzac's name is only mentioned in a general list of names and the reviewer's attitude to his work is nowhere made explicit.

However, what concerns us here is not the possibility of Balzac's direct influence on Gogol, something that has still not been conclusively demonstrated, but the objective typological similarities—and differences—between *Dead Souls* and Balzac's epic, and we chose the word "epic" deliberately, for *La Comédie humaine* does indeed form a single, great epic of the modern world.

"The most realistic thing about Balzac's work is the *plan*, the composition of *La Comédie humaine*, the endeavour to 'embrace all things', as Lev Tolstoy was to say of him". [34] This perceptive comment by Chicherin—which admittedly may not be entirely accurate with regard to certain individual parts of *La Comédie humaine*—does correctly define the significance of the grand design of Balzac's epic composition. This design, proclaimed in the famous foreword, dated July 1842, * relegates to the author the role of "secretary" to that great "historian" which "French society was destined to become".

Balzac and Gogol were equally anxious to embrace as much of life as possible in their writings. "All of Russia will be evoked in it," writes Gogol of the work for which he had still not yet selected the definition "poema" and

---

* Note here the revealing coincidence of dates: the first volume of *Dead Souls* came out in May 1842.

about which he only knew that it would be "something which I still have to consider long and carefully, unlike either a story or a novel, a long, long work, in several volumes, to be called *Dead Souls*" (XI, 77—letter to Pogodin of 28th November 1836).

As his work on the book progressed Gogol was to write on numerous occasions with increasing commitment to this design about his desire to widen the extent of his portrayal of life in *Dead Souls*.

Later, in his *Author's Confession* (1847), in which Gogol looks back on the path he has travelled in writing *Dead Souls*, and written after the fiasco of *Selected Passages from Correspondence with My Friends*, he explains that in *Dead Souls* he wished "to exhibit primarily those noble features of the Russian nature, which as yet are not properly appreciated by all, and above all those low ones which still have not been sufficiently ridiculed and routed" (VIII, 422). From a study of "man in general" he proceeded to the study of the Russian character and Russian society. "I conceived the desire to get to know Russia much better. I ... tried to familiarize myself as much as possible with those experienced and practical people of all strata who are directly involved with all the goings-on inside Russia. I wanted to meet people of all classes and to learn something from each of them" (VIII, 446).

This is the programme of social realism, as it is with Balzac too. But we must also note that Gogol, despite his desire to scrutinize people of all classes, of all professions and ranks, sees his main and final objective as something more general. We refer to the explanation of the "Russian nature", of the "Russian character", with all its merits and shortcomings, in its present decline, in its disorder, with its hidden, its latent potential. For all the author's skill in "dissecting" life right down to its tiniest details, a skill that was so admired by Belinsky, Gogol's "Leviathan", as he jokingly described his book, should, in accordance with his own design, have possessed a certain spiritual *wholeness*.

Both Gogol and Balzac drew on architectural metaphor to define the significance of their monumental works.

Balzac compared *La Comédie humaine* to an "edifice". Both he and Gogol inveigh against those who hasten to judge an unfinished structure by its separate parts. "Why can he (the author—*A. Y.*) not advance pace by pace in his work," exclaims Balzac in the preface to the first edition of *Les Illusions perdues* (1837), "without at every step having to explain that each new book is but one of the stones of the building, that all the stones have to be fastened together and then one day they will form an immense edifice?" Elsewhere he complains of the difficulties he faces, comparing them to those faced by an architect, and expresses his fear that he will not bring to completion his construction of a "magnificent monument". But he attributes this more to material, financial hardship, than to the complexity of his design or the difficulty of studying and generalizing about life.

Gogol, by contrast, is much less prone to blame material circumstances for impeding the construction of his "edifice", although he often lived in a state of near penury. "I am able to bow to my fate. I shall try to endure this hardship, this poverty, to have patience... I have an unshakeable faith in the radiant future, and an unknown force tells me that I will be given the means to complete my work" (XII, 33—letter to Pletnyov of February 6, 1842). However, he is incomparably more concerned by the actual problems of the architectonics of his colossal project. Even before the publication of the first volume of *Dead Souls* he pleads with Pletnyov not to judge his work, which is "important and great", by "that part which is about to appear". "This is no more than the porch of the palace which is being built within me" (XII, 46—letter of March 17, 1842). On May 9, 1842, the very eve of the publication of Volume 1 of *Dead Souls*, he makes this same plea, in even more urgent tones, to A. Danilevsky: "In a week's time ... you shall receive the just-published *Dead Souls*, a rather unimposing threshold to that great epic which is being constructed within me and which shall finally resolve *the enigma of my existence*" (XII, 58; my italics—*A.Y.*). And finally, in his well-known letter to Shevyryov of February 28, 1843, in which Gogol asks him, S. T. Aksakov and Pogodin to take on themselves the obligation of dealing with his routine affairs for the next few years, he gives prominence once again to the idea of the correlation of the various parts of his *poema*.

The design of his work remains something of a mystery to Gogol, a mystery which not only is not cleared up after the publication of Volume 1, but is even somewhat compounded. The reason for this goes far beyond any subjective delusion or prejudice and religious crisis that clouded the last years of his life. Despite the difference in their temperaments, in their personal destinies, for both the French and the Russian writer the national and historical conditions in which they worked were greatly instrumental in directing their creative quest.

In a sense the history of France actually facilitated Balzac's work, enabling him to become indeed the "secretary" of French society.

The French Revolution and the events which followed it, which Balzac himself witnessed—the Hundred Days and the new Restoration of the Bourbons, the 1830 July revolution, which brought the bankers and their "citizen King" to power, the cruelly suppressed uprisings of 1831-1832, the 1848 revolution, and the ominous underground tremors which presaged it—all of these cast into clear relief for such a brilliant thinker and artist as Balzac the minute intricacies of the economic, social and political relations in his country. The changes of the last fifty years in the redistribution of private wealth and political power, in the role of the various classes and social groups, in the beliefs, attitudes and tastes of his fellow-countrymen, were probably more exposed, more apparent, in France at that time than in any other country in Europe. Balzac's epic had for this reason a quintessentially *analytical* character. This is also evident in the remarkable, questionnaire precision with which Balzac forms not only the personal, but also the political biography of his characters. It is also evident in the carefully thought out and strictly logical compositional division of *La Comédie humaine*, set out by Balzac in his preface, into particular sections and subsections, corresponding to those spheres of public life which the author wished to capture, to analyse and to elevate into a system. "Thus depicted, Society must bring with it the reason for its movement," [35] boldly declares Balzac, never for a moment doubting that the secrets of this society are apparent to him or at least suspecting that they might not conceal themselves from his gaze. As he himself states his task is to depict two or three thousand prominent (*saillantes*) figures of a particular age, distributing them accordingly within certain "frames and ... galleries". It is thus he arrives at the division of *La Comédie humaine* into six sections, which he lists in the preface: "*Scenes of private life, of provincial life, of Parisian life, of political life, of military life and of country life.* All the *studies of manners,* which together

71

form the general history of Society, the collection of all its events and doings, are classified in these six books..." [36] In accordance with Balzac's design, this should have formed the foundation, "full of people, full of comedies and tragedies", for the erection of *études philosophiques* and above them *études analytiques*. Not all the parts of this massive design (formulated, moreover, after a considerable portion of the works indicated in it had already been written and published) were carried out. But the logical precision of this system for the analysis of social life is itself impressive.

Gogol's position was somewhat different. Of course he also thought deeply about the history of his country. We know from the memoirs of his contemporaries that the Patriotic War of 1812 was meant to play an important role in the discussions of his characters in *Dead Souls*, Volume 2, as an example of a sweeping popular uprising. The peasant disturbances of his time are reflected, albeit cursorily, in a number of episodes in the work, and the first version of "Captain Kopeikin's Story" of patently rebellious ideas which did not slip past the censors unheeded. The Decembrist movement was still alive in Gogol's mind. Although he tried to present it in a critical light in the extant early version of the first chapters of Volume 2, in his satirical portrayal of the "secret society" which Tentetnikov joins in his naïveté, it is quite probable (once again judging by the memoirs of those to whom Gogol read the destroyed chapters) that echoes of Decembrism might have been far more serious in a later version, in the episodes of Tentetnikov's arrest, his parting from the peasants and Ulenka Betrishcheva's departure for Siberia to join her exiled fiancé. Nonetheless, Russian life, such as Gogol understood and viewed it during the reactionary years of Nicholas I's reign in the thirties and forties, did not give him the opportunity for such trenchant analytical observation as Balzac was able to command. He saw a blatant "wrongness", an opposition of the prevailing mores to human (and for Gogol divine) law. The parasitism of the landowners was now joined by a new peril—the need to "acquire", filthy lucre, the power of which is embodied in the character of Chichikov, but is by no means reducible to this in *Dead Souls*. On the other hand he remembers the heroic feats of the Russian people in the past, he retains his confidence in their pluck, in their strength... The problem was: how to marry these contradictory observations and convictions, how to create harmony from the strident discords which abound in Volume 1 of *Dead Souls*? This was rather a problem of *synthesis*, in search of which Gogol suffered such torments. He did not feel himself to be the "secretary" of Russian society. On the contrary, it seemed to him that this society itself expected him to provide an explanation of the great mystery of its present and future existence, and it is for this reason that the element of prophecy, of solving the historical "riddle" of Russian path of development, has such an important role in Gogol's epic by comparison to *La Comédie humaine*.

Despite all these differences there are indisputable points of typological similarity between Gogol's *poema* and Balzac's *Comédie humaine*. One of the most important of these is the keen awareness, shared by both writers, of the *soul-destroying* role of money, of property, of the need "to acquire". The problem of "dead souls", which Gogol promotes as the title of his work, also runs through *La Comédie humaine*; if the latter work has no buyers-up of deceased serfs, or "souls" still on the census list, it is only for the lack of such in post-revolutionary France.

A good insight to this question can be given by an analysis of *Melmoth reconcilié*, the story that Marx acclaimed as Balzac's "small masterpiece".

In this story, which was published in 1835 and included subsequently in his *Études philosophiques*, we can observe, as in Gogol's Petersburg stories, a direct adherence to the Romantic tradition, and, at the same time, its realistic reconception.

Charles Maturin's novel *Melmoth the Wanderer* gave Balzac not only his fantastic hero, but also the initial situation for his satirical novella.

But Balzac removes Maturin's sinister Romantic wanderer from his Gothic ambience and places him in bustling busy Paris, the very heart of that "civilization" which after 1815 had substituted the principle of "money" for the principle of "honour", and the situation is radically altered. The living human soul, which had been the supremely sacred object in the world where Melmoth had wandered previously, is here not only debased to the position of a commodity, but becomes the object of stock exchange dealing and even rapidly rises in value.

The irony which permeates the entire story is manifested with particular brilliance in its denouement. Melmoth's infernal gift is subsequently acquired by a young clerk, who sells his soul for a mere ten thousand francs: this is the price of a shawl which is supposed to secure for him the favour of the enchanting Euphrasie. The caresses of this courtesan, however, cost him more dearly than he had expected. Falling ill with venereal disease the wretched man undertakes to treat himself and dies, having administered himself an overdose of medicine. His soul fades away in the mercury vapours, and in lieu of the prayer for the dead it is accompanied by the vulgar jokes of mocking clerks, the little devils of modern Paris.

Balzac's story has no literal parallels in Gogol's writing. But in spirit it is very close to the Petersburg stories and, to a certain extent, to *Dead Souls*.

Critics have already remarked on Gogol's direct response to Maturin in several episodes of *Portrait*. But more interesting than these direct analogies (such, for instance, as the portrait of the demonic villain with its magical powers or the staunchness of those pious people, who resist the temptation of the devil) is the switch from a Romantic to a realistic interpretation of the infernal corruption of mercantile society, an interpretation shared by Balzac and Gogol.

In *Melmoth reconcilié* Balzac describes Paris, "this city of temptations", as a "branch of hell", and this theme runs throughout *La Comédie humaine*, sometimes being felt in the subtext, sometimes emerging to the surface of the narrative.

In *La Fille aux yeux d'or*, which Balzac dedicated to the great Romantic Delacroix, the creator of inspired pictures of Dante and Virgil in hell, the opening passage of the story with its magnificent sarcastic portrayal of Paris is constructed in the form of a journey through the circles of the inferno, along which the author conducts his reader. The first circle is the world of the poor toilers. The second circle, which seethes with the busy, thinking, speculating members of the petty bourgeoisie which threshes the interests of Paris and attends to its grain. Then the author informs the reader, his travelling companion, that they have finally reached the third circle of this hell, "which will perhaps one day have its Dante". In this third social circle, a sort of under-belly of Paris, where the interests of the city are digested and where they are condensed into that form called "business", the intestinal gall and spleen move and agitate a mass of lawyers, doctors, notaries, advocates, businessmen, grand merchants, bankers, speculators and magistrates. "It is here that you find the most reasons for the physical and moral destruction... These people have lost their hearts, but where?... I do not know." [37]

This is followed by other circles of the hell of Paris, which know neither labours nor worries, where the twisting golden whirl has gained the heights; but here too, in this privileged world of the rich and noble, human nature is perverted, poisoned by vice and torn asunder by vanity.

There is an obvious similarity between this tragic picture of a soulless and vain existence, which corrupts the very nature of man, and the picture painted by Gogol in both the Petersburg stories and *Dead Souls*.

In Gogol's *Portrait* the "hellish" soullessness of the mercenary world is given a dual interpretation. The moral catastrophe suffered by Chartkov, who destroys his talent and becomes an embittered scourge of true art has, on the one hand, a Romantic motivation: Chartkov is both the victim and the instrument of a Satanic delusion; the cursed gold of the mysterious moneylender, the devil incarnate, has corrupted his soul. The "Melmoth" motif of fatal temptation, which it is the duty of Christian humility and spiritual steadfastness to resist, becomes even more pronounced in the second part of the story, in the account by the artist's son. Here the Romantic interpretation is particularly marked. But the story of Chartkov's fall also has a purely realistic social and psychological motivation for Gogol, which he supports with a mass of ironic and expressive detail. He recounts the melancholy experience of hardship and obscurity, of the temptation to flatter his first lady client, to portray the young coquette as Psyche, easy success, leading to new compromises with his conscience, until his false and flattering style of portrayal becomes an ingrained habit... When viewed in this realistic light, as a typical social parable, Chartkov's story involuntarily recalls the fate of Lucien Chardon, Wenceslas Steinbock, and other victims of spiritual bankruptcy in Balzac's books.

In *Dead Souls* the destruction of the human soul is not presented with such Romantic pathos as it is in *The Portrait*. Here it is a commonplace event which surprises no one—unless in its extremes, as in Plyushkin's maniacal miserliness. But this very universality seems to render it all the more terrible for Gogol. It is as living death that he presents the process whereby the human soul becomes encumbered with egoistic calculations, petty, niggardly concerns or merely vain, empty pursuits, such as Manilov's castles in the sky. In the sixth chapter of Volume 1, the episode of Chichikov's visit to Plyushkin, Gogol expresses the horror of the artist at a picture which he has painted himself with particular force.

In the image of Plyushkin the grotesque portrayal which colours the whole of *Dead Souls* attains great tragic intensity. But the thoughtful reader—and it is for such a reader that Gogol hoped—will also detect a note of horror in the *comic* vulgarity of the meaningless lives of the other heroes. There is comedy, for example, in the scene where Chichikov haggles with the "bear-like" Sobakevich over the price of "non-existent" (as the purchaser cautiously terms them) souls. But there is one passage which is more grim than comic, in which Gogol tries to explain the insensitivity of Sobakevich's "heavy nature": "It seemed as though there was no soul in this body, or perhaps there was one but in quite the wrong place, somewhere, as with the Immortal Koshchei, beyond the mountains and covered with such a thick shell that whatever stirred in its depths made not a slightest tremble on the surface" (VI, 101). It is precisely to Immortal Koshchei—one of the most sinister and terrible images conjured up by the popular imagination—that Gogol turns in order to introduce the "frightening" motif that he requires for his artistic purpose into this primarily comic, or grotesque image of Sobakevich. But, as Gogol himself emphasizes, the problem cannot be reduced to *individual* landowners. Gifted Tentetnikov, who has become a hopeless idler, the wretched, nondescript Khlobuyev, Platon Platonov, who has lost his taste for life, the mechanical bureaucrat Koshkaryov—all these are for Gogol merely varied manifestations of a terrible disease which afflicts society, a disease whose causes he seeks in order to point the way to its cure.

Seen in this light the problem of the "dead souls", destroyed by the conditions of their social existence, points up the direct parallelism between Gogol's book and *La Comédie humaine,* as well as between the concern of both writers to find the path to their resurrection—a quest upon which Gogol is constantly engaged, and Balzac, a more sober and stoical observer of human corruption, only occasionally.

It is natural that we should consider in this context the question of Dante's tradition and its importance to both these writers. In the very title of his work—*La Comédie humaine*—Balzac declares its kinship with Dante's great poem, and also its break with this tradition: for his monumental epic about the modern age is to be "Human" and not "Divine", although the religious idea (as he declares in his preface to *La Comédie humaine*) is for him "the greatest element of Social Order". [38]

The connection between Gogol's work and the tradition of Dante, reassessed, as with Balzac, in the light of the vital problems of the 19th century, is far less evident, but it cannot be excluded. Admittedly the only direct reference to the *Divine Comedy* in *Dead Souls* has a distinctly comic, almost parodistic air to it. This is the episode of Chichikov and Manilov's visit to the town chambers, where "Themis... received the visitors in négligé and dressing gown" and where "one of the acolytes, making his sacrifices to Themis so zealously that both his coat sleeves had burst at the elbows and the lining had long been sticking out of the holes for which in his time he had been promoted to the rank of collegiate registrar, escorted our friends as Virgil once had escorted Dante, and led them into the presentation room... Here our new Virgil was so overcome with awe that he durst not cross the threshold and turned on his heel, displaying a back as threadbare as a bit of matting, with the odd chicken feathers stuck to it" (VI, 144).

But it is with good reason that Gogol assigns such an important role to the grotesque in his book and the intentionally mundane character of this "allusion" does not alter its significance.

We have to bear in mind the fact that Dante's *Divine Comedy* was in its time the very same thing that both Gogol and Balzac dreamt of creating for their own age—a sort of "encyclopedia" of modern times, recorded in its dynamism and development. The great Florentine's epic was the poetic and philosophical culmination of the entire West European culture of the Middle Ages, but at the same time it also partially foreshadows the humanism of the Renaissance. Balzac and Gogol each strove in their own way to create a work of *comparable* culminative grandeur, devoted to their own time, but also—and this is particularly true of Gogol—adumbrating the horizons of the future. Dante's work abounds in lyrical prognoses of the future—both with regard to the fate of individuals and to that of Italy as a whole. This aspect of the *Divine Comedy* would have been especially interesting to Gogol as it was to many of his contemporaries. (We may recall how Byron makes use of Dante's tradition, subjecting it to the problems of the modern age, when in his poem *Prophecy of Dante* he combines echoes of the *Divine Comedy* with a direct address to the Italian people of the 19th century, who languished under the yoke of the Austrians and the Papal throne, and wove together memories of the bitter lot of the Florentine exile and lyrical references to his personal experience as an unrecognized and persecuted poet).

But the *Divine Comedy* contains, in addition to this idea of the eternal movement and development of existence so important to both Gogol and Balzac, its inseparable corollary: the theme of the great potential latent in the human soul. Praise for divine predetermination collides in Dante's poem with the poet's grief over the fate of those people who have perished forever, lost in the mire of sin, often fine and noble people who, it would seem, had been created for a better destiny. Satire, a direct and angry denunciation of bad rulers, both secular and clerical, extortioners and scoundrels, whose proper place is in hell, goes hand in hand with reflections on the only possible, the only "true" path to the salvation of the soul. Furthermore, this last concept, which was subsequently "die-stamped" and misconstrued in religious tracts to mean renunciation of every thing worldly and ascetic self-perfection, has a far broader, even humanistic, significance for Dante. It is important that man should recognize his true calling and should adhere to it: this, in particular, is the gist of the admonitions which Dante hears from Charles Martel in the eighth song of *Paradise*. It is the will of God that people should be endowed from birth with different natural inclinations:

> *Therefore one is Solon born;*
> *Another, Xerxes; and Melchisedec*
> *A third; and he a fourth, whose airy voyage*
> *Cost him his son. In her circuitous course,*
> *Nature, that is the seal to moral wax,*
> *Doth well her art, but no distinction owns*
> *'Twixt one or other household.*

. . . .

Nature ever,
Finding discordant fortune, like all seed
Out of its proper climate, thrives but ill.
And were the world below content to mark
And work on the foundation nature lays,
It would not lack supply of excellence.
But ye perversely to religion strain
Him, who was born to gird on him the sword,
And of the fluent phraseman make your king:
Therefore your steps have wander'd from the path. [39]

Gogol might have found in this something consonant with his own theory of the passions contained in human nature, which can be turned either to evil or to good—depending on circumstances, of the significance of a person's true "calling", which must be ascertained. *The Divine Comedy* also developed the idea, so important to Gogol, of the "transformation" of man. The souls of *Purgatory* undergo a slow and arduous process of cleansing from the pollution of sin (and it is here, Dante thinks, in the circle where the men of pride are undergoing correction, that his own place is being prepared). But the intercession of Beatrice, who initiates him to the secrets of life beyond the grave, can lighten and accelerate this process of spiritual enlightenment for him. The inner *humanistic* import of the *Purgatory* and the *Paradise* is precisely the idea, expressed in mediaeval theological forms and images, of the gradual but constant and infinite spiritual improvement of man, of his upraising.

This aspect of *The Divine Comedy* was also perceived to some extent by Balzac; however, as we shall see below (see Chapter Two), Balzac was relatively more concerned with the process of degradation of human nature, while Gogol, who also closely scrutinized this side of reality, was sustained by his faith in the possibility of enlightenment, of "resurrection" even of the "dead souls" of his age.

Perhaps it is for this reason that direct, "infernal", allusions and metaphors are so frequent in *La Comédie humaine* and practically unattested in Gogol, although the gloomy picture of Russian life that he paints is perfectly comparable to Balzac's vision of France. In an entry in his diary for July 29, 1842, Herzen brilliantly expresses the contiguity of horror and hope that is so typical of Gogol and makes a direct comparison between *Dead Souls* and *The Divine*

Comedy. Mentioning the arguments provoked by Gogol's work ("Slavophiles No. 1 say that this is the apotheosis of Russia, our *Iliad*, and praise it ... others are enraged, saying that this is the anathema of Russia and carp at it"), Herzen continues: "It is ridiculous to see apotheosis, and unjust to see nothing but anathema. There are words of conciliation, there are presentiments and hopes of a full and triumphant future, but this does not prevent the present being reflected in all its repulsive reality. Here, as you move from the Sobakeviches to the Plyushkins, you are filled with horror: with each step you will sink deeper into the mire. A lyrical passage enlivens the scene, brightens it up, only to be replaced once again by a picture which recalls to us the ditch of hell we are in, like that which made Dante wish he could see and hear nothing—but the comic words of the *cheerful* author ring outloud." [40]

We do not have any documentary evidence of the extent to which Gogol may consciously (like Balzac) have turned in his mind to the plan, ideas and images of *The Divine Comedy* when working on *Dead Souls*. It is worthy of note, however, that he responds with rapturous approval to a letter from Shevyryov in which the latter informs him that he has commenced a translation of Dante's poem. "So you're at Dante! Oho-ho-ho!" exclaims Gogol, carefully explaining to Shevyryov why he should be "so delighted" at this "enormous undertaking" (XI, 247—letter of September 10, 1839). While living in Rome and working on *Dead Souls* Gogol constantly read and re-read his favourite passages from *The Divine Comedy* and Gnedich's translation of the *Iliad*, as well as Pushkin's poetry. Gogol knew Italian well enough to read Dante in the original.

By contrast to *Dead Souls* Balzac in his *La Comédie humaine* makes a far more precise differentiation of social categories. Following the actual logic of French history Balzac systematically reproduces in the various parts of his epic the successive stages in the development of bourgeois France. In the examples of his individual heroes he creates the biographies of entire classes, showing how some fall into decline and ruin, and by what means others grow rich, and come to power and glory.

Gogol's situation was somewhat different. Of course, observation and study of reality were of decisive significance in his work too. Like Balzac he also proceeded from facts and endeavoured to use them to test the plausibility of his images. It is not surprising, therefore, that Gogol's notebooks abound in remarks about popular customs and turns of phrase, about the routine of farmwork and the life of government clerks. It is with good reason that he made such a close study of travellers' accounts of Russia, of works on land use, descriptions of the soil and vegetation of different areas of the country, and took such a lively interest in statistics. But while reflecting on the past, present and future of his people he does not assume the role of a "secretary" who merely records what is dictated to him by society. When compared to this practical and exaggeratedly modest description which Balzac gives himself, thereby emphasizing the realistic character of his social epic, the images which Gogol employs in *Dead Souls* and the relevant letters to describe his role as writer ring with a different, far more romantic note, that of a special prophetic mission placed upon him by fate, by God, or, perhaps, by his own country.

He also expresses differently the organic bond between the writer and his country and people. Balzac dearly loves France, knows all its nooks and crannies, its people and its nature. With Gogol, however, this love is much less tranquil and balanced. His feelings for his country are in constant turmoil; even his landscapes are full of contradictions— deliberately bathetic prosaisms and an off-hand, satirical tone suddenly give way to lyrical dithyrambs and dazzling poetic pictures. Whether Gogol is writing about the manners of his fellow-countrymen or about the earth on which they live and which feeds them, he is not concerned merely to convey to his readers something which he already knows only too well. His concern is to reveal the hidden meaning of the commonplace and everyday, to penetrate deep into hitherto unrevealed mysteries, to discover the unknown. This discovery is depicted as the sacred final goal of the very process of writing an epic: to achieve the completion of the epic means to divine the great mystery of the life of the people, to become one of them and at the same time to influence their present and future.

The "majestic lyrical flow" of *Dead Souls*, as Gogol himself described the movement of his work, by no means excluded a critical or satirical attitude to life. It is precisely in the close interweaving of these principles that we find the special quality of his epic work. As with Balzac, Dickens and Thackeray, in *Dead Souls* the awareness of the profound injustice of society is expressed, in particular, in the unusual significance accorded to the theme of crime in the actual definition of the plot. Chichikov's shady dealings, just like Vautrin's transmutations, Rebecca Sharp's escapades, Pecksniff's machinations, Uriah Heep's swindling and other such activities, are of course more than just "relapses" of the picaresque novel, although the realists of the nineteenth century were very well acquainted with picaresque literature, particularly in its Enlightenment interpretation. Gogol's naïve critics were indignant at the improbable ease with which Chichikov is able to carry out his own fraudulent scheme; occasionally they pointed out that in accordance with existing legislation he would have been unable to effect his deeds of purchase, nor could he have mortgaged "non-existent" peasants. But this sort of trifling detail was not important to Gogol. He was concerned not with the combat of an individual cheat against the entire world, as in a picaresque novel, but with the total corruption of society.

In his notebooks for 1841-1844 we find detailed remarks about all the varieties of bribery in a provincial town. These are subdivided under the headings: "Public prosecutor's bribes", "Governor's bribes"; and followed by the sarcastic note: "The masks donned by governors" (VII, 353-355). In the drafted sections and final chapter of Volume 2 we find such remarkable lines as: "Everyone wants to live on state money, to derive profit from their government service, to turn the state into an almshouse required to feed them all. Hence the general ambition to become civil servants and administrators" (VII, 275). In general the theme of crime should have been developed more widely and in greater variety in Volume 2, as we can see from the surviving fragments.

The situation arising after the death of the decrepit "triple-millionaire", Khlobuyev's aunt, whose will, as we can guess, was forged by Chichikov, is described in a manner that is straight from Balzac. "Relations materialized whom no one had ever heard of. Like vultures diving down on carrion, so did they all swoop down on the incalculable fortune left behind by the old lady: there followed denunciations of Chichikov, of the last will as a forgery, denunciations of the first will too, accusations of theft and embezzlement of money" (VII, 105). We should note the indicative expression: "so did they all swoop down". The author's finger is pointed not at Chichikov alone: the whole of society is corrupt. Not only the "first officials of the town", even "the governor himself" prove to be involved in "this most dishonourable affair", to rank amongst "thieves and ne'er-do-wells" (VII, 119).

It would be appropriate at this juncture, while discussing the genre of *Dead Souls* in comparison to Balzac's epic, to emphasize that in both cases the "criminal" plot line is not regarded as an end in itself, but, to employ Gogol's favourite word, it "transforms" or symbolizes the deep-reaching depravity and corruption of society, and thus has a particularly vital *organizational* role in grouping the characters and events.

It would be superfluous to list all the works in *La Comédie humaine* that are based on a "criminal" plot. It is sufficient for our purposes to recall *Le Père Goriot*, *Les Illusions perdues*, *Splendeurs et misères des courtisanes*, *La Cousine Bette* amongst many others.

Balzac represents criminal machinations in far greater variety than Gogol, they are set out in far greater detail, in accordance with the analytical character, discussed above, of the epic narration of *La Comédie humaine*, and the author, like a preliminary investigator, makes detailed reference to documents, to the cunning legal dodges and traps used by his swindlers and frauds. The story of the bankruptcy of the ill-fated César Birotteau, exclaims the author, would have filled all 14 volumes of Richardson's *Clarissa*. Gogol confines all Chichikov's earlier shady dealings to the last chapter of Volume 1, where he gives a cursory retrospective account of his embezzlement of public funds in the "building commission", his contraband operations in the customs, etc. It is probable that Balzac would have developed all this with a mass of detail, close description of all the machinations, and lists of documents and figures. But despite these differences in their narrative manner, both writers are anxious to reveal to their readers the essence of a new and vital discovery: the criminal nature of all pursuit of gain, the corrupting, dehumanizing role of lucre. Gogol perspicaciously describes the first signs of bourgeois predation, then making its initial inroads in the backward Russia of serfdom. Balzac describes processes which were already quite apparent on the surface of public life in France. You will not find in Gogol's work the sort of meticulous analysis of the *mechanics* of banking speculation that is presented in Balzac's *La Maison Nucingen*. But both writers depict the universal adulation of a millionaire as a horrifying sign of the times and approach the subject with an equal dose of irony and indignation.

There is no character in Gogol's work comparable to the Romantically-hued colossus Vautrin, "le Cromwell du bagne" and denouncer of the world of bourgeois "legality". But the essence of Vautrin's mordant sarcasm is expressed—and sometimes in the very same words—in Gogol's narrative, demonstrating how similar the two writers are in their realistic observations and conclusions.

"Steal a million and you will be regarded as a virtue in all the salons," exclaims Vautrin. The pursuit of millions "has its various areas": "some pursue dowries, others liquidation; a first will fish for souls, a second will barter his sponsors", * binding them hand and foot. He who returns with a well-filled pouch will be saluted, fêted, received in good society... "To the infamous millionaire ... Paris will stretch out its arms, will run to his banquets, eat his dinners and toast his infamy."

In the eighth chapter of Volume 1 of *Dead Souls* we find an ironic account of instant wealth as the surest means of winning favour in society, which is perhaps less impassioned but no less profound than the diatribes of Vautrin. The deeds of purchase secured by Gogol's hero give rise to rumours and speculation which initially "have the most favourable consequence which Chichikov could have hoped for. For rumours circulated that he was no more or less than a 'millionaire' ", and thus, although the inhabitants of the town "had grown to love Chichikov dearly in any case, now, after these rumours, they loved him more dearly still" (VI, 156). Ladies who had previously had little to say about Chichikov, now discovered new virtues in him. "Moreover, the ladies were by no means merely motivated by mercenary interests: it was all the fault of the word 'millionaire', and not the millionaire himself, just the actual

---

* We may note the direct concurrence between Balzac's metaphors here and images employed in *Dead Souls*: people are a commodity, souls, an object of speculation... This similarity is not of course the result of verbal coincidence. It is a manifestation of the similarity of the thought processes of the two writers, whose attention is drawn to similar social phenomena equally disturbing to them both.

word; for in the very sound of this word besides any sack of money, there is something which affects people, whether scoundrels, or neither one thing nor the other, or good people; in short it affects everyone. A millionaire has the advantage that he can observe baseness of an entirely unselfish nature, pure baseness, unmotivated by any calculation: many people know perfectly well that they will receive nothing from him and have no right to expect anything, but they will invariably come scuttling forth to meet him, prepare to smile and to doff their hats; they will do their best to be invited to a dinner at which they know the millionaire will be present" (VI, 159). In Volume 2 (the final chapter in the original version) Chichikov himself displays this same "kind disposition towards baseness" (VI, 159) in his conversation with Murazov. They are talking about the weather. " 'We could do with a drop of rain for the sowing,' comments Murazov. 'Yes, a drop of rain would do no harm,' said Chichikov, who had absolutely no need of any rain, but how pleasant it was to agree with a man who had a million" (VII, 237).

The transformation of a man's personal worth into a measurable price—a tendency noted by Marx and Engels in the *Communist Manifesto* as one of those significant changes brought about in nineteenth century life by the hegemony of the bourgeoisie—equally disturbs the author of *La Comédie humaine* and the creator of *Dead Souls*. But Balzac sees the extent and the incontrovertibility of this process. For all the contempt in which he may hold the Nucingens, du Tillets and Taillefers, the more attractive Kellers, and the totally despicable Claparons, the very dynamics of the massive economic, social and political upheavals that altered the entire aspect of France in a single generation's lifetime, he is still impressed by their grandeur. The rapid ruin of some, the new prosperity of others, the intrusion of new social forces into such "strongholds of feudalism" as, for example, such out-of-the-way place as Gueranda in *Beatrice,* the "astonishing changes" as a result of which "grocers become the peers of France", Gobseck's place is taken by sophisticated money-lenders of high society, and the country estates, like Aigues in *Les Paysans*, are divided up by their new peasant-proprietors—all this arouses in Balzac a combination of elegiac sadness, stoical contempt and—above all—the keen desire of an artist with a perceptive historical mind to bring into his epic all this turbulent material, recording it in its true dimensions. Balzac does not fawn before millionaires; but he is the citizen of a country where millions—particularly after 1830—have firmly come to power. He is well aware of the might of capital, and, whilst despising the capitalists, he sometimes seeks out the right emotional tones to convey the enchantment and magnetic force of enormous fortunes.

Balzac himself does not, of course, subscribe to the new dogma of the capitalist age. But nonetheless the clink of gold, the dizzying effect of swift exchanges of enormous sums of money, the ease with which even some of his positive heroes—such, as, for example, Modeste Migron's father or Maximilien de Longueville, who rises from shop-assistant to millionaire and peer of France (*Bal dans Seau*) —attain this "omnipotence", stirs his imagination, just as he is impressed by ranks and titles, by the fashionable glitter of aristocratic balls and salons, however well he may know their seamier side . . .

This contradiction is not found in Gogol's work. For him vulgarity is always vulgarity, whether he is dealing with dim-witted Korobochka or with her "aristocratic sister", who leafs through fashionable novels and conducts empty society chatter in her sparkling urban residence. The governor's ball is no less wretched and ridiculous than the description of the way servant Petrushka lives or of Chichikov's confidential conversation with the waiter at his inn. In Volume 2 of *Dead Souls* the mythical honestly earned millions of Murazov flash by, but they are not manifested as a real force anywhere in the extant pages of the book.

In this respect the Gogol of *Dead Souls* is perhaps closer to the Thackeray of *The Book of Snobs* and *Vanity Fair,* in which we also find no place for any illusions either about the aristocracy or the bourgeoisie, and where vulgarity is unable, in any of its guises, to escape the ironic scrutiny of the artist.

5

Soviet critics have frequently remarked on the fundamental similarity between Gogol's realistic method and that employed by the author of *Vanity Fair.*

Gogol in *Dead Souls* and Thackeray in *Vanity Fair,* as the critic Chicherin argues, "followed one and the same path, stood at the same stage of critical realism ... and the themes of dead souls and of stifling human vanity are essentially one and the same.

"Similarly the object of portrayal—the decline of the landed estates and their owners—and the philosophical ideas, and the nature of realism with its element of grotesque satire naturally define the common area encountered in the work of two writers as different as Thackeray and Gogol." [41]

A comparative analysis of the satirical-realistic portrayal of several characters in *Dead Souls* and in *Vanity Fair* was presented in a dissertation by D. S. Yakhontova. "Gogol and Thackeray mark the same stage in the development of literature. Chernyshevsky regarded Gogol's greatest service to be the introduction into Russian literature of its satirical—or, as it would be more correct to call it—critical tendency. Chernyshevsky's comment applies equally well to Thackeray: he is also the originator of the satirical and critical tendency in English literature of the same period. The similarity of their characters is thus easy to understand. Both writers described typical images of landowners with due account for the specific features of their respective countries. Thus too does Tolstoy think of them together: 'Thackeray and Gogol are loyal, angry, artistic, but not kind'." [42]

These remarks are quite correct. However, if we compare this entry from Tolstoy's diary for May 26, 1856, [43] quoted here by Yakhontova, with another well-known remark by Tolstoy about Thackeray in his *Tales of Sebastopol*, the picture becomes rather more complex, and a divide between the two writers will be apparent.

"Why did Homers and Shakespeares of this world speak about love, glory and suffering, while the literature of our age is nothing but an endless tale of 'Snobs' and 'Vanity'?" Tolstoy puts this question to himself in the *Tales of Sebastopol* ("Sebastopol in May"), and the historical context in which it is formulated renders it even more meaningful.

For *Vanity Fair* deals not only with "snobs", but also with glory and with suffering and love. Does poor Amelia not love her George Osborne, and does he not die a hero's death at Waterloo? And does she not receive more than her fair share of suffering, as do her aging parents, and Osborne's haughty father, who disowns his son after the latter's marriage to his dowryless bride?

But Tolstoy's mind still held fresh pictures of a stirring popular glory and suffering, measured on quite a different epic historical scale. He himself witnessed and participated in the heroic defence of besieged Sebastopol, whose defenders might have succeeded in their valorous fight for their native land had they not been let down by the incompetence and treachery of the rearguard commanders— added to the decay and corruption of the entire administrative machine of state, the inaptitude of the high command, the stupid arrogance of Nicholas I ... His experiences in Sebastopol during the desperate battles against the allied armies besieging the city gave Tolstoy moral right to pass judgement on the "literature of our own age" and to measure it with a stern yardstick. A decade later he himself answered the question he had asked in the *Tales of Sebastopol:* answered it with the creation of *War and Peace.*

But even Walter Scott, who did so much to assist the triumph of realism in the European novel and who was free, in Pushkin's words, of any "slavish predilection for kings and heroes", [44] was felt by Thackeray to subscribe to certain Romantic illusions and be too far from the truth. In his humorous *Miss Tickletoby's Lectures on English History* and *Rebecca and Rowena* (a parodistic continuation of *Ivanhoe*) Thackeray ridicules Scott's idealized view of feudal chivalry.

We should note, too, the ironic and bitter sub-title to *Vanity Fair:* "A Novel without a Hero". The entire regiment commanded by the old warhorse Major O'Dowd demonstrate great bravery and loyalty to their oath during the battles against the Napoleonic guard. Young ensign Tom Stubble courageously defends the regimental colours; Lieutenant Osborne goes to a valiant death. But all the same Thackeray does not wish to promote any of them or others like them to the status of "heroes". Perhaps the reason for this is that, with whatever "feelings of exultation and gratitude, bereavement and sickening dismay" [45] the news of Waterloo may be greeted at home in England, the victory did little, in Thackeray's opinion, to alter either the actual structure of society or its morals. England remained the same as before, and the same vanity fair threshes away on its boards.

Thackeray saw his mission as an artist of integrity to judge events not in terms of their official victorious reports, parliamentary speeches or court chronicles. He was concerned with the deep connection, imperceptible to the official historiographers, between the extravagant deeds of historical figures and the everyday destiny of ordinary, inconspicuous people. "In the month of March, Anno Domini 1815, Napoleon landed at Cannes, and Louis XVIII fled, and all Europe was in alarm, and the funds fell, and old John Sedley was ruined." Following in Scott's footsteps Thackeray concentrates on the ironic contrasts between the appearance and the reality of historical facts, but he interprets these contrasts more deeply and fully, showing how they are manifested in the destiny of ordinary people. But Thackeray does not deliberate about the *movement* of history, about the forces which might propell it, about the *poetry* of the people's life and struggle (a poetry which for Scott constituted an inalienable and extremely important part of his interpretation of the historical process). It is thus understandable why he should be so fond of expressing his sombre philosophy of life with the bitter words of Ecclesiastes: "Vanity of vanities, all is vanity."

The ruin of old man Sedley, Amelia's widowhood, the bereavement of her son—all these, in Thackeray's eyes, are no less significant events than the deeds of generals and monarchs, to glorify which is the sole concern of official historiography. By leading the reader behind the scenes of the dazzling spectacle of history, Thackeray shows at what cost to the involuntary ordinary participants in any historical drama its brilliant trophies are bought. Even the figures of aposiopesis which Thackeray employs so effectively, are full of denunciation import. He refuses to accompany the troops onto the battlefield at Waterloo, preferring to concentrate on events in the back lines of the allied forces, in Brussels. And the picture of general panic and uncontrolled speculation which unfurls in the novel is eloquent illustration of the egoistic and predatory instincts concealed beneath the veneer of official "patriotism" sported by both the nobility and the up-and-coming bourgeoisie. With ironic deference he is reluctant to follow his enterprising heroine into the royal palace, where she awaits an audience with George IV himself, "the first gentleman of Europe". But this deferential restraint holds within it a withering sarcasm, which we find as well in his satirical portrayal of the English grandees, MPs, pillars of the church, diplomats and other men of state, an entire line-up of whom, presented not in their grand, official roles, but in their true, prosaic flesh-and-blood, can be found in the pages of *Vanity Fair*.

We see before us, as it were, a model of English society, represented both by its ruling classes and by those who, like Rebecca Sharp, would also like at any cost to join these upper echelons. The self-interested, vain and egoistical motives which reign supreme in this vanity fair do not escape Thackeray the satirist's keen scrutiny, however well they might be disguised. Even the names of his characters often embody the age-old time-serving traditions. Each of the scions of the pedigree Crawley family was christened in honour of the political figure who held power at the time, so that the Crawley family tree has imprinted on its pages an indiscriminate list of the names of all the main favourites and prime-ministers for the past several generations, and here we can read the author's protest against "genuflecting" history. "I am for having her rise up off her knees, and take a natural posture: not to be for ever performing cringes and congees like a Court chamberlain, and shuffling backwards out of doors in the presence of the sovereign. In a word, I would have History familiar rather than heroic," declares Thackeray in his historical novel *History of Henry Esmond, Esq.* (1852): this programme he had already carried out in his *Vanity Fair*.

This conception of the role of the artist who portrays the life of society forms the pledge of the critical sharpness of Thackeray's realism. But at the same time it harboured the danger that the writer's vision would become too confined. We may recall that Tolstoy heeded this danger.

In *War and Peace* (the action of which refers, incidentally, to the same era as *Vanity Fair*) Tolstoy was able to demonstrate that a nineteenth century novelist could find in the depths of popular life a source of true heroism and epic greatness, and that an unadorned portrayal of the "doings of life" can, without detriment to historical or artistic truth, be wedded to a portrayal of "heroic feats".

Thackeray's social scepticism determined both the strong and weak sides of his writing.

Together with the Romantic illusions of his English predecessors—Byron, Shelley and Scott—he also rejected the sort of elevated heroic poetry which is found in their work

90

as an echo of mighty popular movements. A severe critic and unmasker of human foibles, in his contempt for the parasitism and futility of the "vanity fair", he reflects to a large extent the people's own attitude to the ruling classes. But the people are not actually present in Thackeray's novel, nor are they taken into account, although both the writer's letters and journalistic writings show that he was in touch with the subterranean stirrings of revolution which threatened the status quo, and in particular, closely studied the activities of the Chartists. Nevertheless, in the end his disconsolate and sceptical view of the hopelessness of the historical process comes out on top. "I can't find the end of the question between property and labour," writes Thackeray in a letter to his mother of March 10, 1848. *"One goes round in a perpetual circle* of grief, pain, starvation, there seems no way out..." (my italics.—*A.Y.*).

It is indicative that the historical novel *The Virginians*, which treats the period of the American war of independence, should have been one of Thackeray's weakest works. Thackeray not only fails to reveal the progressive historical significance of this war of liberation, he even appears not to be interested in it. The "daily affairs" of the Warrington brothers, who more through force of circumstance than conviction find themselves in opposite camps, entirely obscure the "heroic feats" of the men fighting for their independence. Thackeray remained indifferent to the cause which had inspired Byron and Cooper before him, and which much later was to inspire such an inveterate satirist as George Bernard Shaw *(The Devil's Disciple)*.

When we return to *Dead Souls* after *Vanity Fair* it is impossible not to feel that, despite the similarity of their respective satirical condemnations of the status quo of social as well as private life, the position of the two authors, and consequently both the structure and tone of their narrative are strikingly different in many respects.

Gogol and Thackeray belong to the same stage of the development of critical realism in nineteenth century European literature. This general thesis can only be accepted, however, with the proviso that we emphasize the remarkable originality that distinguishes Gogol the author of *Dead Souls* as precisely a *Russian* writer.

The first and most general observation with which it would be appropriate to begin, consists in the fact that the critical satire of Gogol's view of the world is not absolutized, is not transformed into a universal and hopeless scepticism, as it is with Thackeray.

Thackeray looks down on his characters from above, with the ironic view of a wise and all-seeing sceptic and moralist, and he introduces them to his readers just as the Manager of the Performance, presents his puppets from his fairbooth; their grimaces and gestures can amuse for a while, although "the general impression is one more melancholy than mirthful".

The novel begins with the Manager's speech "Before the curtain", and it ends with a similarly ironical reminder of the vanity of all existence and of the revelation that everything that has already been depicted is no more than a puppet play, acted out in *Vanity Fair*.

"Ah! *Vanitas vanitatum!* Which of us is happy in this world? Which of us has his desire? Or, having it, is satisfied?—Come, children, let us shut up the box and the puppets, for our play is played out." [46]

The novel thus takes on the appearance of a closed structure, within which the author—the Manager of the Performance—controls the appearances of his actors and the changes of scene with total authority. He is guided by his bitter experience of life and no secret motives or inner contradictions harboured by his characters escape his sceptical scrutiny. Thackeray the Manager of the Performance frequently reminds the public of his omniscience. When he completes the last pages of the novel the reader should feel that he has learnt all it is worth knowing about the intrigues of Rebecca Sharp, the naïve egoism of Amelia, about the Osbornes and Steynes, about Crawley and Dobbin and about the society to which they belong.

There is no trace of this "closedness", this feeling of completeness, of such a self-contained model of society in Gogol's work. This is not only because Volume 1 of *Dead Souls* should have been followed by a second and third volumes. The very standpoint of the author vis-à-vis the life he reproduces is radically different from that held by Thackeray.

Like Thackeray, Gogol views the squalid prose of life with an ironic curl of the lip. But beyond the melancholy fragmentation of his characters, beyond the desiccating wretchedness of their egoistic interests, he detects another, as yet historically undefined, but nonetheless *possible* life.

At first glance the author of *Vanity Fair* may appear

to think in far more concrete and precise historical terms than the creator of *Dead Souls*. But the omniscient Manager of the Performance is not concerned with the hidden, deep meaning of his country's past experiences and future destiny, nor is this touched on in his play (although we do know that in his letters Thackeray anxiously compared his country with slave-holding Rome during its period of decline, on the eve of its destruction). Nor is he concerned here with the problem of the national character of his fellow-countrymen (an issue which, we may recall, so persistently engaged the attention of Walter Scott).

In *Dead Souls* the author does not deem it necessary to designate exactly the time in which the action of his book is set. But many details make it possible to date its beginning to the second half of Alexander I's reign. In Volume 1, chapter 10, in which the town officials put forward their suggestions as to Chichikov's identity, the author lets slip the remark: "We should remember, incidentally, that all this took place soon after the glorious expulsion of the French. At this time all our landowners, government officials, merchants, shop assistants and all manner of literate and even illiterate people became, at least for the next eight years, passionate politicians" (VI, 206). It is for this reason that in their enthusiasm they are almost prepared to take Chichikov for Napoleon, released by the English from St. Helena and now secretly hiding in Russia!

The "Captain Kopeikin's Story" is also directly connected with the 1812 Napoleonic War. Reminiscences of 1812 were also intended to form part of Volume 2, initially in the comic episode where Chichikov, carried away by his own fictions, assures General Betrishchev that Tentetnikov is engaged in the composition of a "history of generals" who participated in the 1812 campaign, and then in the quite serious scene of the dinner at Betrishchev's, where Tentetnikov is to move both the host and his daughter Ulenka with an impassioned speech about the patriotic upsurge of all the people, which secured Russia's victory over Napoleon. * General Betrishchev himself, with the "striking contradictions" of his character, who is retired as a result of "numerous troubles in his service", appears in Vol-

---

* This scene has not survived, but we know of it from the memoirs of L. I. Arnoldi, who heard it read by Gogol himself.

ume 2 of *Dead Souls* as one of "those picturesque generals who were so plentiful in the illustrious year of 1812" (VII, 37-38).

Echoes of real historical events of the twenties, and then of the thirties, can be felt in many passages in surviving parts of the volumes 1 and 2—in mentions of the peasant risings, the secret society to which Tentetnikov belonged, the critical situations in the administrative apparatus, which was riddled with bribery and corruption, and powerless against the collapse of the economy (the poor harvest and famine in Volume 2) and alarmed by the growth of "disturbances" amongst the people ...

But in order to establish the historical import of *Dead Souls* it is necessary to go beyond the precise allusions to the time which we find here, and to take into account the more elusive lyrical strain that runs through the entire work, a *lyrical* divination, a vague and intuitive, but nonetheless profoundly sincere and anxious understanding of the historical experiences of Russia not only in the past and present, but in the future also.

A special role was assigned to the *lyrical* principle in the divination and reproduction of as yet undeveloped historical processes, of unresolved conflicts, in the aesthetics of Romanticism. Thus Shelley, explaining why he describes *Hellas* as a "lyrical drama", writes: "The subject in its present state is insusceptible of being treated otherwise than lyrically, and if I have called this poem a drama ... the license is not greater than that which has been assumed by other poets who have called their productions epics, only because they have been divided into twelve or twenty four books ... The glorious contest now waging in Greece being yet suspended ... I have, therefore, contented myself with exhibiting a series of lyric pictures and with having wrought upon the curtain of futurity, which falls upon the unfinished scene, such figures of indistinct and visionary delineation as suggest the final triumph of the Greek cause ..." [47]

This understanding of lyricism has much in common with that held by Gogol. We might also note the free use both writers make—in the name of this sacred lyrical principle—of formal definitions of the limits of genres. Shelley explains why he called his *poema* a *lyrical drama*. In the final chapter of Volume 1 Gogol promises the reader that his *poema* "will acquire a majestic lyrical flow".

Here too we can see more distinctly the divide between Gogol and Thackeray (and to a certain extent, between Gogol and Balzac, and Dickens, who belong to the same stage of the development of critical realism in European literature—in the broad sense of the term "critical realism"). Both Balzac and Dickens assign a larger role to "poetic" principle than does Thackeray; but it is a different role than that given it by Gogol.

As far as the author of *Vanity Fair* is concerned, in this respect he is particularly distant from Gogol.

We should recall in this connection a letter from Nekrasov to Turgenev of December 18, 1856, in which the Russian poet exclaims: "No! Even the wise Thackeray does not know everything yet, he has not dwelt in the soul of a Russian writer". [48]

By contrast to the self-contained *Vanity Fair* Gogol's work has a markedly open structure. This openness is linked with Gogol's increasing awareness, as he worked on Volume 1, that volumes 2 and 3 were already taking shape, to which the first volume would play a role no bigger than an entrance to a palace. That openness was already manifest in the first volume of the *poema,* both in the amazingly unfettered structure of the narrative and in its motivations.

With Thackeray the upheavals taking place in the "big world" are manifested through the private life of the puppets brought out onto the proscenium of his theatre. The novel begins with the departure from boarding school and entry into the world of two girl-friends, Amelia Sedley and Rebecca Sharp, and their subsequent destinies form the substance of the story. The denouement is provided by the second, happy marriage of Amelia and the disgrace of Rebecca, who, nevertheless, manages through underhand machinations to secure capital and the reputation of a distinguished lady totally immersed in pious and charitable affairs.

This sort of ironic outcome might equally have been used by Gogol to conclude his "Adventures of Chichikov", enabling him to realize his cherished dream of a village idyll, with a comely wife and a brood of children. But while the "exploits" of Miss Rebecca Sharp, although they do not entirely exhaust the content of *Vanity Fair,* largely determine its development and demonstrate the debt that this book owes to the picaresque and, in particular to the satirical novel of mores of the Enlightenment, the "exploits" of Chichikov have a far more subservient role in the general design of Gogol's work. Gogol and Thackeray both adhere equally to the principle of "harnessing a rogue", casting him and not a positive character, in the limelight. Rebecca Sharp is perfectly comparable to Chichikov as a stereotype, embodying all the baseness of a society founded on venality and self-interest. "If this is a novel without a hero, at least let us lay claim to a heroine," exclaims Thackeray, sarcastically maintaining that Wellington himself did not possess the greatness of spirit on the eve of Waterloo that is displayed by this vixen.

In contrast to *Vanity Fair* Gogol's work has two true heroes, who are presented without any irony.

The first of these is a collective and unnamed hero, but one who is always present in the author's mind: the Russian people. The second is the author himself.

He is constantly by the reader's side. His voice can be heard throughout the narration, as, incidentally, can the voice of the author of *Vanity Fair*. But the latter adheres strictly to the role he adopts at the beginning of manager and commentator of his puppet play. The tone of his comments to the public can change: at times he speaks in witty asides, at others with caustic irony, and on rare occasions he utters indignant denunciation.

But the image of the English novelist and his role in the book are predetermined—even graphically so: Thackeray placed a self-portrait on the cover of the first edition of *Vanity Fair,* in which he depicts himself in a jester's cap complete with bells, standing on the stage of a fair booth. This jester is the "moralist" (as Thackeray describes himself), and his function is to tell people the bitter truth which is all too apparent to him.

"If this kind of composition, of which the two years' product is now laid before the public, fail in art... it at least has the advantage of a certain truth and honesty, which a work more elaborate might lose... It is a sort of confidential talk between writer and reader, which must often be dull, must often flag... And as we judge of a man's character, after long frequenting his society, not by one speech, or by one mood or opinion... but by the tenor of his general bearing and conversation; so of a writer, who delivers himself up to you perforce unreservedly, you say, Is he honest? Does he tell the truth in the main? Does he seem actuated by a desire to find out and speak it? Is he a quack, who shams sentiment, or mouths for effect? Does he seek popularity by claptraps or other arts? ...

"I have found many thousands more readers than I ever looked for. I have no right to say to these, You shall not find fault with my art, or fall asleep over my pages; but I ask you to believe that this person writing strives to tell the truth.

"If there is not that, there is nothing." [49] Thus Thackeray writes, with restraint but a dignity and a deep awareness of his responsibility, of the writer's task in the foreword to his novel *The History of Pendennis*. This statement has much in common with some of Gogol's authorial asides, above all in the severity with which Thackeray, and the author of *Dead Souls*, condemn all literary "quacks", and in his firm allegiance to truth as single principle of his art.

But we are also struck by the extraordinary and deliberate restraint of this confiding remark to his readers. It is as if Thackeray were afraid to give too open an expression to his feelings, and shunned any lyrical outbursts— perhaps because such outbursts had been so shamelessly misused in the verse and prose of those feeble imitators of Romanticism he so ridicules. His truth, as presented in his early essays, in the *Book of Snobs* and in *Vanity Fair*, is caustic and severe. It is only in his later works, in *The Newcomes* and *The Adventures of Philip,* that we find any small measure of sentimentality, and that is not in the author's own passages.

He, the author, is only too aware of all his characters' awful and shameful secrets. It was none other than Thackeray himself who turned the expression "a skeleton in the cupboard" into a popular idiom, for while it is also used by Dickens it appears time and time again in Thackeray's novels, as if to proclaim the fatal law of life: in every respectable house, in every family, however irreproachably virtuous they might appear, there is bound to be some shameful secret, some awful "skeleton" carefully concealed in a cupboard, which sooner or later will come to light. But, in contrast to Gogol, who is concerned to discover the as yet unknown, Thackeray in advance knows everything about all these "skeletons". However, there are other secrets, secrets which so engaged Gogol's mind, the secrets of the future of his country, of its possible resurrection and cleansing of all venal corruption, which the author of *Vanity*

Fair either prefers not to think of, regarding this as idle speculation, or on which he at least keeps his own counsel. And the range of his colloquies with his readers, for all their biting satire, is far narrower than that of Gogol. Thackeray the Manager of the Performance remains to the very end exactly as he was at the beginning.

The author of *Dead Souls* cuts a quite different figure in the readers' eyes. He reveals himself gradually, and his own scale changes as suddenly as the tone and message of his utterances. Initially he appears to be a good-natured, albeit derisive, friend and interlocutor, a master of the sly, off-the-cuff narrative, who feels quite at home in this element of commonplace and petty vulgarity. However, a gradual distance between the chronicler and his characters grows. His worldly-wise irony, profundity of observation, frequently presented in the guise of an apparently casual reference, become increasingly prominent after the scene of the governor's soirée.

At the same time the image of the author is amplified by incidental personal reminiscences, as in the memorable comparison he draws between the bewilderment of the officials under the impact of rumours about Chichikov, and that of a schoolboy, on whom his schoolmates play the trick of blowing snuff up his nose whilst he is still asleep. In this picture there is such a vivid evocation of his personal childhood experiences, bringing to life the author's schooldays in Nezhin, and the sunny Ukrainian countryside with its "newly awakened forest", bird song, glinting stream, and "naked children, urging one another into the water" (VI, 189).

Many other significant digressions in Volume 1 are similarly full of this autobiographical lyricism. Such, for example, is the writer's bitter reference to his harsh and lonely destiny (VI, 134), or the sudden, dazzling pictures of Italy, which burst into the sombre vistas of the Russian provinces, that "wondrous, beautiful afar", where Gogol was in fact living at the time he wrote *Dead Souls,* Volume 1 (VI, 220).

Gogol also employs the device, favoured by Thackeray, by Fielding before him, and, still earlier, by their common mentor Cervantes, of engaging the reader in a direct discussion of the secrets of the writer's craft.

Like them too, he defends his right to portray life as it is, repudiating the arguments of his opponents and preempting their objections. But we cannot but be struck by the difference in the actual *tone* of these authorial interpolations in *Dead Souls* and the remarks addressed to the reader by the English satirists.

There had already been precedents for regarding the very act of creative perception, study and reproduction of the world as the object of *artistic* portrayal. In Sterne's *Tristram Shandy* the *subjective* aspect of the creative process is thrust into prominence: the author recounts the peripeteia of his book's nativity with as much enthusiasm and just as extensively as he does the birth and upbringing of his hero. However, this intrusion into the narrative, which is made not only by the author's own person, but also and primarily by his creative mind with all its contradictions, fanciful associative moves and occasionally, impasses, serves not only a constructive purpose, but also undoubtedly to destroy through travesty those narrative traditions which Sterne the sentimentalist regarded as both too rational and too cumbersome. Romanticism, by further elaborating these Sternian tendencies and sometimes even absolutizing them, developed the principle of Romantic irony which Gogol follows in the Petersburg stories.

Our attention is caught by something else in *Dead Souls*. The freedom with which the author, without relinquishing the position of realistic narration, will suddenly interrupt his narrative to reveal to the reader the innermost workings of his mind, his artistic quest, his bewilderment and his vision, is very far from both the fervent mockery and parody of Sterne and the Romantic irony of Hoffmann.

The abrupt contrasts between the prose of life, and the inspired authorial digressions at the beginning of the sixth, seventh, and in the middle of the eleventh chapters and in the celebrated ending are evidence not of the relative nature of our impressions (as is the case with Sterne), nor of the capricious duality of existence (as with Hoffmann). Far from rending the work asunder they actually reveal, or, more precisely, afford a glimpse of, its hidden depths, which correspond to profundity of Russian life, which Gogol has not yet fully explored, but about which he "divines". One of the organic components of his epic narration at this point is the lyrical theme of the poet's civic role, as prophet, diviner and judge, a theme that resounds so forcefully in Russian poetry, notably that of Lermontov and Pushkin.

The word "digression" is only formally applicable to these impassioned monologues. They do not lead the reader aside from the main theme, but deeper within it, to the hidden secrets that Gogol senses and divines in the national character of his people and their history. The verb "to divine" is highly appropriate to the entire arrangement of these monologues. We might recall how often Gogol employs "ugadat" (to divine), in his letters, when discussing his literary designs. In the Author's Confession he identifies as special talent, and one he has possessed since early youth, the ability "to divine a person" (VIII, 439).

The motif of a *secret* or *mystery* awaiting solution also occurs in the draft for Volume 1 of *Dead Souls*. "Life sinks into the Stygian murk, with the mystery of death unrevealed" (VI, 692). This motif emerges most persistently and powerfully, even ominously, in those author-inspired monologues which more than anything else elevate the narration of "Chichikov's adventures" to the level of a true poem, and not mere work of comic irony.

Such great contemporaries of Gogol as Balzac, Dickens and Thackeray all believed in their mission as writers. But none of them described this mission with such ardour as the author of *Dead Souls*, in words which "stirred the soul", and "burst forth from the heart".

He sees poetic inspiration as a miracle which infinitely extends the artist's horizons, revealing to his vision things hitherto unseen. The creative act itself entails for him a great, almost ecstatic élan; the study of the truth of life is not merely the writer's civic duty, demanding great self-denial and sacrifice, it is also a great miracle of discovering the unknown, a miracle whose significance he is already able to appreciate with his artist's sixth sense.

The intense severity of Pushkin's poem *The Prophet* and the majestic symbolism in which he cloaks the notion of poetic creation as an exalted and self-sacrificing exploit were closest of all both in their spirit and their message to the author's monologues in *Dead Souls*.

> There came to me the gentle flutter
> Of angels' wings, I heard the vine
> Push through the earth and skyward climb,
> The deep-sea monsters in the water
> Like fishes glide ... *

---

* Translated by Irina Zheleznova.

The Gogol that we encounter in the authorial asides of his *poema* would appear to stand on the very threshold of just such an illumination. He is full of presentiment of those still sacred truths, of that secret meaning of Russian life, which, as he knows, will be revealed to him at a moment of the supreme exertion of his spiritual forces, at the apogee of his flight of inspiration. This foretaste of an as yet unknown, but perceptible, secret first finds expression at the end of chapter three of Volume 1, where it is conveyed in an off-hand manner, interrupting speculation about Korobochka's aristocratic sisters and the vacuity of their existence: "But enough, enough! Why talk about it? But why is it that amidst such thoughtless, gay, carefree moments suddenly another string should sound, of its own volition? The smile has not yet faded from your face and you are already quite another person amongst the same people and your face is illuminated with quite another light..." (VI, 58).

Later on he develops this allusion further and the same idea is expressed with a persuasive and impassioned, even prophetic fervour in the programmatic introduction to chapter seven, in which Gogol the realist defines his view of the purpose and destiny of a "writer who had dared to make crystal-clear all that constantly lies open to the view but is unseen by the indifferent eye, all that awful quagmire of little things that entangle our lives, the inner world of frigid, fragmented and commonplace characters" (VI, 134).

It is precisely here, hard on the heels of his stoical acceptance of the misunderstanding, condemnation and solitude that lay in store for him (how close Gogol is here to another, this time Lermontov's *Prophet*!), that a sudden shaft of light from a radiant future breaks through the clouds: "For some invisible power has ordained that I am to walk for many a day side by side with my strange heroes, view the hurtling advance of life, view it through the laughter that is there for world to see, and tears unseen and unknown by it! And the time is still far off when, a tearful tempest of fresh inspiration will burst forth from a mind endowed with awe-inspiring power and vision and capable of giving birth to a majestic chorus of other voices..." (VI, 134-135).

We find the same impassioned image of inspiration as a peal of thunder, cleansing spate of the elements, in the eleventh chapter, in the author's address to his country:

"And I stand motionless, in utter perplexity, with a storm cloud, heavy with rain, gathering above my head, and my mind is benumbed by the vastness of your space... Your mighty space encompasses me, to find reflection in all my inner being, and light my eyes with supernatural power: ah! what a breath-taking, marvellous and unexplored vistas you unfold to the view! Russia!.." (VI, 221).

There is no passage in any of the works of Dickens, Balzac or Thackeray comparable to these inspired apostrophes, full of prophetic revelation, in which the author addresses not the reader, nor himself, but—his most cherished audience—his country itself. Interrogative intonations become dominant, and with them we seem to draw ever closer to the great mystery he strives to unravel. "Russia! What is your demand on me? What is that mystic bond that exists between us?.. What is the promise held out by the immensity of your spaces?.." (VI, 221). And the entire memorable finale of Volume 1 bursts with such urgent questions, forecasting the historic greatness of Russia: "Are you not also like that, my Russia, as you dash headlong onwards, a swift troika that no one can overtake?.. Russia, whither do you hasten? Answer!" (VI, 247).

These anxious questions, so charged with presentiment of the future destiny of his country and its people, have no analogues in any work by the major critical realists of West European literature, who are so comparable to Gogol in many other respects.

This does not of course mean that these authors were not also searchers after the truth, like Gogol, that they did not ponder over the mysteries of life. But they gave to their search and their thought a different form.

In his letters and articles Balzac occasionally talks of the high mission of the artist, who looks into the future and brings closer its realization, and he is filled with the same prophetic inspiration as Gogol in the lyrical digressions of *Dead Souls*.

"We are the new priests of an unknown future, whose work we are preparing. The eighteenth century has proved this proposition," he exclaims in his open letter to the French writers of the nineteenth century (1834).

At an earlier date, writing in a review of P. L. Jacob's derivative novel *Deux fous*, Balzac had expressed the same thought in insistent terms. He censures Jacob for his failure to prophesy the future development of society.

Sometimes Balzac compares the act of creation directly to prophetic *revelation*. While working on *Le médecin de campagne* he writes to Evelina Hanska that his work will be a new Gospel of modern times.

But in the novels and stories which together make up the magnificent edifice of *La Comédie humaine* Balzac usually opts for the objective manner of a chronicler of mores —a manner in which both indignation and emotion are moderated by humorous wisdom.

Balzac projected himself in the diverse images of his heroes—the righteous, incorruptible and wise writer d'Arthez; Claës, propelled by an insatiable thirst for knowledge of the "absolute"; the courageous toiler David Séchard, wresting from nature its secrets: and finally, the brilliant clairvoyant Louis Lambert, whose superhuman abilities, that raise him above the world of commonplace understanding, in the end destroy his own humanity ... Each of these and other characters can to some extent be regarded as hypostases of the author, although Balzac never entirely fuses with any one of them. He always retains the right to address the reader directly; his views are profound, witty and acute; but, as a rule, he remains throughout the person he declares himself to be in the foreword to *La Comédie humaine* —the "secretary" of the "historian" he held French society to be.

As for the contradictions in the history of this society, the dangers which beset it, and the direction its future development might take, Balzac does not confine himself to a mere depiction of typical and actual conflicts, but willingly leaves the floor to his characters. Debates about the past, present and future of France constantly resound through the pages of *La Comédie humaine,* in contrast to *Dead Souls,* whose characters are people of few words, at least in Volume 1, and if, on the odd occasion, they might "argue, shout and talk about everything, about politics, even about military matters, they expressed such irreverent views that they would have thrashed their own children had these expressed them" (VI, 151), they are only provoked to do so by the persuasive influence of wine.

From many corners of Balzac's epic we hear the voices of prophets, each of whom is giving vent to his own store of wisdom. But Balzac leaves it up to the reader to draw his own conclusions.

The "moi" of his novels is "not without danger for the author," remarks Balzac in the foreword to *Lys dans la vallée*. The writer's "personal sentiments" should not, in his view, interfere with the portrayal of "imagined sentiments". We should not bridge the chasm that divides the outward physiognomy of a work from "the most cherished treasures" of its creator's heart. "If some poet is to embark on such a double life let this be by accident and not design, as with Jean-Jacques Rousseau." Rousseau's *Confessions* provoke an ambivalent reaction in Balzac: he "admires the writer ... but the person arouses his horror".

Scholars single out "Facino Cane" as perhaps the only story by Balzac in which the author violates his own rule by appearing in person on the boards of his *Comédie humaine*. It is worth noting that this story was published in 1836, several years before its position as one of the *Scènes de la vie parisienne* had been decided. "Facino Cane" begins with an authorial digression, in which Balzac recalls the years of his literary apprenticeship, when he led the life of a recluse, dividing his time between work in his wretched attic and the library. The reminiscences which follow these, about how "listening to people" enabled him to "espouse their life", and how their desires, their needs, all these passed into his soul, are interesting in themselves, and also remarkable for their closeness to certain autobiographical confessions made by Gogol. Balzac describes as "second sight" his gift "of living the life of other people", just as Gogol in his *Author's Confession* describes how, as an artist, he was attracted by the great variety of folk life. "I already knew what rich possibilities lay hidden in that suburb, that hot-bed of revolutionaries, cultivating ground of heroes, of inventors and self-made men, of rogues and swindlers, of men of virtue and men of vice—and they are all abased by poverty, oppressed by need, obfuscated by drunkenness..." But we are also struck by Balzac's *analytic* method of studying his people, a method which he emphasizes himself: "At this time I had already divided up the elements of this heterogeneous mass which is called the people, and I had analyzed it in such a way as to be able to evaluate its good and bad qualities."

In Gogol's *poema* this analysis is far from complete, and the author initiates the reader in the sacrament of its process. Gogol strives to achieve the very thing that Balzac describes in this extract: in some respects their views coincide exactly. But the author of *Dead Souls* is still deeply involved in his quest, he is still "on the road", he listens attentively to the songs echoing across the distant spaces of Russia and peers into the infinite distance... He is still asking, and not affirming and summarizing, as does Balzac. Behind the precise observations, which constitute the archetypal images of *Dead Souls,* the reader can discern the hidden possibilities of Russian social development, not yet encapsulated in thought and formed in word and image, but deeply disturbing the artist's imagination, and still awaiting their realization in life and in art. Thus the characteristic features of both the fundamental harmony and the differences of Gogol's and Balzac's brands of realism become apparent even in this isolated example—the author's image as depicted in "Facino Cane".

In general Balzac preferred to confine outside the narrative proper—in forewords, afterwords and articles—any expression of his artistic principles, polemics with his opponents, or defence of his own perception of the world and of his selection of themes and characters—in other words, all things which for Gogol form such an organic part of the very fabric of his artistic work. This deliberate restraint on the part of an artist with such a stormy temperament as Balzac, would appear to reflect an inner polemic with the aesthetics of Hugo's Romantic prose, in which the author's philosophical monologues sometimes form entire chapters of his novels.

In Dickens's novels the author's lyrical voice is also heard more frequently, and his emotional range is broader than Balzac's.

As Dickens himself says, he stands invisible at the reader's side; he incessantly interrupts his narrative with exclamations of surprise, joy, or indignation. Sometimes he addresses a question to the reader and engages him in a good-natured discussion: "If you should happen, by any unlikely chance, to know a man more blest in a laugh than Scrooge's nephew, all I can say is, I should like to know him too. Introduce him to me, and I'll cultivate his acquaintance." [50]

When the plot reaches some particularly dramatic moment Dickens is prepared to depart from the role of an objective narrator and intrude into the action, in order to give heart to an over-timid hero or to restrain another who is deluded by pride and arrogance.

We should also note other lyrical digressions by Dickens, in which he addresses himself not to his "friend the reader", but to those people who arouse his utmost anger and contempt—the authorities, lords and spiritual pastors of England, responsible for all the misfortunes of their people. Such a grave accusation, for example, concludes the forty seventh chapter of *Bleak House,* in which poor Joe departs this life—a homeless, hunted urchin from the London slums: "Dead, your Majesty. Dead, my lords and gentlemen. Dead, Right Reverends and Wrong Reverends of every order. Dead, men and women, born with Heavenly compassion in your hearts. And dying thus around us every day."

Thus too in the eighth chapter of Book III of *Our Mutual Friend* Dickens interrupts his account of the inheritance of the Golden Dustman. Taking his rubbish heap as a symbol of the pointlessness and paltriness of the bureaucratic fuss of legislators and administrators, he rounds on them in anger:

"My lords and gentlemen and honourable boards, when you in the course of your dust-shovelling and cinder-raking have piled up a mountain of pretentious failure, you must off with your honourable coats for the removal of it, and fall to the work with the power of all the queen's horses and all the queen's men, or it will come rushing down and bury us alive."

However, despite the variety of these authorial digressions both in terms of their content and their emotional ardour, they differ from Gogol's lyrical monologues. Like Gogol Dickens knows with whom he sympathizes, whom he despises and whom he shall ridicule. But he generously shares with the reader observations made long before and well-confirmed, and a spiritual wisdom which no longer harbours any problems for him. Even in his most subjective and largely autobiographical novel, *David Copperfield*, he does not for a moment consider revealing to us the writer's inner world, the concealed life of his imagination and thought in their quest for new truths, although this novel is constructed as an account of the *novelist's life.*

Perhaps this is why Belinsky criticizes Dickens for having so little that is personal and subjective. "Why does he have to be closer to Walter Scott, than to Byron!" [51]

In order to find anything in West European literature comparable to the image of the author conjured up by a reading of *Dead Souls* we would have to turn not to critical realism, but to the Romantics, from Byron to Carlyle.

It is indicative that in precisely those works in which Dickens is closest to Carlyle as an artist—in "The Chimes" or *A Tale of Two Cities*—he is also closest of all to the theme which engages Gogol throughout his own great work: the connection between the historical future and the past and present. In "The Chimes" two contradictory versions of the future come into conflict. One of them is that which proceeds from the social forecasts made by those Malthusian economists and Tory zealots of the old order, who are so hateful to Dickens, and which bodes nothing but disaster, ignominy and death for his heroes—poor labourers, who have the audacity to dream about happiness. The other is that based on the logic of the good fairy-tale, which glorifies honest poverty and generously endows it with all sorts of bright joys, warmed by the cosy fire of the home hearth. The spirits of the old church bells, who intrude on New Year Eve into the life of a humble errand-man, Toby Veck, embody, as it were, the voices of the past and the future, instilling in the people a belief in their own worth. It is precisely in this light that their fabulous revelation is received by Toby Veck, whom the author brings out of his role for a moment, in order to pronounce the main social idea of the story in a flight of prophetic inspiration (so inappropriate, it would seem, to this down-trodden and ridiculous man): "I see the spirit of the Chimes among you! I know that our inheritance is held in store for us by Time. I know there is a sea of Time to rise one day, before which all who wrong us or oppress us will be swept away like leaves. I see it, on the flow! I know that we must trust and hope, and neither doubt ourselves, nor doubt the good in one another." [52]

A Tale of Two Cities is devoted to events which have become the property of history. We are, however, struck by the metaphor and symbolism with which Dickens expresses the concealed interaction of the present and the future, which already lies latent within it, a future which is familiar to the reader and the author, but as yet unknown to the heroes. These symbolic scenes proclaim the great upheavals to come in the Romantic language of indistinct, but menacing prophetic allusion. Thus the wine spilt from a broken cask onto the pavements of St. Antoine, prefigures the torrents of blood which are soon to flow down the streets of Paris in revolution. An even more enigmatic and ominous portent of the future can be heard in the echoing footsteps in the quiet London mews where Dr. Manette lives—the sound of a crowd of people in a deserted place. These are the first drops of rain in the still before a storm; and the author concludes this chapter with a sign to his heroes: "Perhaps. Perhaps, see the great crowd of people with its rush and roar, bearing down upon them, too." [53]

As an artist Dickens's imagination is more often attracted, however, to a different kind of "secret", which correspondingly occupies an important place in the structure of his novels.

In his early books (such as, for example, *Oliver Twist,* or *Nicholas Nickleby*) these secrets tend to be connected, as Belinsky was quick to note, with the provenance of their rejected and persecuted heroes.

In his later novels, beginning with *Dombey and Son,* and in particular in *Bleak House, Little Dorrit* and *Great Expectations,* all of which remained unknown to Belinsky, the "secret" itself and the process of its revelation acquire a new, profounder and more significant import. At the same time the novels are constructed in accordance with a new principle. Dickens moves on from the novel of travels, or adventures (compositionally closer to *Dead Souls)* to works of a different kind, in which the threads of different human destinies prove—irrespective of the will of the heroes, and often, without even their knowledge—to be connected in a single, tangled knot.

Society is thus revealed as a complex, contradictory and at the same time intricately interconnected whole, and not in gradual stages, as its successive layers are explored by the itinerant hero. The aristocratic Edith Granger, who cynically marries Dombey for his money, thus proves to be no better than her cousin, the convict Alice Marwood, sad daughter of the slums, corrupted and destroyed by the very same Carker who is to disgrace and ruin Mr. Dombey. By establishing these hidden inter-connections between the upper and lower echelons of society Dickens penetrates its most shameful secrets: if we refuse to allow ourselves to be taken in by its respectable façade and peer still closer within we shall see that it is quite eaten away by incurable and ignominious social diseases.

Thus too in *Bleak House* Dickens reveals the hidden ties that connect the estate of the glittering Lady Dedlock and the slums where the father of her daughter, the penniless and unknown writer Nemo, takes his own life, or between the Chancery and the filthy, cluttered shop run by the owner of these slums, the rag-dealer Krook.

In exactly the same way the reader of *Little Dorrit* is gradually and painfully acquainted with the secret circumstances which connect the wretched Bleeding Heart Yard and Marshalsea debtors' prison with the Clennams' gloomy house, the dapper new house of Merdle the banker and the Ministry of Circumlocutions, which is administered by the aristocratic and high-ranking Barnacles. Poverty and riches occasionally swap places. The multi-million speculations with which Merdle, financial "genius", hopes to benefit mankind, burst like a bubble of soap, ruining tens of thousands of his creditors. The Clennams' house, which has been eroded from its roofbeams to its foundations by the relentless chisel of Time, collapses, and in its rubble lies buried for ever the memory of the injustices and crimes perpetrated under its roof. The only ones unaffected are the Ministry of Circumlocutions and the barnacles, who have firmly latched onto the ship of state.

Anticipating the secret which must ultimately be revealed to the reader of these novels, Dickens, like Gogol, boldly employs symbolic images and introduces lyrical motifs into the narrative, which refer distantly to real circumstances to be revealed in closer detail later on. The remorseless, murderous cold which holds Mr. Dombey's house in its grip is not only an attribute of their living conditions, but also a presage of the dramatic conflicts in which this self-centred man with his "frozen" soul is shortly to find himself. The mists, autumn twilights and mire—the symbols which haunt the first chapters of *Bleak House*—help "transform", in Gogol's expression, the tragic content of the novel, which as yet remains shrouded in mystery.

But although Dickens's narrative manner brings him closer in this respect than Balzac or Thackeray to Gogol, we must also note the essential differences between them.

Dead Souls retains in its subtext the memory of a civil, patriotic ideal of "comradeship", so vividly embodied in *Taras Bulba*. Gogol dreams about the word "Forward!", which would awaken and direct towards a united goal the great forces latent in Russian society. In his view this word "Forward!" entails the transformation of individual and public morals in Russia. For Dickens, even the Dickens of the late, maturest novels, revealing the secrets of social injustice, of the moral responsibility of the upper classes for the misfortunes of the lower classes and of the futility of the contemptible fetishes of riches, nobility and power, leads to a single conclusion: man can become worthy of his exalted mission in any, even the humblest sphere of his *private* existence—and above all in precisely this sphere. Thus the supreme wisdom of Jarndyce and Esther Summerson, the wisdom of Clennam and his trusty Little Dorrit are manifested not in any public activities, but in their kindness and stoic resignation.

The words addressed by the ill-starred bankrupt Mr. Jellyby to his daughter: "Never have a Mission, my dear child," have a comic sound in the context of the *Bleak House*. But the fact remains that this is an echo of what we might term Dickens's positive programme (although Dickens would probably have rejected the concept of a "programme" with scorn).

It would only be an exercise in pedantry to attempt to illustrate how well Dickens, the creator of Sam Weller, Pickwick, Mark Tapley, the two Peggotties, Joe Gargery and a host of others, understood the English character and with what affection he regarded it. But as a rule Dickens takes it as something given, something stable and firmly established, a trusty support in times of sorrow as well as joy, a combination of good-natured, even eccentric spontaneity with genuine compassion and great staunchness. But neither these heroes, nor their biographer are normally prone to reflecting on their Englishness, or on the reason for their national character. On the contrary, the question of what is English and not English is discussed, noisily and arrogantly, by precisely those characters whom Dickens holds in unconcealed, withering contempt. The most notable of these is the flourishing dealer Mr. Podsnap, whose importance as an archetype is carefully underlined by Dickens, with the derivation from his name of the abstract concept "podsnappery", which has taken its place in the English language in a way comparable to Gogol's coinages *manilovshchina, nozdryovshchina,* etc., in Russian. This is the title Dickens puts to his chapter in *Our Mutual Friend* which displays in close-up this zealot of the English, *bourgeois* way of life.

The question of England's development is one that is usually deliberated in Dickens's novels by such characters as the snobs who gather at Lord Dedlock's house, a veritable English Museum of Antiquities. "What follows? That the country is shipwrecked, lost, and gone to pieces (as is made manifest to the patriotism of Sir Leicester Dedlock), because you can't provide for Noodle!"[54] This motif runs throughout *Bleak House*: " 'Then upon my honour, ... then upon my honour,' " exclaims Sir Leicester, apoplectic with rage, "upon my reputation and principles, the floodgates of society are burst open and the waters have—a—obliterated the landmarks of the framework of the cohesion by which things are held together!" In response to this his ". . . 'debilitated cousin thinks—Country's going—Dayvle—steeplechase pace'."[55]

But meanwhile, notes Dickens with irony, although "England has been in a dreadful state for some weeks, Lord Coodle would go out, Sir Thomas Doodle wouldn't come in and there being nobody in Great Britain (to speak of) except Coodle and Doodle, there has been no Government . . .", it appears nonetheless that "England has not appeared to care very much about it, but has gone on eating and drinking and marrying and giving in marriage, as the old world did in the days before the flood."[56]

This brings us to one of the most essential differences between Dickens's realism and that of the author of *Dead Souls*.

In Dickens's view it is private life—that little world which "has gone on eating and drinking and marrying and giving in marriage"—that provides not only the trustiest refuge, but also most favourable soil for the flowering of true humanity. The fire of the home hearth, about which he wrote so often and with such affection, glows from the pages of his novels like a guiding star for all the toiling, oppressed folk of his time. The worst disaster befalls those who fail to appreciate properly the warmth of the home, of domestic comfort—Ralph Nickleby and Dombey, the Dedlocks and Gradgrinds, and many, many others.

His sombre social epics are somewhat brightened by this lyrical warmth.

Similarly, Dickens's favourite heroes are those who value these joys and take inspiration from them. From the author's point of view, the most stirring deeds are those little, everyday actions which are performed here, at the fireside, in the name of one's nearest and dearest. Little Dorrit, the poor seamstress who every day takes her humble dinner to her father in the debtor's jail; the illegitimate orphan Esther Summerson, who becomes an indefatigable, bustling housewife, the fairy godmother of Bleak House, and who transforms it into the very opposite of bleak; Lizzy Hexam with her calloused hands, roughened by pulling on the oars, and her tender loving heart, who all her life has sacrificed herself for her severe father and ingrate brother—such are the people to whom Dickens imparts a poetic aura, and on whom in the end he confers their just reward. The seasoned reader of Dickens knows that the arrogant Dombey's most carefully checked calculations and plans can collapse, but the toast to which the two old eccentrics Captain Cuttle and Gills drink in the "Wooden Midshipman", is bound to come true. Just as the pictures of a happy future which appear to Lizzy Hexam in the flames of a dying fire are bound to come true, although neither at the time, nor in the way, she hopes.

It is impossible simply to dismiss these tendencies, which continue even in Dickens's later, mature novels, these contrasts between the little world of home comfort and the big world of selfish gain and hypocrisy, as a mere manifestation of the writer's philistinism or limited vision.

The jubilant description of steaming punch and good ale, roast beef, pies and so forth, in which his heroes indulge beside the hearth—almost Rabelaisian in their tone, with the necessary adjustments for Dickens's more prosaic nineteenth century—were often intended as a direct challenge. He aimed particularly to challenge not only the hypocrisy of those of whom Heine wrote in his "Deutschland":

Ich weiß, sie trunken heimlich Wein
Und predigten öffentlich Wasser, *

but also the very status quo which, with the sanction of the esteemed politicians and economists, lowered the life of the poor to the level of a starvation "norm".

But these unusual Romantic corrections which Dickens, both in love and in anger, introduces into his portrayal of

---

* "I know in secret they drank wine, But publicly preached water."

112

the life of the English people, also caused certain defects in his realism. Happily listening to the soft trilling of the cricket and the kettle singing on the hob Dickens occasionally insists that these are far more important to him than the voice of the tempestuous winds of history raging over the vast expanses outside the windows of his cottage.

Witness the sarcasm with which he writes in "The Battle of Life" about the fierce battle which was fought "once upon a time, it matters little when, and in stalwart England". He does not even want to know what the participants in this great battle were fighting for. For, to quote one of the dramatis personae of his tale, Doctor Jeddler, "not half a hundred people were the better for the gain or loss. Not half-a-dozen men agree to this hour on the cause or merits; and nobody, in short, ever knew anything distinct about it, but the mourners of the slain". [57] It is enough for Dickens that merciful nature should have erased the traces of this great conflict. Peaceful fields and orchards now lie where once so much blood was shed and girls dance gaily over the grass beneath which lie the bones of the fallen warriors.

The rather long-winded and improbable plot of his story is designed to reinforce the author's main idea: the most heroic of "life's battles" are those which are fought not in the battlefields, but within the peaceful walls of our own homes. The sacrifices of Marion Jeddler, who breaks her vow and hides from her father's house for six years in order to secure happiness for her elder sister when the latter falls in love with Marion's own fiancé—this is Dickens's version of the thousands of "bloodless battles that are some set-off against the miseries and wickedness of Battle-Fields".

It would of course be unjust to promote "The Battle of Life" as a model of all Dickens's work. But it is undoubtedly true that it displays in clearest relief a tendency inherent in all his books. For all the breadth of his epic narrative, for all the variety of social institutions and types he portrays, for all the perspicacity of his diagnosis of the grave social ills afflicting his country, the author's imagination, like that of his favourite characters, is subject to a sort of centrifugal force, drawing it out of the world at large into the little domestic world, to the flickering fire of their one and only family hearth—be this even the wretched cell in the Marshalsea Debtor's Jail, about which Little Dorrit sighs from her safe but hateful "afar".

However difficult the life of his heroes the road they travel along at the end of the day always leads *home,* and it is this certainty that both for Dickens and his heroes redeems all the hardships that precede the attainment of their cherished goal.

Exceptions are rare: little Nell finds peace only in the grave; but even here, at the end of *Old Curiosity Shop* we feel the same motif of a longed-for refuge, at last, from the treachery of enemies and the vanity of earthly life. The old church, the cemetery, the isolated guard-house into which Nell and her demented grandfather move shortly before her death—this is their final and most secure place of refuge.

Dead Souls is characterized by the directly opposite conception of rest and motion, of the "road" and "home" in their metaphorical sense.

No one was better equipped than Gogol, the author of *Village Evenings Near Dikanka,* to portray the naïve charm of a folk festival, noisy betrothals, evening get-togethers, sing-alongs and other forms of jollification. There are few more convivial characters in literature than his Doppelgänger narrator, Ginger Panko, who heartily invites the reader to pay him a visit, singing the praises of his house, his garden, and the delicious Ukrainian confections with which his good wife will ply their guests.

But in this humorous "skaz" * frame to the *Village Evenings,* as in the poetic portrayal of folk life in *Sorochintsy Fair,* or *Christmas Eve,* two of the stories from the collection, we can detect a measure of Romantic stylization. By the time we get to the story of *Ivan Fyodorovich Shponka and His Aunt* the angle is shifting, and shifting rapidly. The poetry of home comfort, of cordiality and hospitality gives way to irony as gradually the writer's focus moves to a portrayal of the real, earthly life of smallholders; and as if to taunt the readers the author scornfully breaks off the story of Shponka and his aunt at the

---

* "Skaz"—a mode of narration in which the author introduces another narrator, in the frame to his story, who then actually recounts the story. Employed by Gogol in *Village Evenings,* "skaz" was extensively used by Leskov (1823-1892) and has been much favoured by Soviet writers too.—*Tr.*

very point where, in accordance with another tradition, parodied by Gogol, it should have been wound up by a suitably happy and cosy, nuptial ending.

What in the story of Ivan Fyodorovich Shponka is the subject of gentle irony is closely scrutinized by the author in *Old-World Landowners,* whose patriarchal heroes are both tenderly loved and severely judged by their creator. There is surely no other piece by Gogol which is at one and the same time so Dickensian and so anti-Dickensian as this humorous and yet melancholy story. The quaint old couple who are the heroes of Gogol's tale would seem to have stepped right out of the pages of a Dickens novel, with their childlike good nature, old-fashioned hospitality, innocent weaknesses and infinite goodness which shines from their every look. There is so much of Dickens in the comic portrayal of their patriarchal mores, their tumbledown cottage with its cosy warm rooms and singing doors, the bountiful feasts and kitchen bustle, which consists in "incessant opening and closing of the pantry, salting, drying and preserving untold quantities of fruits and plants." Recall too the extraordinary drozhki which rattles along with all the noise of an entire orchestra, and the coachman who "... was forever at work over a brass alembic concocting infusions of vodka, and peach leaves, birdcherry blossom, knapweed, cherry stones, and towards the end of this process was quite unable to control his tongue ..." [58] There is an unmistakable and striking similarity between these details of old-world life and the idyllic patriarchal estate of Dingley Dell, where the inhabitants eat and drink with equally gay abandon, entertain their guests just as cordially and similarly do not burden themselves with unnecessary spiritual anxieties. But Gogol's portrayal of this patriarchal idyll, in contrast to Dickens, remains ambiguous. The story's ending is disturbed by the tragic motif of the "terrible inward sense of emptiness" (II, 37). The force of habit, which has so subjugated the peaceful and inert existence of the old couple, is not merely touching, it is alarming in its power. In addition, the gentle humour with which Gogol recalls these kindly old people— the Philemon and Baucis of the nineteenth century, goes side by side in *Old-World Landowners* with an ironic and caustic intonation, such as Dickens never employed when depicting the "holy of holies" of his own world, the cosy domestic hearth.

Soviet scholars writing about Gogol have already remarked on the surprizing strength of feeling with which the author depicts the reverse side of this carefree, hospitable, but *parasitic* way of life *: the "terrible plunder", the chopped-down forests, the lopsided peasant huts, the degeneration and greed of the household staff. "The bailiff, who was in cahoots with the headman, mercilessly robbed the old couple"; immense quantities of food was eaten "by staff and livestock, beginning with housekeeper and ending with pigs" and as much was stolen... "the proceeds from which all made their way to a common destination, namely, the local tavern".

Dickens prefers to keep right out of the *economic* details of the way Wardle, proprietor of Dingley Dell, manages his affairs. The entire set-up of this blissful estate, along with its emblematic embodiment, Joe "the fat boy", who eats when he's not asleep and sleeps when he's not eating, constitutes for Dickens a part of that particular Romantic myth which is admirable for the very reasons that it cannot by definition be subjected to analysis by Gradgrind's system of "facts, facts and facts".

Even in *Old-World Landowners* Gogol mercilessly undermines the very fundaments of such a myth. Henceforward the idyll of domestic bliss only flashes again for the briefest instant, in an unconnected digression, in the drugged dreams of the unfortunate Piskaryov (*Nevsky Prospekt*). There is no place for it in *Dead Souls*. Neither the unnatural conjugal tenderness of the Manilovs, nor the hospitality of Sobakevich, Korobochka or Petukh, who eclipses them all in his largesse, arouse Gogol's pleasure or his approval. All this is just as vain, vulgar and egoistic as Chichikov's dreams about his "comely wife and little Chichikovs", which Gogol recounts with such obvious scorn.

It is not the *home* but the *road* which is the key notion in Gogol's *poema*. In his interpretation the image of the road is extremely ambiguous and capacious.

It ranges from a metaphorical designation of the path of life in general—"our, often bitter and dreary road" (VI, 134)—to the highroads and by-roads of Russia along which Chichikov travels in his *britchka* with Selifan at the reins,

---

* See, in particular, V. V. Ermilov, *Geniy Gogolya* (The Genius of Gogol), Moscow, 1959, pp. 139-140 (in Russian).

carrying out his shady business. To some extent these latter roads form the compositional core of the work—to the extent to which it is arranged around Chichikov's travels. "Wheresoever he might decide to go, thereto must we also wend his way" (VI, 241). And insofar as the reader gains them together with Chichikov his impressions of the journey are for the most part cheerless and redolent of the vulgarity which surrounds all the activities of Gogol's hero. The author writes of these Russian roads unable, as it were, to resist a scornful and at the same time sad smile: "No sooner had the town receded behind them than there appeared the usual *claptrap* and *farrago* on both sides of the road: hillocks, fir-trees, dumps of squat young pines, the charred trunks of old pine-trees, wild juniper bushes and *such-like rubbish*. They came upon long, straggling villages, their buildings like bundles of old faggots covered with grey roofs... A few peasants in their sheepskin coats sitting on benches before the gates yawned in their customary way... Their womenfolk, with fat faces and swathed bosoms, gazed out of the upper windows while out of the lower there peered a calf, or a pig thrust out its blind snout. In short, the usual sort of picture" (VI, 21-22; my italics.—*A.Y.*). And further on we read: "Roads crawled off to right and to left, like crayfish shaken out of a sack." The road is distinguished by a building that looms in the distance. " 'Now what is that building?'—'Just the tavern.' " (VI, 60).

At the same time this apparently "prosaic" account of N after a three-day absence is unexpectedly interwoven with strands reminiscent of the grotesque symbolism of the *Arabesques,* and in particular, of *Nevsky Prospekt*. Note the picture of Chichikov's arrival in the town: "Dusk had already set in. Light and shade were intermingled to such an extent that the objects themselves became unrecognizable. A striped turnpike acquired an altogether vague colour; the whiskers of a soldier standing guard appeared to sprout from his forehead well above his eyes, and he seemed to have no nose at all" (VI, 130). This confusion of appearance and reality, in which the most commonplace thing becomes unrecognizable, seems to foreshadow the ensuing peripeteia of Chichikov's dubious enterprise, the essence of which the reader has not yet entirely grasped and which is destined to throw the officials and philistine inhabitants of N into great confusion. But a far more significant and melancholy thought lies concealed in the following cursory account of the town's nocturnal life: the noise of soldiers, cabbies and workmen talking and arguing, drunken oaths, prostitutes flitting across the road, a picture in which all the commonplace vulgarity is thrown into deliberate contrast by the inclusion of a day-dreaming youth, returning from the theatre; in his thoughts he is "in heaven and has just paid a visit to Schiller—when suddenly fateful words ring out above him like a clap of thunder and he sees that he is back on earth, indeed, in the town square, and even near the tavern, and once again the familiar scenes of life resume their strutting parade before him" (VI, 131). Just like the streets of nocturnal St. Petersburg in *Nevsky Prospekt* the road here is presented to us through the prism of the *author's* mind, at the acute apex of two intersecting planes: the exalted romantic dream and the commonplace scene of dirt and vulgarity. In this grotesque clash of dream and reality it is the latter that emerges victorious: for the dream is too naïve (a street in Spain, "night, an enchanting female apparition with a guitar and lovely curls. . ."—VI, 131).

It is important that the author's subjective presence, which is concealed in a variety of disguises, constantly surfaces with unmistakable clarity in the image of the road. The road is not only where the reader comes across Nozdryov, Sobakevich and Plyushkin, and, on making detour, drops in on Korobochka. It is not merely a convenient and traditional pretext for a story, or a way of mustering a string of episodes. . .

With Gogol the road is also an image of the author's mind, which not only eagerly gathers impressions of life's realia, but also gives these impressions meaning, endeavours to grasp their profound essence. We see the very process of artistic thought—and not only in such direct authorial digressions as, for example, the beginning of chapter 6, or of chapter 7 of Volume 1, or the traveller's reflections in chapter 11, but everywhere, throughout the book. It is conveyed to us, loudly and clearly, through the sometimes ironic, sometimes admiring intonations of the real author— and not some faceless "narrator"—with his innermost thoughts, his laughter through tears invisible to the world, his premonition of the profound significance of the mysteries of Russian life to which he is about to initiate the reader. We could adduce numerous examples. . . Suffice it to recall the author's sad lyricism which informs the passage contrasting the wretched village and Plyushkin's dilapidated home and garden with the picture of aristocratic squandering also conveyed through the resplendent and lyrical landscape (VI, 120). The author takes up his stand, unseen, at the reader's side, and a few pages on even addresses him directly: "But is this true to life?—Indeed, everything is true to life, anything can happen to a man... Be sure to take with you on your journey all your human sentiments, do not abandon them on the road for you may be unable to pick them up again later!" (VI, 127).

This inner bolstering of the image of the *road*, as the source of the author's artistic creation, is given its most explicit expression in chapter 11: "Oh Lord! how fine you are at times, you long, long road! How often, in my dejection and despair, have I reached out for you, and every time you have sustained and saved me! How often, as I travelled your length, have I been visited by wondrous thoughts and poetic dreams, how often have you brought me marvellous impressions!" (VI, 222).

And it is here, in this same chapter with its inspired finale that the two main meanings invested by Gogol in his image of the *road* are at last fused into one: in a burst of lyrical inspiration the author's mind divines the hidden meaning of his country's historical *movement*. The flight of the troika contains both a subjective and an objective element—both the "hurtling advance of life" of the Russian people and the inquiring impulses of this life, the tireless, searching mind of the artist. The lyrical and the epic interpretations of the world stand before us as equal forces.

NOTES

[1] Prosper Mérimée, *Etudes de littérature russe*. Texte établi et annoté par Henri Mongault, œuvres complètes, t. 2, Paris, 1932, p. 13.

[2] Thus, for example, the American scholar Donald Fanger, who devotes a long chapter to Gogol in his comparative work *Dostoyevsky and Romantic Realism,* begins it with the assertion that the author of *Dead Souls* is "more elusive perhaps than any other great writer of his century" (Donald Fanger, *Dostoyevsky and Romantic Realism. A Study of Dostoyevsky in Relation to Balzac, Dickens and Gogol.* Cambridge (Mass.), 1965, p. 101.

³ N. V. Gogol, *Collected Works* in 14 volumes, Vol. XI, Moscow, 1952, pp. 73-74 (in Russian). Subsequent references to this edition will be given on the line, citing only the volume and page number.

⁴ A. V. Chicherin, *Vozniknovenie romana-epopei* (Rise of the Epic Novel), Moscow, 1958, pp. 27-28.

⁵ V. Kozhinov, "K metodologii istorii russkoi literatury" (Towards a Methodology of the History of Russian Literature), *Voprosy Literatury*, M., 1968, N. 5, p. 78.

⁶ Ibid., p. 80.

⁷ Barbey d'Aurevilly, "Nikolai Gogol (with commentary by M. P. Alexeyev)" (in Russian). In: *N. V. Gogol. Materialy i issledovaniya* (Materials and Analysis), Vol. 1, Moscow-Leningrad, 1936, p. 264.

⁸ V. G. Belinsky, *Collected Works,* Vol. VI, Moscow, 1955, p. 419 (in Russian).

⁹ Ibid., p. 217.

¹⁰ Ibid., p. 222.

¹¹ V. V. Gippius, *Gogol,* Leningrad, 1924, p. 140.

¹² H. Fielding, *The History of Tom Jones a Foundling.* Vol. II, London, 1962, p. 16.

¹³ Karl Marx, Friedrich Engels, *Werke,* Bd. 29, S. 603.

¹⁴ T. Smollett, *The Adventures of Roderick Random,* London, 1944, p. 3.

¹⁵ *N. V. Gogol. Materialy i issledovaniya,* Vol. 1, p. 260.

¹⁶ Prosper Mérimée, *Etudes de littérature russe,* Vol. 1, 1931, pp. LXXVI-LXXVII.

¹⁷ Donald Fanger, *Dostoyevsky and Romantic Realism.* A Study of Dostoyevsky in Relation to Balzac, Dickens and Gogol; Cambridge (Mass.), 1965, p. 102.

¹⁸ Ibid.

¹⁹ H. Fielding, *The History of Tom Jones a Foundling,* Vol. I, p. 394.

²⁰ H. Fielding, *The History of the Adventures of Joseph Andrews and His Friend Mr. Abraham Adams,* London, 1931, pp. XXVII-XXVIII.

²¹ H. Fielding, *The History of Tom Jones a Foundling,* Bungay, Suffolk, 1959, p. 311.

²² H. Fielding, "The Journal of a Voyage to Lisbon", *Works,* Vol. XIII, London, 1775, p. 222.

²³ *Zerkalo sveta,* St. Petersburg, 24th July, 1786, Part II, p. 231.

²⁴ T. Smollett, *The Expedition of Humphrey Clinker,* London, 1938, p. 325.

[25] H. Heine, *Werke und Briefe,* Bd. 5, Berlin, 1961, S. 137.

[26] V. G. Belinsky, Op. cit., Vol. VI, p. 258.

[27] Ibid., p. 254.

[28] Ibid., p. 415.

[29] Ibid., p. 414.

[30] Ibid., p. 417.

[31] A. V. Chicherin, "Sootvetstvia v istorii raznykh literatur" (Correspondences in the History of Different Literatures), *Voprosy literatury,* 1965, No. 10, pp. 175-176.

[32] Ibid., p. 176.

[33] Leonid Grossman, "Balzac v Rossii" (Balzac in Russia). In: *Literaturnoye nasledstvo* (Literary Heritage), Vols. 31-32, Moscow, 1937, p. 322.

[34] A. V. Chicherin, *Vozniknovenie romana-epopei* (Rise of the Epic Novel), Moscow, 1958, p. 8.

[35] Honoré de Balzac, *Œuvres complètes,* Vol. 1, Paris, 1956, p. 82.

[36] Ibid., pp. 87-88.

[37] Op. cit., Vol. 9, Paris, 1959, p. 331-332.

[38] Op. cit., Vol. 1, Paris, 1956, p. 82.

[39] Dante Alighieri, *The Divine Comedy,* London, 1901, pp. 316-317.

[40] A. Herzen, *Collected Works* in 30 volumes, Vol. II, Moscow, 1954, p. 220 (in Russian).

[41] A. V. Chicherin, Op. cit., p. 174.

[42] D. S. Yakhontova, "Novatorstvo tvorcheskogo metoda Tekkereya v romane *Yarmarka tshcheslaviya*" (The Innovatory Method of Thackeray's Novel *Vanity Fair*), Lvov, 1965, Yakhontova is led to these conclusions, in particular, by her detailed comparison of the images of Gogol's Plyushkin and Thackeray's Sir Pitt Crawley.

[43] L. N. Tolstoy, *Collected Works,* Vol. 47, Moscow, 1937, p. 178 (in Russian).

[44] A. S. Pushkin, *Collected Works,* Vol. 5, Moscow, 1954, p. 303 (in Russian).

[45] W. M. Thackeray, *Vanity Fair,* London, 1963, p. 340.

[46] Ibid., p. 666.

[47] P. B. Shelley, *Poetical Works,* London, 1901, p. 432.

[48] N. A. Nekrasov, *Collected Works,* Vol. 10, Moscow, 1952, p. 305 (in Russian). This reproach follows an extremely enthusiastic appraisal of Thackeray. "After you he is my favourite writer," Nekrasov informs Turgenev, fresh from the experience of reading *The Newcomes.*

[49] W. M. Thackeray, *The History of Pendennis,* Boston, Co., n.d. p. VII.

[50] Charles Dickens, *Christmas Books*. "A Christmas Carol in Prose", L., 1915, p. 56.

[51] V. G. Belinsky, Op. cit., Vol. XII, p. 446.

[52] Charles Dickens, Op. cit., "The Chimes", p. 158.

[53] Charles Dickens, *A Tale of Two Cities*, L., 1924, p. 103.

[54] Charles Dickens, *The Bleak House*, L., 1906, p. 135.

[55] Ibid., p. 479.

[56] Ibid., pp. 471-472.

[57] Charles Dickens, *Christmas Books*. "The Battle of Life", L., 1915, p. 324.

[58] Nikolai Gogol, *A Selection*, Moscow, Progress Publishers, 1980, p. 24.

CHAPTER TWO

THE PROBLEM OF CHARACTERS

> Even in a monster you can perceive the
> ideal creation of which this monster is
> a travesty.
>
> *Gogol to A.O. Smirnova*

1

The words we have taken as our epigraph to this chapter are of key importance to an understanding of Gogol's
views of human nature, and thus to an identification of the
principles underlying the creation of the characters of *Dead
Souls*. First uttered in his letter to A.O. Smirnova of June 6,
1846 (XIII, 76) and then repeated with minor stylistic
alterations in *Selected Passages* (VIII, 317) they should
not, however, be regarded as a mere manifestation of Gogol's
spiritual quest at this critical time in his life. Despite the
comments of Turgenev's Bazarov about the "nasty kind of
feeling" aroused in him by Gogol's letters to "the Governor's lady of Kaluga", * we do sometimes detect through the
forced, didactic sanctimony of these letters the voice of an
earlier, inquiring Gogol, eager to master the true "science
of life". Thus it was in this case too.

This observation about the monster in which we can
perceive the ideal creation which it travesties, a paradoxical
idea which is in fact dialectically very profound, expresses
one of Gogol's most cherished beliefs, namely, that there
are conflicting possibilities latent in human nature, the dominant passions which, depending on circumstances, can be
turned towards good or evil.

Gogol constantly pondered over this in his youth and in

---

* Ivan Turgenev, *Fathers and Sons*, Moscow, 1958, p. 201.

his mature years, when writing *Dead Souls*, Volume 1 and still only planning its continuation. In the actual text of Volume 1, in the direct lyrical addresses to the reader, the author repeatedly refers to this immense *potential* of man, of his power and his passions. This might be in the form of an impassioned warning to young people just embarking on life's journey, to consider carefully the terrible example of Plyushkin, tragically dehumanized by his own avarice: "To what depths of paltriness, wretchedness and obnoxion can a man sink! *To think that he could change so!* But is this true to life? Indeed, everything here is true to life, *anything can happen to a man.* The fiery youth of today would be horrified if you were to show him his portrait as an old man. As you pass from the gentle years of youth into harsh and embittering manhood, be sure to take with you on your journey all your human sentiments, do not abandon them on the road, *for you may be unable to pick them up again later!*" (VI, 127; my italics.—*A.Y.*).

Later on, in the memorable digression in chapter 11, when engaging the reader in a discussion about Chichikov's character, the author gives this topic a more general application. The activities of his "hero" are decidedly nefarious. "But wise is he who does not detest any other man, and instead confronts him with a searching look and seeks to perceive the mainsprings of his nature. For everything in man is rapidly transformed; before you can look round a terrible worm grows up inside you and will tyrannically absorb all your life juices" (VI, 242).

In his portrayal of Plyushkin, the living corpse, "a gaping hole in mankind" (VI, 119), who not so long before was a "thrifty master of his estate", whom his neighbour would visit to partake of a full meal, to listen and learn from him how to manage one's estate and the wisdom of parsimony, until this *wisdom* grows excessive and turns into a madness, a tragicomic mania, deadly not only to himself and his family, but also to his household serfs—in this portrait Gogol shows with particular clarity the immense divide between the reasonable and unreasonable development of one and the same passion. Speaking of Chichikov with his inexhaustible patience, will-power and energy, Gogol confines himself in Volume 1 to mere allusions to the fact that the activity of this great "acquirer", which has hitherto been exclusively directed towards the augmentation of his own wealth, might still—who knows?—be given a new direction: "perhaps the passion which draws Chichikov along is not in fact his own and perhaps his cold nature contains something that will afterwards reduce man to dust and bring him to his knees before the wisdom of heaven" (VI, 212).

But the entire context of the work (not to mention the attempted continuation) is designed to lead the reader to the thought that it is concerned not with Plyushkin and Chichikov alone, for the author's real objective in the creation of *Dead Souls* was to bring to life the great powers which lie dormant or have been put to evil purpose in millions of his fellow-countrymen.

The idea of the omnipotence of experience and habit, the belief that the character and destiny of man depend on his education and other circumstances, became in one form or another the common property of all Enlightenment philosophy and literature. In his book *The Holy Family* Marx evaluates highly the progressive impact of this entire complex of humanitarian Enlightenment ideas, most consistently developed by the eighteenth century French materialists. "There is no need for any great penetration to see from the teaching of materialism on the original goodness and equal intellectual endowment of men, the omnipotence of experience, habit and education, and the influence of environment on man, the great significance of industry, the justification of enjoyment, etc., how necessarily materialism is connected with communism and socialism. ...If correctly understood interest is the principle of all morality, man's private interest must be made to coincide with the interest of humanity. ...If man is shaped by environment, his environment must be made human. If man is social by nature, he will develop his true nature only in society, and the power of his nature must be measured not by the power of the separate individual but by the power of society." [1]

Eighteenth century Enlightenment literature could not and did not give *systematic* expressions to these remarkably far-reaching and consistent conclusions derived from the suppositions of their humanist thinkers. But many of the arguments summarized by Marx had at that time already formed the basis for the portrayal of various types of human character.

Gogol could draw on the rich tradition of eighteenth century Russian Enlightenment literature with regard both to the reproduction of the people's destiny, and to the deforming "brutalizing" influence of the serf system on the characters and morals of landowners. Novikov's articles, Fonvizin's plays, Radishchev's *From St. Petersburg to Moscow*, explore the disastrous effect of this system with differing degrees of consistency, but all with a sharp satirical thrust rarely encountered amongst the West European Enlightenment writers. However characters like Fonvizin's Skotinins (from "skot", animals) and Prostakovs (from "prostak", simpleton), or the despotic blockhead landowners portrayed by Novikov and Radishchev, lacked the plastic expressive qualities which distinguish the dramatis personae of *Dead Souls*. Gogol's reference to the "*inner world* of the frigid, fragmented and commonplace characters" (VI, 134; my italics.—A.Y.) which faces the readers of *Dead Souls*, is deeply significant. The characters in his book, whilst remaining comparable in many respects to the characters encountered both in Russian and West European works of the eighteenth century Enlightenment, possess entirely new artistic properties and appear before the reader in a different, new artistic perspective, when the significance of the *typical* once more is prominent and obvious.

These fundamental differences, which constitute the peculiar essence of the characters of *Dead Souls,* will, it is hoped, become more apparent after a detailed comparison of the first with their Enlightenment counterparts, and then with the characters created by Gogol's contemporaries—the West European critical realists Balzac, Dickens and Thackeray. Holding the view that man has infinite potential for self-betterment and re-education, Gogol no longer relies on a representation of the individuals who together make up society. He thinks in the far broader categories of popular destiny, national character and historical development, which had only been fully assimilated by European literature with the flowering of Romanticism, and then acquired at the hands of the critical realists a more concrete social interpretation.

In his review of Semyon Poroshin's *Notebooks* (Poroshin was a remarkable public figure and thinker, who worked as tutor to the Tsarevich Paul and died young), Belinsky quotes a comment by Poroshin that particularly struck him: "If His Highness were a private individual and could dedicate himself utterly to the pursuit of the mathematical sciences, through his keenness of mind he might well become our Russian Pascal." This observation about the natural talents already manifest in a ten-year-old boy, which regretfully were doomed never to grow to fruition, for he was destined for the throne and not science, can be regarded as a typical Enlightenment view (which was given an ironic twist by the subsequent inglorious and tragic death of Paul I). Here everything is decided by "chance", by the particular correlation between the individual and his circumstances.

In a laconic epigram "Chaadayev's Portrait" Pushkin encapsulates within four lines of verse not only Chaadayev's personal tragedy, but also a hint of the unjustness of a social order which can find no worthy application for civil valour and statesmanship.

> By God's will born in chains, he serves the tsar;
> A Brutus he'd have been in Rome,
> A Pericles, in Athens—
> > here, at home,
> He's a hussar. *

In the sixth chapter of his verse novel *Eugene Onegin* the author's reflections about the possible variations on the premature death of Lensky are permeated with the same philosophical sense of history—on this occasion directed towards the modern age. The suggestion that Lensky might in future ages be celebrated as a great poet is supplemented in the omitted 38th stanza by different and highly varied hypothetical ends to the young hero's life:

> *Teaching some and duping others,*
> *To the thunder of applause or imprecations,*
> *He could have forged a triumphant path,*
> *To breathe his last breath*
> *In sight of those majestic trophies,*
> *Like our Kutuzov, or Nelson,*
> *Or like Napoleon in exile,*
> *Or, like Ryleyev, to be hanged.*

But this list of heroic possibilities, based on historical precedents, concludes with a final, bitterly ironic hypothesis, perhaps the most probable of all, comparing Lensky's

---

* Translated by Irina Zheleznova.

fate to that prepared for the majority of landowners like him—the fate of Manilov, the fate of Tentetnikov:

> *Or this, perhaps: a humble lot*
> *Would have awaited the poet.*
> *The years of youth would have passed,*
> *And with them his ardour would have cooled.*
> *In many ways he would have changed.*
> *He would have been happy, in the country,*
> *Wearing horns and a quilted dressing gown.*
> *He would have learnt what life was really like,*
> *Would have had the gout at forty,*
> *Would have drunk and eaten, grown bored, fat and decrepit.*
> *And finally, have passed away*
> *In bed, surrounded by his children,*
> *Tearful women and physicians.*

Gogol's view of the *Russian* nature in its *potential* and actual state has much in common with these reflections by Pushkin. Admittedly, Gogol's portrayal of characters lacks the keen *political* thought which permeates the above-quoted lines. But the ethical and social content of their reflections, once divested of its figurative costume, can be seen to be very similar. In these lines Pushkin moves from exalted heroic possibilities to the wretched and typical realities of life. When he portrays this reality Gogol ponders over the unrealized potential latent in the characters he brings forward, and considers how best to bring this potential to life.

The idea of the development both of man and of society is contained in the subtext of these reflections.

Gogol expressed this idea long before *Dead Souls* in his remarkable early article, "Several Words on Pushkin", which he included in the collection *Arabesques*, appending to it the date 1832.

"Pushkin," he wrote, "is an extraordinary phenomenon and perhaps a unique manifestation of the Russian spirit: he is a Russian person at the stage of development Russians might reach two hundred years hence. In him the Russian nature, Russian soul, Russian language, Russian character are reflected with all the purity, all the purified beauty of a landscape reflected in the convex lens of an eye-glass" (VIII, 50).

In order to have expressed this idea Gogol must have had both a profound understanding and love of Pushkin, and at the same time have understood the Russian character and had an unshakable faith in the future history of his people.

In a paper read to the Gorky Institute of World Literature in Moscow in 1970 Professor Walter Dietze, a prominent East German scholar, speaking on "The image of man in Goethe's work", began his analysis of Goethe's humanism by quoting this same remarkable observation by Gogol, that Pushkin was a Russian person at the stage of development "Russians might reach two hundred years hence". Professor Dietze maintained that this succinct idea of Gogol's accords closely with Goethe's world view, that of a man who had intimately understood the dialectics of existence and perceived the ability to "metamorphose" not only as a law of the vegetable and animal kingdoms, but also as a law of man's social existence, and, consequently, of the development of human characters. Dietze compares to Gogol's conception the view of man projected by Goethe in his *Faust*, from the "Prolog im Himmel", where he counters the sarcasm of Mephistopheles, who compares man to a cicada, "Die immer fliegt und fliegend springt... Und läg er nur noch immer in dem Grase!" ("forever flying and leaping in the air ... Would he only lie still in the grass!"), with the impassioned assertion of man's moral worth given by the Lord Himself:

Und steh beschämt, wenn du bekennen musst:
Ein guter Mensch in seinem dunklen Drange
Ist sich des rechten Weges wohl bewusst. [2]

("And shame on you if it need be explained to you: A good man in his obscure aspiration, Knows himself the right path to take.")

Professor Dietze's typological comparison of Goethe's and Gogol's views of human nature and moral character supports our own hypothesis that the problem of "brutalized" man and his "resurrection" engaged Gogol's mind to the same extent that it did the minds of West European writers and philosophers of his time, and determined a great many of the features he invests in his characters.

Connected with this is the above-quoted remark by Gogol about the "inner world of the frigid, fragmented and commonplace characters"—a remark that might at first seem inconsistent with his general philosophy. The point is that he refers here to the depth of *generalization*, by dint of which the characters of *Dead Souls* are perceived as types and their names have given rise to new collective concepts which have enriched the Russian language and remain in use to this day: *manilovshchina, nozdryovshchina*, etc. At the same time he has in mind the profound potential which he wished to "illuminate", to awaken in his fellow-Russians.

Just as the theme of humanity is developed by Goethe in the constant dialectic argument between Mephistopheles and Faust, in the confrontation of the former's evil scorn and the latter's untiring surges of thought and feeling, so too in *Dead Souls* is the satirical grotesque inexorably bound up with the ideal of human nature. In our Chapter One we have already discussed the immense role of the lyrical digressions in determining the genre structure of *Dead Souls*. Here, with reference to Gogol's portrayal of characters, we must stress that this ideal is present in the subtext of even the most satirical and grotesque portraits, scenes and dialogues. The grotesque is never an end in itself for Gogol—as it is, for example, in the eighteenth century comic-epic or satirical novel of mores. However comic his grotesque images, comparisons and descriptions, their effect is never limited to comedy: they are also terrible, since they demonstrate the entire range of monstrous deviations from the "ideal creation of which this monster is a travesty", i.e., from the ideal of human nature, such as it should and must become.

Connected with this is the tragic pathos which (as, for example, in the description of Chichikov's visit to Plyushkin) "interrupts"—apparently quite unexpectedly, but in fact in full accordance with Gogol's design—the comic description of the absurd and outrageous behaviour, appearance and habits of the degenerate miser Plyushkin.

"The pale reflection of feeling", fleetingly expressed on Plyushkin's lifeless face at the mention of his schoolday friendship with the present chairman of the Civil Chamber, provides the impetus for an expressive extended metaphor: thus does a drowning man suddenly appear on the surface of the water, writes Gogol, "but in vain do his rejoicing brothers and sisters throw him a rope from the bank and wait for another appearance of his back or arms, exhausted by their struggle. Everything is still, and the now calm surface of that unanswering element seems all the more terrible and desolate" (VI, 126).

This sense of tragedy innate in Gogol's brand of grotesque realism distinguishes it from the grotesque of such Enlightenment novelists as Fielding and Smollett, as well as from the grotesque of Thackeray.

The grotesque, which plays such an important role in Gogol's portrayal of characters in *Dead Souls,* has frequently given rise to the mistaken interpretation of this work as a work of fantasy, "unreal", or even "surrealistic", with little or nothing in common with actual Russian life.

Such an interpretation of Gogol's characters, widespread amongst Western scholars, traces its lineage back to the antirealistic conceptions of his work formulated by the Russian decadents and symbolists. Valeri Rozanov was the first to proclaim in his "Dostoyevsky's Legend of the Grand Inquisitor", that "the great mystery" of Gogol's works consists in the fact that "essentially there is nothing concealed" behind the apparent lifelikeness, the sculpture-like reality of the "outer forms", "there is no soul, there is no one who could take on these hollow forms". [3] "Gogol looked on life with a dead gaze and saw nothing but dead souls in it," claims Rozanov. Ignoring Gogol's vital idea of the living human potential of the "dead souls" he depicts, Rozanov declares Gogol's characters to be pure caricatures, and thus lacking any relation to real life: "A caricature takes only one feature of a character and its entire figure reflects only this—both through the grimace of its face and the unnatural convulsions of its body. It is false and it is remembered for ever. Such too is Gogol." [4]

In direct contradiction to the facts Rozanov maintains that "not one of Gogol's works has any *development* of passion, character etc. in man; all we have from him are portraits of a person in statu, immobile, unchanging, growing neither larger nor smaller. This too, it seems, was his attitude to nature". [5] Meanwhile it is precisely the tragic *decline* of a person, his profound moral degradation, which Gogol presents in the figure of Chartkov (*The Portrait*) and in that of Plyushkin; the development of Chichikov's character, as well as that of Tentetnikov, are explained by the circumstances of their education and position in society.

The authorial digressions in *Dead Souls* are interpreted by Rozanov just as perversely as he does the book's characters. Irony and pity are all he can detect in Gogol's lyricism, which he dismisses as "the fruit of a sick imagination". The prophetic insights of Gogol the artist, his painfully sustained faith in the future of Russia, his irate sarcasm and agony over the squandered dignity of man —all this is rejected by Rozanov. He only detects in Gogol's *poema*, permeated though it is with profound and impassioned humanistic beliefs, an absence of "trust and respect for man" and he castigates the great realist for having "corrupted our souls with his imagination".

Thus Gogol crudely and maliciously was presented in the Decadents' own manner. His work is forcibly divorced from life; the powerful social criticism and humane beliefs of his literary quest and generalizations are declared a fiction, an "illusion", and by Rozanov even "an insuperable barrier" to the unification of people.

Recent attempts to repudiate or refute Gogol's realism, undertaken abroad and most frequently in the USA, belong to this same tradition. Erlich's book *Gogol* (1969) positively bristles with quotations from Rozanov. Erlich accepts the latter's "deduction" that Gogol's heroes are incapable of movement, development or growth. He dismisses as a trivial "cliché" the view that Gogol's "laughter perceptible in the world" and "tears unseen and unknown to the world" permeated with sympathy for man's scorned humanity, display a "satire tempered by compassion or pity". "This cliché," writes Erlich, "I submit, may have some applicability to a truly humanitarian and at times downright sentimental 'humorist' such as Charles Dickens, but it is profoundly misleading with reference to Gogol. ...His satire demeans its targets by reducing them to psychic automatons dominated by an idée fixe, forever distorted by a physical or moral deformity, scarcely worthy of our tears." [6] About the only thing in Erlich's book which is not found in Rozanov is the former's anxiety to present Gogol as a sort of nineteenth century existentialist: the denunciatory element of Gogol's work is, in Erlich's view, "a matter of an existential nausea rather than of social protest". [7] He accordingly chooses to see in the image of the author himself, as revealed in the intense lyrical digressions, nothing more than a conventional "Romantic poet, wacky, exuberant, dreamy, grandiloquent", [8] and even Gogol's love for Russia is declared to be "strident, compensatory patriotism", an artificial psychological compensation for Gogol's voluntary alienation from his native land. [9]

This carefully constructed existentialist "model" is thus reft of everything which constitutes the living soul of Gogol's work. All that remains of the realism of *Dead Souls* is an "intermittent illusion of realism"; the impassioned finale of Volume 1 is regarded as a mere "sleight-of-hand whereby the dismal subject dissolves into, and is superseded by, dazzling verbal magic." [10]

In this Erlich directly echoes his predecessor Vladimir Nabokov. The latter, furthermore, does not even trouble to inquire into the problem of Gogol's realism: he takes as the point of departure for his analysis of *Dead Souls* the unacknowledged assertion (first made, in fact, by Rozanov) that the author did not in fact know Russian reality at all and the world he depicts is a mere figment of his imagination. The characters of Volume 1, according to Nabokov, are all equally "subhuman" and all live "in the bosom of Gogol's demonocracy," so "it does not matter a damn who judges whom". [11]

Dead Souls, Volume 1 is, in Nabokov's opinion, a "kaleidoscopic nightmare which for years to come simple souls were to accept as a 'panorama of Russia' (or 'Homelife of Russia')" born of Gogol's "hypnotizing himself". [12] It is precisely "Chichikov's fundamental irreality in a fundamentally irreal world" as depicted in Volume 1 which, according to Nabokov, constitutes the pledge of the artistic wholeness and expressiveness of Gogol's work. The failure of Volume 2 is attributed in the terms of this anti-realistic conception to the artist's fatal error in attempting, to his own misfortune, to undertake the collection and study of "facts", and, then, worse still, to interpret them—for "a writer is lost when he grows interested in such questions as 'what is art?' and 'what is an artist's duty?' " [13]

Furthermore, in accordance with the "logic" of the irrational demonic nightmare which he follows in his interpretation of *Dead Souls* in general and of Chichikov in particular, Nabokov considers the burning of Volume 2 a symbolically proper conclusion to Gogol's design: so "little blue flames" devouring the manuscript were Chichikov's "native element", his "humble hell" out of which he was born and to which he was duly restored. [14]

In accordance with this conception Korobochka, who drives into town in a carriage which is more like a round water-melon on wheels, loaded with pies and a mass of cushions, turns out to be no more than a grotesque "hypostasis" of Chichikov— of that round soap-bubble. Sobakevich is declared to be the most poetic character of *Dead Souls*—if only because from the description of his pumpkin-like physiognomy a wonderful butterfly is born, as from a hideous cocoon, and flutters away in the form of the image of a light balalaika, of the "pride and joy of a dashing youth, ladies' man, first and dandy..." (VI, 94). On the other hand, the poetic portrayal of the face of the charming blonde (the governor's daughter), whose oval circumference is "like that of a freshly-laid egg," and like such an egg was white with a sort of translucent whiteness when held against the light by the swarthy hand of the hen-keeper (VI, 90), Nabokov regards as a repellent, monstrous caricature, substituting for a live human face this lifeless, noseless, eyeless oval...

However absurd and misleading such conceptions of Gogol's characters and of their portrayal in *Dead Souls*, they still merit our critical attention not only because of their widespread currency abroad but also because they partially capture—but then falsely interpret—certain key features of Gogol's realism which evade those scholars who limit themselves to a too general, and thus superficial sociological definition of *Dead Souls* as a mirror of Tsarist Russia in the days of serfdom.

Gogol's realistic generalizations grow out of life. But there are *special* principles for the creation of the typical characters which he follows in his realism.

On the one hand, the images of the "heroes" of *Dead Souls*, particularly in Volume 1, are much *larger* than life. When he depicts Nozdryov, Sobakevich, Korobochka and others like them, Gogol makes his readers aware of the vulgarity and fragmentedness of their characters, the pettiness of their interests, and at the same time adheres to his principle of "transforming" isolated, particular phenomena to the point where they are significant and typical, and thus extends the limits of his narrative, "measuring" the characters he portrays against other spheres of Russian life. Thus, alongside the eminently concrete Nastasia Petrovna Korobochka, a hard-headed and cowardly landowner of the backwoods, we have the images of her town sister, "unattainable behind the protective walls of her aristocratic house ... who yawns over an unfinished book as she awaits the time for an entertaining social call, when she will have the chance to display brilliance of wit and to express her learned by heart views..." (VI, 58), and even images of other public figures no less hard-headed than Korobochka.

Thus too does Nozdryov—an eminently concrete and clearly individuated character—function at the same time as a type, whose range of reference is far wider than the reader would at first think. "Nozdryov will not disappear from the world for a long time to come. He is everywhere amongst us, except that, perhaps, he merely goes about in a different caftan; but people are frivolous and unperspicacious, and a man in a different caftan seems to them to be a different man" (VI, 72).

In the image of Sobakevich the individualized characteristics of a parochial *kulak* landowner are similarly extended into the far broader and more capacious archetype of a "born *kulak*", who would remain himself even if he were "set going" in St. Petersburg. He would be even more dangerous: "he would soundly thrash" subordinate officials, or "would embezzle ... state funds".

This treatment does not of course blur the distinct social and historical outlines of Gogol's characters. But, whilst remaining entirely concrete they are still transformed in Gogol's interpretation into more general types, who have acquired a proverbial significance and outlived the old Russia of serfdom.

This "class-transcending" breadth of generalization, inherent not so much in the portrayal as in the *interpretation* of the characters of *Dead Souls*, illustrates the typological similarity of Gogol's realism to that of the Enlightenment. But Gogol's characters are more complex and possess a greater force of artistic expression.

Gogol's grotesque satire is largely instrumental for this. Endowed with immense archetypal stature, Gogol's characters acquire in addition a mass of apparently trivial, but in fact extremely expressive, details, which complement one another and in their totality create an integrated and multivalent image. The mention of the "distinctive smell of his own", a kind of stale air of stuffy rooms, which Chichikov's factotum Petrushka carries about him, ironically recalls to the reader Chichikov's own fastidious habits, with his intimate knowledge of the best sorts of foreign soap and custom of scrubbing himself on Sunday "from head to toe with a wet sponge" (VI, 21). Master and servant complement and illuminate one another in this and many other aspects: recall, for example, the old playbills and battered volume of the *Duchesse de Lavalière* which constitute the entire library of the "erudite" Chichikov, and the "noble thirst for enlightenment" of Petrushka, prepared mechanically to read everything that falls into his hands "with equal attention", from a child's primer or prayer book to a text-book of chemistry (VI, 20).

A profound archetypal significance also underlies many of Gogol's grotesque "zoological" metaphors. Witness how frequently we encounter the word "fly" in a variety of contexts in *Dead Souls,* Volume 1! In an extended metaphor the author compares the tail-coated officials jostling one another in the Governor's ball-room to the swarms of flies that gather on a summer's day around the lumps of sugar. And without any didactic commentary this comparison alone is sufficient to arouse in the reader a contempt for the indolence and vanity of these officials and philistines, described as "dense squadrons" of flies, who are satiated with food and "have gathered with no intention of eating, but merely to show themselves off, to promenade up and down the mound of sugar, rubbing their hind or front legs ... or scratching themselves under wings ... only to turn around and fly away and come back again..." (VI, 14).

Further on, while reflecting on the various "shades and nuances" of behaviour and manners found in Russia, and how these express various measures of baseness and sycophancy, Gogol depicts such a grotesque "metamorphosis, as even Ovid could not have imagined". "A Prometheus," says he about a chancellory superior amongst his subordinates, but before one slightly superior to himself he becomes "a fly, less even than a fly", he shrinks to the size of "a grain of sand!" (VI, 49-50).

At the same time we find the image employed in quite a different way, with reference to the serfs, in the phrase: "they die like flies", which casts its ominous reflection on the description of the futile "fly-like" existence of their masters—a reflection rendered all the more ominous by the fact that the "sympathy" and even "slight palpitation of the heart", with which Chichikov receives this news, is a manifestation not of any compassion, but of the most sincere delight felt by this buyer of dead souls.

"Gogol's grotesque is immersed, like a magnet in iron filings, in the world of things and of the minutest details. which in their turn give his creation its form and serve as a sure guarantee against schematism," [15] writes Soviet critic Yuri Mann, describing the realistic essence of Gogol's grotesque satire.

2

Employing another metaphor favoured by Gogol, Fielding takes the image of a *mirror* to reveal the satirically didactic significance of his characters. He sets himself "general and noble purposes: ... not to expose one pitiful wretch ... but to *hold the glass to thousands* ... that they may contemplate their deformity, and endeavour to reduce it" [16] (my italics.—*A.Y.*). This Enlightenment programme of *purposeful* study and generalization of life in the hope of changing it through the force of artistic conviction has clear affinities with Gogol's own attitude, as exemplified in the characters of *Dead Souls*.

The English author, in creating his "comic epic-poem in prose", as yet lacked the concepts of national character and the historic destiny of his people. But Fielding did confront the problem of the corruption of human nature by its deadly egoistic passions, and he illustrates it in the images of numerous petty and big-time extortioners—from the land-grubbing Parson Trulliber and the greedy innkeeper Mrs. Tow-wouse to the Great Swindler Jonathan Wild, in whose image Fielding wished, to quote his own memorable phrase, to describe "not individual, but a species", presenting it as a broad satirical symbol of the universal corruption undermining the country's very foundations.

There is an obvious similarity between these satirical images in Fielding's work with their widely allegorical application and the underlying principle of *Dead Souls*. For all the difference between the content and artistic structure of Fielding's and Gogol's works, the two authors are guided by an identical striving after a "transformation" of trivial, individual facts into significant and disturbing phenomena of a universal scale.

Admittedly, with the exception of the image of Jonathan Wild himself, we rarely encounter such broad generalizations amongst Fielding's characters (indeed, his book about Jonathan Wild occupies a special place in the history of the English Enlightenment novel). But we can detect the seed of the conception of *Dead Souls*, scattered over a number of characters who people the pages of Fielding's "histories"—the theme of the corruption of human nature by grasping egoism, self-interest and pettifogging greed. In the process the author's ironic reflexions provoke the reader's own mind, making him match his initial impressions against his latest. In *Tom Jones* the author initially presents his rogue Blifil as a meek, considerate and virtuous young gentleman, although certain of his exploits do awaken our doubts; thus too does Gogol emphasize with ironic insistence the remarkable benevolence and good breeding of his Pavel Ivanovich Chichikov.

In contrast to Gogol Fielding does not cast any doubt on the actual legitimacy of the grasping ways of the English gentry; but the democratic intuitions of a true man of the Enlightenment inform him that money—even that which has been obtained with the very best of intentions— might be the "dirtiest money in the world" and that material prosperity, an honorable reputation and success in society, cannot serve as a reliable yardstick for the moral worth of a man.

We encounter throughout Fielding's comic epics a great number of grotesque characters—bestial people in whom greed, avarice and cupidity have ousted any trace of humanity. Such, for example, is Parson Trulliber in *Joseph Andrews*, who regards his swine more dearly than all his pastoral flock; he sees every visitor as a potential buyer, and has become so like his own animals as to resemble a fattened boar in his gestures, manners and appearance. Another such is the inn-keeper Mrs. Tow-wouse, a grotesque figure in whom every feature expresses the repulsive spiritual squalor and miserliness of their owner. At the same time Fielding is quick to emphasize that he is describing "not an individual, but a species". Mrs. Tow-wouse has, in this collective role, been present in the world for thousands of years, and "I will not scruple to affirm," declares Fielding, "she hath likewise in the revolution of ages sat on a throne". [17] Recall Gogol's question, when presenting to us Korobochka in all her unique detail: "Indeed, is the divide too immense between her and her sister, unattainable behind the protective walls of her aristocratic house with wrought-iron staircases, shining brass, fine wood and carpets...?" (VI, 58).

However, there is an important difference between Gogol's and Fielding's various interpretations of the characters they create. Fielding, with a typically Enlightenment ahistorical view of human nature sees the malicious and niggardly Mrs. Tow-wouse as unchanging over the centuries. Thus too does he interpret the character of Jonathan Wild the Great, on several occasions likening him satirically to Julius Caesar, and to Alexander the Great, and to all the other "great" men of history who became illustrious through their conquests, massacres and cruelty.

Gogol thinks in historical terms and projects his characters not into the depths of history, but in the cross-section of Russian society of his own day, taking them from one social sphere into another, apparently of higher station, but distinguished by the very same vices. This is how he achieves the satirical juxtaposition, referred to above, of the slow-witted and useless, backwoods landowner Korobochka and various men of state and aristocratic ladies.

Through the novels of Tobias Smollett there files a similar succession of grotesque monsters, comparable in many respects to the satirical figures of *Dead Souls*. "Animal" features abound in the physical and moral aspect of Smollett's heroes, and are far more prominent than in Fielding's works. The small allegorical tale prefaced to *The Adventures of Roderick Random* narrates how a certain young artist depicts on a canvas a conversation between a bear, an owl, a monkey and an ass: his inquiring spectators are quick to recognize themselves in these portraits. This fable is highly typical of Smollett's style in general. "Animal likeness" serves as a permanent characteristic of his dramatis personae. In *Roderick Random* the hero's grandfather is compared to an "old shark"; the parson to a "black beaver"; the teacher, who is beaten up by his pupils, roars "like a mad bull", and Random himself looks "like a cousin to an orangutan". The brother of the charming Narcissa, the die-hard squire Orson Topehole, is given the sobriquet Bruin (cf. Gogol's Sobakevich), Captain Whiffle "is more like a baboon than one of the human race", the old woman Miss Withers, besotted with Random, hurls herself upon him "like a tigress".

The majority of Smollett's characters are endowed with whimsical grotesque features. They are all monstrosities, each in their own way. Some are distinguished by their actual physical and moral hideousness, others by idiosyncrasies of appearance and behaviour. Smollett makes much freer use of caricature than Fielding, frequently employing it as an end in itself. The portraits of most of his heroes have caricature features. Such, for example, is the surgeon Mr. Crab, Random's employer. Captain Weazel appears in the same novel in "the shape of a little thin creature, about the age of forty, with a long withered visage, very much resembling that of a baboon, through the upper part of which two little grey eyes peeped...". [18]

This sort of exaggeratedly grotesque portrayal of Smollett's characters is connected with the writer's bleak view of the moral aspect of the people he portrays. As Sir Walter Scott said of him: "He was ... a searcher of dark bosoms". [19] This remark is most indicative. Swindlers, rogues, confidence tricksters, gamblers and all manner of crooks and shysters all jostle for space on the pages of Smollett's novels. Nevertheless, although Smollett's view of the world is far more jaundiced and misanthropic than that of other authors of the English Enlightenment, even he does not lose faith in the possibility of correcting and effecting the moral "resurrection" of those of his characters who have been subjected to the corrupting influence of the world they inhabit.

In this sense Smollett's novels, like Fielding's comic epics, and more extensively the works of other writers of the English Enlightenment, have affinities with *Dead Souls*. The fickleness of human character, its ability to become "brutalized", and, if the right conditions are at hand, to be corrected and ennobled—this conception is shared by the creator of *Dead Souls* and the writers of the Enlightenment. However Gogol stands divided by an enormous historical distance from Fielding, Smollett and their fellow authors.

In the context of nineteenth century realistic literature the problem of transforming and directing to good purpose Chichikov's inexhaustible enterprise, of resurrecting his own "dead soul" to a new life, as well, perhaps, as the souls of his colleagues, would appear not so much titanic (as Gogol held it to be) as utterly chimerical, if not a reactionary delusion. Nevertheless, this problem, whose insupportable weight eventually crushed the talent of Gogol, writer and citizen of the nineteenth century, had been frequently posed and explored in the writings of the Enlightenment a mere century before.

The corruption of human nature under the deadly influence of a bad upbringing, the blandishments of luxury, prejudice, bad example, hardship and—in a broad context—social injustice in all its various forms constituted one of the common features of the novels of Defoe, Fielding, Smollett and the other writers of the English Enlightenment.

In contrast to the picaresque writers, these Enlightenment authors were concerned in their description of their heroes' adventures to illustrate not only their paradoxical variety, but also their psychological motivation. They were interested not only in the dizzying peripeteia in their hero's material well-being, but also in the shocks and upsets in his spiritual world. The elucidation of the hidden potential of human nature—of those redeeming moral resources which man can still draw on, to whatever depths of humiliation and despair he has been reduced by circumstances, or however in his arrogance he might elevate himself above the entire world—constitutes the nerve centre of many classics of the English Enlightenment, starting with Defoe's *Robinson Crusoe* and *Moll Flanders*.

Robinson Crusoe is a perfectly ordinary, albeit enterprising, planter and slave-trader, who discovers miraculous funds of energy, ingenuity and patience when he is shipwrecked on a desert island. Before adapting to his extraordinary new situation he undergoes a painful spiritual crisis; but his moral education, which takes place amidst arduous labours and peril, eventually transforms him into a "natural philosopher", tempered by life itself, who wisely and humanely, in the spirit of the Enlightenment ideals of the eighteenth century, arranges the lives of the other people shipwrecked on his island.

Defoe's other heroes experience similar inner revolutions: notable examples are Moll Flanders, who lives by theft and prostitution, the murderer and pirate Bob Singleton, and the pickpocket "Colonel Jack". Defoe does not let slip the chance to show the full range of potential latent in these people, who have been "lost" since early youth. Circumstances pervert their rich talents; habit completes the job begun by bitter necessity. Inveterate criminals all, they symbolize

141

through their own activities the bitter enmity that divides all society—the society that has corrupted them—and they do not return to the path of virtue before they have extracted from their chosen criminal trade every possible profit. Nevertheless this return is, in the writer's view, entirely possible. Colonel Jack becomes the owner of plantations, Moll Flanders ends her days in peace and quiet, performing charitable deeds and contritely recounting the misdeeds of her youth as a lesson for future generations; Singleton the pirate returns to his home, starts a family and savours the peaceful joys of the family hearth. There is something ironic in these happy endings, in which yesterday's rogues and murderers are converted to the "true path", retaining however, a little nest-egg of their ill-gotten gains. But Defoe, if he was aware of this irony (something that is disputed to this day by his commentators), nevertheless insisted on genuine happy endings. He was convinced of the possibility of mending men who had been deformed by circumstances, and this was how he endeavoured to prove the possibility of such correction.

As far as Richardson is concerned, he took a much surer and heartier approach to the problem. Admittedly, Lovelace is incorrigible in his diabolical pride. But the dissolute and obstinate Mr. B is easily reformed in Pamela's school. While the "divine philanthropist" Grandison, who so unceremoniously interferes in the life of his nearest and dearest, performs miracles by dint of rational conviction: he marries some, divorces others, dissuades duellists and gamblers to mend their ways, saves mortgaged estates and squandered fortunes—and with them the lost morals of their owners.

Fielding, the most profound of all the English Enlightenment realists, is considerably more reserved in his estimation of the real possibilities of educating and reforming human nature. Admittedly, he too is convinced that it is often enough to reach out a helping hand in time to one who has slipped and he may be returned to the true path. (This, incidentally, is the point of the story about poor Anderson, a harmless philistine, good family man, who becomes enmeshed in debt and in despair resolves to take up crime, in order to save his sick wife and little children.)

But Fielding does not endeavour to reform Blifil, or Trulliber, or Peter Pounce... With regard to them and other acquirers like them the purpose of his art can only be to render them less dangerous by exposing their moral squalor. Neither does he leave any loop-hole, any possibility for repentance and correction for his Jonathan Wild the Great: this master of theft and embezzlement, even while standing on the scaffold, with the noose about his neck, manages to steal a corkscrew from the pocket of the dozing, drunken priest.

But Fielding is more optimistically inclined towards those who sin frivolously, without pursuing material gain. Vanity, futility, and depravity, however they might stain a person's character, can still be overcome. Frequently we encounter in the pages of Fielding's works highly dramatic situations: the writer shows how a beneficial moral revolution can be effected in a person through the influence of reason and conscience. Occasionally this situation is shifted into the past: thus, in *The Adventures of Joseph Andrews* the respectable gentleman farmer Wilson relates the story of his own depraved youth. With the noble help of Harriet Hearty, who frees him from prison and subsequently becomes his wife, Wilson is able to find in himself the strength to start life anew. And the scrap of earth on which he works together with his servants, looks like an oasis of peaceful and noble labour amidst the landed estates, ruled over by the fools and arch-rogues so vividly portrayed by Fielding.

Moral enlightenment is also attained by the libertine Tom Jones at the end of his story—and also in prison, when under the influence of fictitious evidence he is prepared to believe himself guilty of murder and incest and bitterly regrets his earlier frivolity.

In Fielding's *Amelia* we meet another wild madcap: William Booth, a kindly man, but weak and easily led astray, who languishes in a debtor's jail, and undergoes a spiritual drama. In this novel we see the crisis that had affected Fielding's free-thinking humanistic philosophy: the moral resurrection of this fallen sinner is given an unmistakably religious explanation.

Smollett is far more morose and jaundiced than Fielding, but even he preserves his Enlightenment belief that it is sufficient to remove the adverse conditions in which so many lost people live in order to bring them back to the path of virtue. The spoilt young nobleman Peregrine Pickle has to learn the bitter lesson of experience in order to shed his egoism and depravity: only material ruin and a long prison sentence teach him to appreciate the friendship and love of the people he has spurned. Elsewhere the help of kind people enables others to climb from the mire of corruption when it seemed they were lost for ever. Thus the young harlot Nancy Williams (*The Adventures of Roderick Random*) and the robber Edward Martin (from *The Expedition of Humphrey Clinker*) manage to reform their lives. In this latter novel Smollett appears to be particularly concerned to demonstrate how relative people's views are of one another and of themselves, and how much potential lies hidden within them. The old vagrant Captain Lismahago changes before our eyes, acquiring both a home and a family. Lismahago's character is compared to an old, desiccated raisin: when cooked in a pudding it becomes soft and sweet again. The main protagonist also changes: the jaundiced grumbler Matthew Bramble, totally obsessed by his real and imaginary complaints, comes to the conclusion that he was wrong to seek happiness in indolence, isolation and peace. Finally overcoming his laziness he busies himself with the lives of those around him, developing an active, and by no means feigned, philanthropy, and rescues Mr. Baynard, from imminent ruin. (This sub-plot of Smollett's novel graphically illustrates how simple these and other problems, which utterly confounded Gogol, appeared to the Enlightenment writers.)

Here, as in other novels by Smollett, which we have mentioned above, the reader binds himself amongst the ordinary English people of the novel's day. But Smollett also wrote an experimental novel, in which he boldly combines a realistic picture of everyday English life with foreign customs and improbable events, creating the image of a rogue of the highest order in order to demonstrate through his example the sacred Enlightenment thesis of the "perfectibility of man". This novel is *The Adventures of Ferdinand Count Fathom*.

It is indicative that the first English reviewer of Gogol's *Dead Souls* compared Gogol's work to precisely this composition of Smollett's. [20]

Eighteen years later Smollett's readers were to meet up with Count Fathom again, in *The Expedition of Humphrey Clinker*—a comic novel, quite dissimilar in its sunny warmth and colours to the gloomy, ill-boding account of Ferdinand Fathom. Nevertheless, like some alien from another world, the impostor count figures in this novel, in the guise of the retiring country apothecary Grieve. Under this motivated name, which symbolizes Fathom's break with his past, he leads an inconspicuous, hard-working life in a remote corner of northern England, where he is "universally respected among the commonalty of this district, as a prodigy of learning and virtue" [21] until the novelist brings him together with the people who had once been his principal victims. Risking his own life to save the Count de Melville from robbers, Grieve-Fathom gives graphic proof of his repentance and makes at least partial amends for his shady past.

It is not hard to imagine that if "The Adventures of Chichikov" had been created by one of the English Enlightenment novelists, the plot would have been given the necessary twist to bring it to a happy conclusion. Once "corrected", Chichikov would have retired to his little country house, obtained by hard if dishonest toil, where he might on occasion even have recounted the tale of his past misdeeds to a visitor. And the author, having thus fulfilled his literary mission, would suffer no more pangs of conscience.

This, however, would have been impossible for Gogol.

Even in eighteenth century England, which led the rest of Europe in social development, the Enlightenment thinkers regarded society as a conglomerate of freely operating individuals. And although certain of the more farsighted amongst them had doubts about the legitimacy of pursuing material gain (witness here Fielding's curious remark about a rich man, foreign to charity, a swindler), social contradictions were as yet insufficiently pronounced or apparent for realist writers to have to come to terms with them, and they continued to secure happy endings for their wayward heroes. Vice and virtue lay so close together that one small step seemed to suffice to return from the treacherous, slippery path of the former to the highroad of the latter.

Gogol's position was quite different. In an age of developed historical awareness and acute social contradictions, a writer who was already concerned with the destiny of an entire people, and country, rather than the destinies of individuals, could not but employ a different measure of realism.

Chichikov's life could have been brought to a happier conclusion. Moves in this direction can be seen in the surviving fragments of Volume 2. He could buy Khlobuyev's estate for a small price; he could follow the exemplary Kostanzhoglo's advice and revive an abandoned farm; he could wed himself to a good "wench" of a wife and produce little Chichikovs, and spend his days in warmth and comfort, listening to the spring nightingales, as he does when visiting Kostanzhoglo, amidst the "laughter of the attractive hostess", with a cricket singing in the corner and "merry candles" burning, and the "spring night ... spangled with stars" peeping in through the door... (VII, 74). But no, Gogol could *not* have ended *Dead Souls* like that. This is partly because Chichikov is totally incorrigible, and is already beginning to hatch designs about how to deceive both Khlobuyev and Platonov—and even Kostanzhoglo... Another fundamental reason is that, however charming this idyllic conclusion might be, in which Chichikov would have his own, not "dead" but living, souls, and his own land, it did not appeal to Gogol.

All Gogol's efforts to convince others—and, above all, himself!—that by working for his master a peasant is performing a godly deed, were unavailing, and founded on his own doubt. As E. A. Smirnova quipped, "all the time he expounds his labour programme Kostanzhoglo is in fact talking about the peasant's labour, while he himself is, in Gogol's expression, a sort of a barnacle to a peasant. What does the following statement by Kostanzhoglo really tell us, for example: 'It's quite simple for me: if a carpenter is wielding his axe I'm happy to stand and watch him for two whole hours, I so enjoy hard work'? (VII, 73). Thus, even against Gogol's own wish the true performer of the hard work overshadows his figure of a 'hard-working' landowner and thereby assumes the position that rightfully is his." [22]

Gogol would like, on the one hand, to smooth out the social contradictions of his time, to find some true path to the "resurrection" of the "dead souls" of Russia—the path to the resurrection of human nature in general, as interpreted by the Enlightenment. But, on the other hand, as an artist and realist of the new age Gogol cannot fail to be aware of the shortcomings of this Enlightenment programme. What could Chichikov (even a "repentant" Chichikov) have in common with these stalwart fellows, whose lives he ruminates over as he reads the list of fugitive souls he has bought! Let us submit, for the sake of argument, that Plyushkin once again becomes a diligent landowner, that Chichikov finds "honest" ways of turning a fast rouble, that the inveterate rake Nozdryov mends his ways—what effect will all this have on the lives of the people? This is the fundamental difference between the "Adventures of Chichikov" (typologically cognate with the Enlightenment and even picaresque novel) and the philosophical epic *Dead Souls* with its concern with national history,* a work that even prefigures, in its enquiry, Tolstoy's *Resurrection*.

Gogol was not the only Russian writer of his time to examine the question of the enlightenment or "illumination", as he termed it, of man. The painter Alexander Ivanov spent practically half his life battling over a similar problem, endeavouring to capture in his monumental canvas "The Appearance of Christ to the People" the instantaneous transformation of people of diverse, but equally oppressed backgrounds, when suddenly confronted by the supreme purpose of life. And another Russian painter, Fedotov, was able to discern fine features (this is most apparent in his sketches) in the debauched physiognomy of an official who has drunk himself into a stupor ("The Official's Morning"), celebrating his receipt of a decoration. But all of them, Ivanov, Fedotov and Gogol, were to encounter in their quest the true agonies of creation and a tragic, although not identical, end.

If the literature of the eighteenth century was at all able to present, in impressive and artistically convincing images, the resurrection of "enlightened" human nature, it was only able to do so on the soil of Romanticism. It was thus, for example, that Shelley achieved the chimerical final act of his *Prometheus Unbound,* in which the sun, moon and stars, resurrected to a new life, rejoice alongside transformed mankind. Thus too does Charles Fourier dream, in his *Theory of the Four Movements*, about a social utopia, in which all, even the most repugnant and destructive, passions will be turned to a good purpose. Thus does Charles de Coster introduce a fantastic vision into the finale of his *Légende d'Ulenspiegel*, in which the Seven Deadly Sins are transformed in fire and blood into their respective opposing Virtues.

---

* It is indicative that practically all the poetry of *Dead Souls* is either devoted to a portrayal of Russian nature, of its wide expanses and roads, or to a description of the plucky national character, while all the sombrest prose belongs to the landowners' and Chichikov's lives—the sphere of "The Adventures of Chichikov".

"De ces cendres sortirent sept autres figures; le premier dit:

—Je me nommais Orgueil, je m'appelle Fierté noble. Les autres parlèrent aussi, et Ulenspiegel et Nele virent d'Avarice sortir Economie, de Colère, Vivacité; de Gourmandise, Appétit; d'Envie, Emulation; et de Paresse, Rêverie des poètes et des sages. Et la Luxure, sur sa chèvre, fut changée en une belle femme qui avait nom Amour.

...Ulenspiegel et Nele entendirent alors mille voix d'hommes ... chantaient:

> *Quand sur la terre et quand sur l'onde*
> *Ces Sept transformés règneront,*
> *Hommes, alors levez le front:*
> *Ce sera le bonheur du monde."* [23]

Was this not also the subject of Gogol's dreams?

But with this we leave the confines of Enlightenment realism and approach the problems of the Romantic novel.

3

In his foreword to Russian edition of the novel *Notre Dame de Paris* Dostoyevsky wrote that the idea which Hugo advances in this work is "the fundamental idea of all nineteenth century art, and Victor Hugo was almost the first artist to proclaim it. It is a Christian idea, a notion of high morality; its formula is the resurrection of a fallen man, crushed by the injust yoke of circumstances, the stagnation of the centuries and of social prejudices". [24]

The moral transformation of Quasimodo, this rejected, hideous, embittered and obtuse creature, is effected in the Romantic logic of Hugo's novel instantaneously and miraculously. In the chapter "Une larme pour une goutte d'eau" Hugo initiates his readers to this miracle. While the crowd is mocking Quasimodo, who has been exhibited for their derision and is imploring someone to give him a mouthful of water, the young Esmeralda (whom he had tried to abduct the day before) climbs up to him in a moment of sudden compassion and lifts a flask of water to his parched lips.

Similarly, in his novel *Les Misérables*, Hugo presents the moral resurrection of Jean Valjean as a miracle wrought by human (and at the same time divine) mercy. In contrast to *Notre Dame de Paris*, here the initial situation is less exceptional, and the image of Jean Valjean is socially and psychologically more typical. A poor man, caught stealing bread for his starving nephews, he increases his "guilt" in the eyes of society by attempting to escape and only returns home after nineteen years of penal servitude, which have left him embittered by the injustice caused him and, still worse, by the mistrust, fear and hatred he encounters on all sides immediately it becomes known to his interlocutors that he is an ex-convict. The very circumstances seem to compel this industrious, strong and skilful worker, faced by universal rejection, onto the path of crime and ruin. The miracle is effected when he crosses the threshold of the humble home of Bishop Myriel. This poor country bishop, who piously observes the apostolic simple life, correctly interprets the conflict in the soul of his malevolent nocturnal visitor. This moment marks the beginning of Jean Valjean's spiritual transformation, setting this man, who is racked with despair and hatred of all society, on the path of a now life, a life of heroic philanthropy and self-sacrifice.

In some respects this denouement can be compared to Gogol's utopian dreams about the liberation of the human soul from the "thick, earthly skin of egoism" that encloses it. Hugo's Bishop Myriel achieves what, we may assume, should have been achieved in *Dead Souls*, Volume 2 by Murazov, through similar Christian precept and admonition to Khlobuyev and Chichikov. But, for all the undoubted similarity between the humanistic ideals of the two writers, we must also note the essential differences both in the initial situations and, accordingly, in the principles of character portrayal followed by Hugo in his Romantic novel and Gogol in his realistic *poema*.

In his well-known foreword to *Les Misérables* Hugo himself explains the social significance of the three primary problems which form the substance of his work. The destiny of the proletarians, the fate of women condemned to prostitution, the suffering of children deprived of their childhood—he describes these problems as a manifestation of "l'asphyxie sociale", and inveighs against it. This novel, which was published in 1862, twenty years after *Dead Souls*, Volume 1, manifests the profound influence of the lessons of the workers' movement in France and echoes of the 1848 revolution: the social contradictions are far more clearly identified, far more clearly perceived by the author himself, as well as by his characters, than those in *Dead Souls,* and besides, the actual historical content of the novel is quite different from that of Gogol's work, which depicts pre-reform Russia "shortly after the glorious expulsion of the French" (VI, 206). Jean Valjean stands as a collective Romantic embodiment of the French worker who has fallen sacrifice to the injust legal system, and who defies this system to recover from near ruin, performing his feat of recovery in the name of true human justice. As such Jean Valjean partially embodies the revolutionary experiences of the French people.

Hugo and Gogol share a faith in what Dostoyevsky describes in the quotations above as "the fundamental idea" of the "resurrection of a fallen man". The two writers follow a similar path in turning to Christian mercy and the propagation of good deeds as a means of arousing the human soul. We might also note that Hugo employs the expressive metaphor of "the purchase of souls", with its obvious parallels with *Dead Souls*, but in *Les Misérables* it is given the opposite meaning: Bishop Myriel "buys" Valjean's soul in order to make it good again (*"C'est votre âme que je vous achète"*). [25]

With this the typological similarity between Hugo's and Gogol's works is exhausted. There is much in Hugo's novel to remind us of Gogol's polemic in the famous authorial digression in Volume 1, chapter 7, where he berates writers of a Romantic persuasion for "ignoring characters who are tedious, repugnant, and notable for their sorry plight", in favour of characters "who embody the supreme worth of man"; writers who select "from the great whirlpool of images that revolve about us daily only the rare exceptions" (VI, 133). The task of "revealing ... all the terrible, shocking mire of petty trifles which choke our lives" (VI, 134), which Gogol sets himself, was not undertaken by Hugo. The hopelessly "dead" souls of the Chichikovs and Plyushkins of this world, which Gogol wishes to restore to life, do not belong to the *"misérables"*, but to their masters, to their grasping oppressors. As he studies them the writer creates a panorama of Russian life that is not Romantic and conventional but highly realistic, and inspired by a lyrical striving into the future. Even in Volume 2, insofar as it is possible to judge from the surviving fragments, the realist and satirist is still so strong in Gogol that all Murazov's rhetoric, directed not only at stirring Chichikov's Christian conscience, but also at touching the most sensitive chords of his egoism and vanity, can only move the "dead soul" of Gogol's hero for a short time. The miracle which is effected so effortlessly by the laws of Hugo's Romantic poetics, eludes Gogol the realist, whose characters develop in accordance with other laws and obey the objective logic of real life.

The problems of the "fall" and "resurrection" of lost souls engaged the attention of another French Romantic, Eugène Sue. His novel *Les Mystères de Paris*, whose intricate, convoluted plot is largely concerned with precisely these issues, created a sensation in France and abroad. Both Belinsky and Marx wrote critiques of it,* at practically the same time in 1844, and, as Soviet scholars have already remarked, their critical analyses of Sue's novel have many points in common.

As Belinsky shows, *Les Mystères de Paris* was in many ways a "speculative" intercession for common people which had already shown its true colours in the recent history of French society, designed to earn it acceptance as a growing force. Both Belinsky and Marx indignantly detail how Sue and his favourite hero, the utterly implausible vulgar and bombastic Prince of Geroldstein, acts in total defiance of the vital logic of Fleur de Marie's character, crushing her natural high spirits and joie de vivre, depriving her of all earthly happiness and destroying her soul, that has supposedly just been resurrected, by foisting upon her a hypocritical religious penitence and monastic vows. An equally dubious moral transformation is ascribed to Chourineur, when he becomes Rodolf's lieutenant and hangman...

If Sue's melodramatic novel with its larger-than-life and stilled characters, placed in contrived and imaginary situations, can in any way be compared to Gogol's *Dead Souls* (primarily to the author's intentions for volume 2), such comparison is largely negative: it shows the perils that Gogol faced as a great realist, and which he successfully

---

* Belinsky's article "Les Mystères de Paris" was published in the journal *Otechestvennye zapiski* (1844, Vol. XXXIII, No. 4) in the spring of that year (the censors' approval was obtained at the end of March). *Die heilige Familie oder Kritik der kritischen Kritiker. Wider Bruno Bauer und Gesellschaft*—Marx and Engels's first joint work—came out in 1845, having been written in September-November 1844. Chapters 5 and 8, in which they mount a satirical polemic against Sue and the interpretation of him given by Scheliga, one of the "critical critics", were written by Marx.

evaded. It is however noteworthy that Gogol took an interest (at precisely the time when, after the fiasco of *Selected Passages*, he was casting around for a way of returning to *Dead Souls*) in works like *Les Mystères de Paris*. In a letter to A. O. Rosset on the 11th February 1847 he begs her to send him "only those books which have at least a whiff of Russia, even if it is malodorous", and enlarges: "Any accounts of St. Petersburg and the provinces, *mysteries* and so forth" (XIII, 211; my italics.—*A.Y.*). The word "mysteries" is a clear allusion to the numerous imitations of Sue's novel which proliferated in Russia and elsewhere in Europe. However, even Sue's most lifelike characters ultimately degenerated into vulgar melodrama, becoming improbable and pretentious eccentrics. This sort of Romanticism did not lie within Gogol's orbit.

4

If we now move on to a comparison of Gogol's characters and those in the works of his contemporaries who belonged to the critical realist school, i. e., those who were typologically closest to him, namely Balzac, Dickens, Thackeray, we shall have to begin by clarifying a few essential points.

The numerous characters created by these above-mentioned writers who have affinities with Gogol's own protagonists are, in fact, only part of an entire system of images, and it is only in juxtaposition with other parts that they are fully revealed. These systems are different in the works of Balzac, Dickens and Thackeray. But taken as a whole they can be seen to have even more striking differences from the system of images in *Dead Souls*.

The Soviet critic I. M. Katarsky refers in this context to the "plot asceticism of classical Russian prose", [26] describing Gogol's *poema* as a typical manifestation of this plot "asceticism", which differs so markedly from the complex and convoluted plots of American and West European novels of the time. This term might at first seem ill-chosen: Lev Tolstoy's and even more so Dostoyevsky's plots clearly contradict it. And even the plot of *Dead Souls*, as we have argued above, is far more complex and dramatic than might at first appear if we perceive *Dead Souls* as a mere variation on the picaresque theme. However, Katarsky has correctly identified the fundamental difference between *Dead Souls* and the great majority of West European and American novels of its time. With a few rare exceptions (*Posthumous Papers of the Pickwick Club* is one of the first that comes to mind), these novels were constructed as "the story of a young man". A young man, taking his first steps in life and securing a place in society, gradually shedding his illusions and learning the darker side of reality from his own experience—this was the central figure in these works, but often, as in many of Dickens's novels, by no means their most colourful character; accordingly romance also figured prominently in their plots.

These traditions are violated in *Dead Souls*. This is not only a "novel without love" (if we may apply to Gogol's *poema* Chernyshevsky's description of Godwin's novel *Adventures of Caleb Williams*). Gogol goes much further than this. By depicting the "maelstrom" of gossip and rumours aroused by Chichikov's nefarious business Gogol directly parodies the romantic intrigues of those melodramatic novels, which he counters with his own realistic narrative. Thus he has the ladies of N ascribe to Chichikov not only the intention of abducting the governor's daughter, but also a plan to seduce Korobochka.

Consider how Dickens's novel *The Life and Adventures of Martin Chuzzlewit* would have looked if its entire contents had been subordinated to Pecksniff, with Pecksniff elevated to the rank of main protagonist. Or *David Copperfield*, with Uriah Heep as its central character. Yet these and other characters like them are, of all Dickens's characters, closest in type to Gogol's Chichikov. But their total importance in Dickens's opus is far less than that of Chichikov in *Dead Souls*.

In Balzac's work, as in that of Dickens and Thackeray, a quite different scale of values and perception of vice and virtue obtains than that applied by Gogol in *Dead Souls*. This cannot but affect these authors' character portrayal. Confining ourselves initially to the briefest, most general definition of this difference we might say that Gogol is much stricter and more demanding by nature.

In his moral judgements Gogol proceeds from quite different, more socially oriented criteria; and in this respect his character portrayal often differs sharply from that we find in the novels of Balzac, Dickens and even the more severe Thackeray.

Balzac differs in his portrayal with his scrupulously accurate social, political and economic analysis of all the circumstances of his characters' formation. At the same time, the brief biographies with which, as a rule, the entry of each of his more or less significant characters is accompanied, is not only their personal biography, but the biography of an entire class. Special concordances have been compiled of the characters of *La Comédie humaine*, providing dossiers on each of them, documented with quotations from the works in which they appear, and these compilations are massive volumes. *Dead Souls* would not furnish sufficient material for a "Who's Who" of this sort. For all the variety of domestic and, ergo, social detail provided about these characters, their prevailing passions are only given in the broadest outline, in a synthetic and highly generalized form.

It is instructive to compare, for example, Gogol's and Balzac's portrayal of government officials. With Gogol only a few characters stand out from the crowd. These are, in *The Greatcoat*, the hapless Akaki Akakievich Bashmachkin and the "important personage" who plays such a fateful role in his life. In *Dead Souls*, Volume 1, Gogol gives only a cursory description of the governor, the postmaster (who tells the tale of Captain Kopeikin), the chairman of the Local Chamber, the police chief and the "poor" public prosecutor, who does not survive the furore aroused by Chichikov's mysterious buying up of dead souls; among their lesser brethren, the officials in the treasury, only "jug-faced Ivan Antonovich" stands out. Individual descriptions of the "civic worthies" are rudimentary and the choice of details is itself an indication of the author's deliberate ironic cunning. Thus the governor, "it would appear, like Chichikov, was neither fat nor thin, had the Order of St. Anne round his neck, and, it was said, had even been recommended to another, higher reward; he was, furthermore, a fine chap and sometimes even did the odd bit of embroidery on tulle" (VI, 12). The public prosecutor remains in the reader's memory for his eternally immobile physiognomy, his bushy eyebrows and winking eye, this eye seeming to invite his interlocutor: "come along, friend, into another room and I'll tell you a thing or two" (VI, 15). On the other hand the reader clearly remembers the ironic contrast between the deferential politeness which invariably accompanies all Manilov's and Chichikov's references to these local worthies, and the unceremoniously withering opinion of Sobakevich: "I know them all: they're all rogues; the whole town's like that: one rogue at another's throat and still another rogue behind them. They're all Judases. There's only one honest man amongst them: the public prosecutor, and even he, if the truth be told, is a swine" (VI, 97).

Gogol prefers to operate with more general forms of satirical typisation. Thus, right at the beginning of *Dead Souls* we are introduced to his ironic classification of "thin" and "fat" officials. As the formation of another general law we can take the sarcastic comment, quoted above, about the innumerable "shades and nuances of behaviour and manners", in which Russia has easily overtaken all other countries and which enable a government official to turn from Prometheus into "a fly", even "a grain of sand", depending on whether he is in the company of his subordinates or those whose rank is slightly above his... (VI, 49-50).

Both Balzac and Gogol write about the stultifying, soul-destroying bureaucratic routine, which turns living people into automatons. Balzac's comparison of a ministerial secretary to a well-trained, "constitutional" circus dog—"un de ces aimables caniches constitutionnels, si doux, si bien frisés, si caressants, si dociles, si merveilleusement dressés, de bonne garde, et ... fidèles!" [27] is quite worthy of Gogol's satirical pen.

This "échiquier bureaucratique", described by Balzac, has much in common with Gogol's wretched bureaucratic world. In *Les Employés* Balzac described the ruinous effect of their milieu on "l'être moral contenu dans ces affreux compartiments, nommés bureaux, ou le soleil pénètre peu, ou la pensée est bornée en des occupations semblables à celle des chevaux qui tournent un manège, qui bâillent horriblement et meurent promptement". Like Gogol he shows the appalling spiritual poverty and perversion of the official's life: "la nature, pour l'employé, c'est les bureaux; son horizon est de toutes parts borné par des cartons verts; pour lui, les circonstances atmosphériques, c'est l'air des corridors, les exhalaisons masculines contenues dans des chambres sans ventilateurs, la senteur des papiers et des plumes; son terroir est un carreau, ou un parquet émaillé de débris singuliers, humecté par l'arrosoir du garçon de bureau; son ciel est un plafond auquel il adresse ses bâillements, et son élément est la poussière." [28]

But the similarity of the mise-en-scène and the situation does not extend to the character portrayal. With his customary passion for analytical identification Balzac presents to the reader of *Les Employés* an entire gallery of wretched and nondescript officials, schemers and careerists. They all participate in the novel's action, which in Balzac's hands frequently acquires a dramatic form. Authorial narration gives way to long stretches of dialogue, accompanied by only the most essential remarks. The office is a battle ground of conflicting interests, prejudices, secret and unconcealed antagonisms. The figures which form the background for the story of the luckless Rabourdin's utopian plan to refashion the entire bureaucratic apparatus of France, now jostle one another for the reader's attention, interfering in the course of events, arguing, mocking, reviling or mystifying one another and directly or indirectly influencing the entire plot. Where Gogol would prefer to proceed from the particular to the general, preserving all the colourful detail of his picture of mundane life and describing only the most important elements in close-up, Balzac, like a keen entomologist, wants to demonstrate all his two-legged specimens, firmly convinced that each of these creatures possesses remarkable features entirely worthy of the reader's attention.

He himself provides the reader with a theoretical social justification for the striving after maximal differentiation which distinguishes character portrayal in *La Comédie humaine:* "La constitution actuelle des sociétés, infiniment plus compliqués dans ses rouages que celle des sociétés antiques, a eu pour effêt de subdiviser les facultés chez l'homme," he writes in *Les Illusions perdues.* "Autrefois, les gens eminents, forcés d'être universels, apparaissaient en petit nombre... Plus tard, si les faculté se spécialisèrent, la qualité s'adressait encore à l'ensemble des choses. ...Mais aujourd'hui la qualité s'est elle-même subdivisée. Par exemple, autant de professions, autant de ruses différentes." [29]

This "specialization" of faculties is embodied in many of Balzac's characters. *Dead Souls* has but one Plyushkin, one Chichikov, etc.—Gogol leaves it up to the reader to find representatives of all these types in all walks of life, but only going about "in different caftans" ... In *La Comédie humaine* we find alongside Gobseck Gigonnet, Samanon and others; alongside Grandet père, Séchard senior, the Rogron brother and sister; alongside Nucingen Taillefer, du Tillet, the Keller brothers... As a whole they are all typical of their age, but the social and psychological aspects of each of these people, corroded by their grasping passions, display features of individual "specialization".

Like Gogol, Balzac endeavours to identify in each of his characters that person's dominant passion. Furthermore, in *La Comédie humaine* these passions are revealed in all their dimensions, and often enlarged. In contrast to Gogol Balzac is not troubled by considerations of vraisemblance. He leaves it up to his readers to tie up the loose ends, as they wish, in those places where the sublime Romantic feelings and actions of his heroes apparently or actually conflict with the vulgarity of their immediate ambience. The author of *Dead Souls* pokes fun at the hyperbolic and flowery portrayal of "large scale characters": "hurl the paints with all your might at the canvas—piercing black eyes, beetling eyebrows, the brow furrowed by a wrinkle, a cloak, black and scarlet, like fire, cast across the shoulders—and the portrait is complete" (VI, 23-24).

Meanwhile Balzac is not deterred by such hyperbole. Vautrin, Trompe-la-Mort, appears in some of his reincarnations (as, for example, in *Les Illusions perdues* or at the end of *Splendeurs et misères des courtisanes*) so utterly demonic as to be a creature not only of another world, but even of a different artistic dimension from that inhabited, until Vautrin's arrival on the scene, by the vain provincial Lucien Chardon with all his foibles, vulgarity, obsessions and treachery, or by the Parisian prostitute Esther Gobseck, discovered by this enigmatic stranger in the act of committing suicide in her wretched room in the filthy "house of profit". A demonic light is reflected from the countenance of the former convict even after his secret is revealed to the readers. He is like Mephistopheles; his relation to Lucien and Esther is that of a Satanic contract. He is gifted with "la volonté d'un homme doué du génie de la corruption",[30] which gives him a fantastic power over people.

He is well-matched by his aunt, Jacqueline Collin, the very embodiment of physical and moral deformity. The reader is expected to believe that she is a native of Java, onetime mistress of Marat and the most skilled poisoner of her day. Appearing in *La Comédie humaine* under the sobriquet Asie, or the names Mme de Saint-Estève or Mme Nourrisson, she brings inescapable and mysterious death with her everywhere.

But the matter goes beyond these isolated examples of

Romantic hyperbole. All the action of *La Comédie humaine* takes place in an atmosphere charged with electricity. Gogol gradually initiates the reader to an awareness of the appalling depths hidden beneath the mire of the pettifogging cares of everyday life. It is some time before we see through the humorous tones of his leisurely narration to the "tears unseen and unknown" to the world. The impassioned digressions and highly dramatic image of the author that emerges from them are in sharp contrast to the vulgarity of his "strange heroes". And we have to read deeply into the work in order to divine the author's generalization, the "transforming" significance of his characters.

In Balzac's books all the characters and their author exist in a permanent state of emotional excitement. Thunderbolts heralding storms of passion rend the air from the very first scenes of *Le Père Goriot, Eugénie Grandet, Les Illusions perdues, Splendeurs et misères des courtisanes.* In this atmosphere even nondescript characters have their luminous moments: they make grand and dignified gestures, utter portentous words, and well-turned aphorisms.

Balzac's heroes are as eloquent as their creator. His travelling salesmen, newsboys, policemen, cocottes, sleuths and procuresses sparkle with wit. To quote an old adage, even Balzac's concierges are endowed with genius.

The author of *La Comédie humaine* depicts a world of desperate struggle and rapid transformation. Fortunes worth millions are made and squandered with incredible speed, noble titles and coats of arms acquired by enterprising upstarts, reputations are destroyed or hallowed as a result of secret machinations or fateful coincidences. The field of action of *La Comédie humaine* is presented by the author as a colossal theatre of war, where battles are fought every hour and every minute, in political and private life.

In the fourth chapter of *Dead Souls* Gogol describes the battle between Nozdryov and Chichikov and likens the former to a reckless lieutenant, "whose head is in a complete whirl" and "who has grand ambitions", "not realizing that he is prejudicing the carefully considered plan for the whole attack, ... and that the fateful bullet is already whistling through the air, on its way to close for ever his strident throat" (VI, 86-87). But this entire extended simile is maintained in a humorous key, and consequently the comparison of his antagonist Chichikov to a besieged fortress also sounds comic. "But if Nozdryov called to mind a headstrong, desperate lieutenant laying siege to a fortress, this fortress was by no means impregnable. On the contrary, the fortress was seized with such paroxysms of fear that its heart was in its mouth" (VI, 87). By contrast Balzac presents the collision between Jacques Collin and his pursuers in a martial simile as well, but here the comparison is entirely serious and straightforward.

In *La Comédie humaine*, as in *Dead Souls*, the portrayal of the character's egoistic and soul-destroying passions is permeated with profound irony.

Both writers contrast the apparent decorum of the people and their mores with their actual corruption. The humour that arises from the glaring incongruity between this superficial portrayal of life and the reality "that constantly lies open to the view, but is unseen by the indifferent eye" is full of bitterness and anxiety. Irony is made, both by Gogol and by Balzac, to serve a satirical purpose. Note the dedication of *La Comédie humaine* to Victor Hugo, in which Balzac describes himself as a writer who "castigat ridendo mores" ("through laughter castigates mores"). But with Balzac this irony is frequently tempered by his spontaneous admiration for his own characters, irrespective of whether they sacrifice themselves to their duty, or, as is more often the case in *La Comédie humaine*, transgress all limits and laws in order to satisfy their all-consuming passion.

As he describes in his epic work the historical development and consolidation of bourgeois relations in France Balzac displays a certain ambivalence in his treatment of bourgeois individualism. He abhors the exploitation of labour, the power of money, but at the same time, as a philosopher and artist he is deeply impressed by the far-reaching revolutionizing processes of the emancipation of the individual, which were set in motion in 1789 with the destruction of the feudal-estate system and the foundations of the church. He is fully aware of the corruptive influence of material desires and the search for power on human nature, and knows only too well how soulless and terrible is a world ruled by capital in the person of the Nucingens, Taillefers and others like them. But he takes a truly aesthetic interest in the way the enormous, hitherto suppressed potential of man is set free and his energies, intellect, diverse talents come to life, describing how all the grasping and ambitious desires and passions seethe and bubble in the maelstrom of life.

It is this that gives rise to his ambivalent attitude even to those characters in *La Comédie humaine* who are eaten away by a monstrous cupidity or driven by an uncontrollable thirst for power. He dissects their deformed souls with a remorseless accuracy. But he cannot suppress his own admiration for the grand sweep of their emotions.

Balzac resorts to "Napoleonic" associations when he wishes to convey the scale of his characters. The perverted and rapacious Valérie Marneffe conducts her intrigues with the presence of mind of the great general. One of Balzac's favourite and largely auto-biographical characters, the courageous and stoical writer Daniel D'Arthez, whose literary endeavours are presented as a truly heroic feat, is compared to Napoleon himself.

Reminiscences about Napoleon also play an important role in the eventful story of Lucien Chardon and his "patron", the fugitive convict Jacques Collin, who disguises himself under the name l'Abbé Carlos Herrera. At the beginning of *Les Illusions perdues* Balzac as it were provides a key to Chardon's story, enabling the reader to follow the experiences of this young buck, eager for glory and pleasure and prepared to abandon both his honour and his conscience in their pursuit. Balzac writes: "L'example de Napoléon, si fatal au dix-neuvième siècle par les prétentions qu'il inspire à tant de gens médiocres, apparut à Lucien". [31] The dramatic episode which in *Splendeurs et misères des courtisanes* marks the end of Lucien's career in high society is similarly pointed up by analogy with Napoleon. As he awaits the dénouement Lucien once again recalls Napoleon, but this time Napoleon after his fall. Finally, the self-styled Abbé Carlos Herrera receives a letter from his luckless protégé, now in prison, and writing in valediction before taking his own life. In this letter he calls his patron a descendant of the tribe of Cain, one of those demonic creatures who, in accordance with the whim of God, become Moses, Attila, Charlemagne, Mahomet, Napoleon, Pugachov, Robespierre or Luvel.

Thus the world of dark, criminal intrigues acquires the significance of history and is elevated to the status of high politics.

Remarkably enough, the "Napoleonic motif" also figures in Gogol's writing, applied in *Dead Souls* to Chichikov's machinations—but this time in a purely ironic way.

In Volume 1, chapter ten we read how the perturbed

officials of N puzzle over Chichikov's true identity, and "of all the many perspicacious conjectures there was one, strange though it may seem, that Chichikov might even be Napoleon in disguise", released by the British from St. Helena and now seeking his way to Russia—"in the guise of Chichikov, but not Chichikov at all in fact" (VI, 205-206).

Even Chichikov's benign and seemingly trustworthy physiognomy now started to arouse their suspicions: ". . .it was found that Chichikov's face, if he were to turn sideways, was similar to the portrait of Napoleon". The police chief (who had personally seen Napoleon during the 1812 campaign) "similarly could not but admit that he had been no taller than Chichikov and that in his figure Napoleon was also what you may describe as not exactly too fat, nor really all that thin" (VI, 206). Gogol pokes fun at the obvious ridiculousness of such a surmise. But at the same time, as previous Soviet commentators have already pointed out, the "Napoleonic" associations in a way complement and elucidate the image of Chichikov, at the same time as they explain the artist's own position with regard to the major social tendencies of his day, one of the symbols of which is the name of Napoleon.

> We're all would-be Napoleons;
> You're just a tool, those millions
> Of two-legged creatures—at least, to us, *

writes Pushkin in *Eugene Onegin*. In this socio-ethical sense Chichikov was also "a Napoleon" in his own eyes. And for him, as for all those like him, the men of "enterprise", captains of capitalism, people, whether alive or dead, are merely a tool for the attainment of their rapacious goals. But these "Napoleonic" allusions, which are to be found in Volume 1, are exclusively ironic in character. Gogol invests Chichikov with immense stamina, great experience and knowledge of life, but then subjects him to an entire succession of failures. Moreover, the collapse of Chichikov's so carefully conceived and tested schemes, which he undertook first in the construction commission, then in the customs and finally in the town N, with his purchase of "non-existent" serfs, is due not by any means to the vigilance of the law or the moral fortitude of the people around him.

---

* Translated by Alex Miller.

Chichikov's plans collapse on the slightest trifle, on minor miscalculations and annoying chance circumstances. In the first case it was because "suddenly his employer took a dislike to his face, although God only knows why" (VI, 232); and though at first a number of Chichikov's colleagues are also "pulverized to dust" by the zealous general, these succeed in regaining his favour, but "Chichikov was no longer able to crawl back in" (VI, 233). His contraband dealings, which amassed millions of roubles for their skilful entrepreneur, also come to grief, this time after a ridiculous quarrel with a collaborator: "Some devil messed the whole thing up" (VI, 236).

Finally, the fiasco which ruins the newly-arrived "millionaire", the "landowner from Kherson", in the town N, comes about not through any premeditated and calculated action on the part of his declared or secret enemies (as is usually the case with Balzac), but through what appear to be entirely trivial details. Thus Nozdryov gets drunk at the governor's ball and spills the beans; Korobochka rattles into town from her backwoods in order to ascertain the going price for dead souls; and Chichikov himself, inadvertently casting his roving eye in the direction of the governor's daughter, thereby causes all the ladies of N deep offence, and little suspects what a storm this will generate in the town. While Balzac's heroes operate in an atmosphere of frenzied activity, in which everyone is doing his utmost to achieve his end against an equally determined opposition, Gogol's *poema* is pervaded by a sense of the vanity and futility of existence, choked as it is by trivial and egoistic interests, and the Russian author denies Chichikov—his "little Napoleon"—even the honour of defeat by the strongest opponent. In the ironic digression which concludes the account of the ridiculous conjectures and theories put forward by the officials of N as to the true identity of Chichikov, the author gives an extremely sceptical view of the claim of these men of state to resolution of character and clarity of thought. "And it became quite clear what sort of creature man is: he is wise, knowledgeable and able in all matters concerning others, but not those concerning himself. What well-considered, firm advice he can provide in the difficult moments of life! 'My, what an incisive thinker!' exclaims the crowd. 'What an unshakable character!' But let the slightest misfortune befall this incisive thinker, let him be placed in one of life's difficult moments himself, and so much that character, the unshakable stalwart goes all to pieces and turns into the most pitiful coward, a wretched, weak child, or, simply, a goof, as Nozdryov would say" (VI, 209).

Both volumes of *Dead Souls* close with scenes of tragicomic confusion. In Volume 1 this is depicted in a predominantly comic key, although the death of the public prosecutor, who has been destroyed by Chichikov's ruinous scheme, adds a note of pathos to the tenth chapter. In Volume 2 the tragi-comic turmoil created by the nefarious activities of Chichikov and his collaborators, acquires a sinister air: "The case reached unimaginable proportions... The confusion mounted... People quite lost their minds: one denunciation followed another and cases were opened the like of which the world had not seen before, and cases which had indeed never existed at all... Scandals, corruption and such things all become so intertangled and bound up with Chichikov's story, with the dead souls, that it was quite impossible to make out which of all these cases was the biggest nonsense" (VII, 117-118). But this time it is not only the minor provincial officials who are confounded, but the governor-general himself, representative of the supreme powers. In the final fragment, the prince (the governor-general) makes a speech to the officials he has summoned, and this speech with its angry subtext reveals the impotence of the tsarist bureaucracy against the corruption which utterly consumes it. The prince threatens his subordinates with court martial, he promises that he will "act harshly", that "he therefore must become a remorseless weapon of justice, the axe which is fated to fall on the head of the guilty" (VII, 125).

The chaotic mass of conflicting interests, passions and habits depicted by Cogol leads to unexpected results for every one of the participants in the action, results which ultimately defy their own will. Life moves in accordance with its own ineffable laws, and unpredictable peripeteia persistently confound even those who regard themselves as highly experienced and resolute. Thus, the administration of the province, despite the prudence of the governor-general despatched from St. Petersburg, is fraught with just the same confusion and chaos, only on a much larger scale. Chichikov's accomplice, a legal consultant, "like a concealed magician, invisibly turned the entire mechanism" (VII, 117). And whilst he does not manage to whitewash his protégé, Chichikov does extricate himself from his tight corner, albeit with some loss, and "in a strange situation", confused and discomforted. However, his discomfort is no less than that of the governor-general, at whose feet Chichikov had so recently been grovelling. "Besides the legal administration another administrative body has come into existence, far more powerful than any legal variety" (VII, 126), exclaims this high and mighty official, publicly admitting his inability to untangle through "legal procedures" the rat's nest of fraud, denunciation, intrigue and slander, which has ensnared the province in his charge. "...We are only able to see dimly through it, and we may scarcely..." (VII, 127)—thus his speech abruptly breaks off in the last surviving fragment of Volume 2, breaking off on the motif of chaos and confusion, so characteristic of Gogol's work, of the futility and hypocrisy of life, attempting in vain to pass itself off as real, carefully considered, and worthy of man's highest purpose.

"The maelstrom of misunderstandings"—an image that is also encountered so often in Gogol's correspondence with reference to his own relation to his readers, critics and friends, moves into prominence in the culminating "catastrophes" of both volumes of *Dead Souls*. "Everything started to ferment, and no living soul could comprehend it... The dead souls, the governor's daughter and Chichikov, all mixed and churned together in their heads in the most extraordinary fashion... It was simply: A lot of old balderdash, poppycock and hard-boiled boots! It was simply the devil only knows what!.. The town, that hitherto seemed to be peacefully slumbering, now swirled in a veritable maelstrom!" (VI, 189-190). In this maelstrom of conflicting rumours we catch the occasional glimpse, indistinct and transient, of the real conflicts which jostle together with all manner of imagined and fantastic stories. The natural, spontaneous laws of life prove to be "more cunning" than the plans and calculations of individuals. In Balzac's vision of the world, by contrast, not only Vautrin, the genius of the convict prison, but even the most ordinary people are able to conceive and carry out the most complex stratagems, in which every step has been carefully tested beforehand, and if they do fail it is only because they encounter a still stronger opponent.

The corruption which is eating its way into Russia's bureaucratic system deeply worries Gogol and is frequently depicted in *Dead Souls*. But Gogol prefers to portray his officials as flies, which "swarm over the tasty titbits" "in dense squadrons", "like undisputed masters": a comparison which mercilessly satirizes their paltriness and parasitical qualities, but not that *systematic* predatory energy which Balzac emphasizes in his portrayal of scheming bureaucrats.

In the pages of *La Comédie humaine* we encounter a large number of characters—dissolute rogues and scoundrels, who appear to have affinities with Gogol's Nozdryov. But even they, even these desperate rakes and gamblers, idlers, brawlers and rowdies, all act in accordance with a particular "plan". In comparison to the deliberate fictions concocted by Balzac's scoundrels Nozdryov's inspired lying is, on the contrary, remarkable for its nonsense. He is carried hither and thither by that same "maelstrom of misunderstandings" which plays such an important role in Gogol's world.

With Balzac even those misunderstandings to which his heroes sometimes fall victim, appear to be consciously and carefully planned by other people, whether for a particular purpose, or for mere diversion. As a typical example we can take the story "L'Illustre Gaudissart". The anecdotal dialogue that unfolds between Gaudissart and Margaritis, could be compared in terms of its absurdity to the conversations between Chichikov and Korobochka, or the mad Koshkaryov. But with Gogol this absurdity is the child of life itself. Gaudissart, on the other hand, has been deliberately duped by a local wag, the Duc de Verneuil, who has recommended him Margaritis as a respected banker, one of the pillars of the town, and concealing himself in the neighbouring room together with various friends enjoyed the resulting comedy which was played out by the two unsuspecting actors.

Gogol does not make a fetish of accident, as the Romantics might have done in his place, frequently seeing it as a manifestation of fate. But the unexpected concatenations of circumstances which destroy the plans of his characters (and above all Chichikov) are made to seem like manifestations of the broad and free objective flow of life, whose depths the author's penetrating gaze is just beginning to plumb.

Chichikov's plans now and again misfire—not only in the past, but also in the present. It seems that the very expanses of Russia turn against him. Roads crawl away in all directions like crayfish shaken out of a sack. "The confusion and blizzard" cause him to lose his way. Chichikov goes to see Sobakevich and ends up making an unplanned visit to Korobochka, then Nozdryov (the two visits which are to have such fateful consequences for him); he makes his way to Koshkaryov and ends up with Petukh. At the beginning of the first chapter we overhear the remarks of two peasants, reported in an off-hand, almost flippant manner, who are studying Chichikov's carriage: " 'What do you say,' would that wheel make it to Moscow if it had to?' 'Aye, it would,' answered the other. 'But I wouldn't reckon it'd make it to Kazan.' 'No, it'd never make it to Kazan,' said the other" (VI, 7). Many scholars have commented on the possible symbolism of this episode, which as it were heralds the collapse of Chichikov's designs. But what is even more important is the way Gogol himself, approaching his hero from different aspects in his authorial digressions, at times talks of him as of someone quite clearly-defined and easy to understand: "So there you have our hero, en face, just as he is" (VI, 241), and at others hints at the many unexpected turns of events which lie in wait not only for him, Chichikov, but also for the reader as he follows his adventures. Thus the writer's promise to continue the story of Chichikov and his "dead souls", delivered with a mass of concrete, commonplace detail, is followed a page further on by a passage in an altogether different key, where a character who appeared to be entirely cut and dried turns out to be enigmatic, with a dark side quite unknown to the reader, and perhaps even to the author: "And perhaps the passion in this same Chichikov, the passion that drew him on was not of his own... And why this character should have taken its place in the *poema* written here is another mystery" (VI, 242).

In his portrayal of the heroes of *La Comédie humaine* Balzac frequently sets the reader unexpected riddles. But their solution is never a mystery to the author, he knows it beforehand and imparts it in good time. He willingly has recourse to a device which is alien to Gogol's principles of character portrayal in *Dead Souls*. In *L'auberge rouge, La Maison Nucingen* and *Gobseck* the chronicle of the nefarious doings, the amassing of wealth and "ascent" of the thief and murdered Taillefer, who becomes a financial wizard, of the crooked banker Nucingen and of the moneylender Gobseck is recounted retrospectively as the sarcastic resumé not of the author, but of one of his secondary characters, made in an off-hand way, sometimes even à propos altogether.

In *La Maison Nucingen* a brilliant analysis of the financial and political machinations of Nucingen and his accomplices is given in the form of a casual table conversation between four shrewd *condottieri* of modern commerce, who are seated in a separate room in the restaurant and have no idea that their conversation carries to the next cabinet, where the narrator finds himself unintentionally eavesdropping. In *Gobseck* the story of the recently deceased extortioner is related to the respected Duchess de Grandlieu by his executor, the scrivener Derville, in order to dispel the Duchess's prejudices against her daughter's marriage to the young Comte de Restaud, in whose property dealings Gobseck had been implicated.

In all these cases the underhand dealings have already become part of history: the mystery surrounding them does not exist for the initiated. Worldly wise people discuss them with a shade of cynicism, as an inalienable, inevitable law of the modern world.

Gogol writes of similar tendencies, but these had not yet become so prominent in the Russia of his time. While Balzac analyses in minute detail the links between his Kellers, du Tillets, Nucingens and others like them with political changes in the life of France (*La Maison Nucingen* is concerned not only with the fall of the Bourbons, but also with the weavers' uprising in Lyons) and his financial *condottieri* are presented in brilliant clarity, leaving no room for doubt, Chichikov acts as a perturbing symbol of the time, but a symbol whose meaning is not yet entirely clear. "His parents were of noble stock, but whether theirs was a hereditary or recent lineage—God only knows" (VI, 225). In terms of his position in society and manner of acting he is no landowner nor merchant, nor even pettyfogging clerk—at the same time all their qualities are combined in him, and he engages in his strange negotiations with full knowledge of the correct "form", and dreams of spending his old age as a true landowner, but becomes intoxicated with the thought of other deals worth millions. . .

With application to the conditions prevailing in Russia at that time he can be seen as an embryonic prototype of the same social "species" other representatives of which were studied by Balzac at a time when they had reached the peak of their development. The characters of *Dead Souls* are for that reason more comparable to Balzac's employers and acquirers, depicted in his *Scènes de la vie province* and *Scènes de la vie privée* than those active in the world of big politics, like the big bosses from *La Maison Nucingen* (which forms part of *Scènes de la vie parisienne*).

Such characters as old Séchard, Eugénie Grandet's father and Gobseck are close, both in their social and moral make-up and in the manner their characters are revealed, to Gogol's heroes.

The Soviet critic Boris Suchkov detects features in the image of Gobseck which are cognate with Pushkin's *The Covetous Knight* as well as Gogol's characters. "Like Pushkin's baron," he writes, "Gobseck still possesses power and great stature, although both are already beginning to display signs of Plyushkin-like avarice. They are still *collectors* of capital, and not yet big wheels, and are thus typical of the early stage of bourgeois amassment of wealth. They are the first examples in world realistic art of capitalist predators: their images stand at the fountainhead of 'Chichikovshchina'—the typical feature of that rapacious age, and they are the direct ancestors of Baron Nucingen, the brokers Gundermann and Saccard from Zola's *L'argent,* Shchedrin's Kolupayevs and Razuvayevs, the bankers and financiers from Verhaeren's poetic cycles, right down to the figure of Cowperwood—the hero of Dreiser's *Trilogy of Desire*."

Old Séchard, Félix Grandet, Gobseck and many other less memorable characters from Balzac's works, embody in an extreme form the acquisitive desires, which, to quote Gogol, "are becoming terrible tyrants" (VI, 242) over their characters and actions. In the case of the first two the hunger for profit is manifested in still patriarchal forms. They are good citizens, both until recently craftsmen, whose miserliness does not over-surprise their fellow-countrymen, although it makes them relentless despots in their business dealings and in their family life. In their portrayal, as with that of many of Gogol's characters, comic features initially obscure the tragic deformation of their human nature. The old printer Jérôme-Nicolas Séchard (whose original trade of printer has left him with the expressive nickname "the Bear") has a grotesque appearance, which Balzac describes with the same relish that is displayed by Gogol in such cases. Playing on the old man's professional nickname, Balzac relates how the "old Bear" (le vieil Ours), trying to convince his son against all the evidence of the superiority of his obsolete typographical equipment, operates his press "avec l'agilité qu'aurait mise un jeune Ours". The comic details of this scene, which pertain not only to the manners of old Séchard, but also to his persistent bargaining, have echoes of the memorable account of Chichikov's visit to Sobakevich. Balzac, however, intensifies the drama of this opening episode, which constitutes the mise-en-scène of the first part of *La Comédie humaine*, by having Séchard-père swindle his own son, the talented inventor David Séchard, in whose subsequent career the old man is to play such a fateful role. When he passes the printing press on to his son he now sees him as no more than "un ennemi à vaincre. Cette transformation du sentiment en intérêt personnel, ordinairement lente, tortueuse et hypocrite chez les gens bien élevés, fut rapide et directe chez le vieil Ours". [32]

In the figure of Félix Grandet, a former cooper and subsequently a landowning vintner, who starves his wife and daughter, economizes on coal and candles and dies the possessor of a seventeen-million franc estate, we see the ruinous, soul-destroying force of greed and avarice in a still more sinister form. The animals and other zoological metaphors to which Balzac resorts in his portrayal just as frequently as Gogol are here void of that comic shade which they have in the portrait of "le vieil Ours" Séchard. Old Grandet has "steel claws". In his commercial dealings he recalls both a tiger and a boa constrictor. The very "bredouillement, l'incohérence de ses paroles, le flux de mots où il noyait sa pensée" are a deliberate device employed by Grandet to disable his listener. (Thus too does Chichikov cultivate an intentionally flowery manner of speech, full of inference and insinuation.) Like Gogol Balzac recognizes the intelligence and will-power of the old miser, who so skilfully plays the part of a simple fellow. If he had had but a little more ambition, "si d'heureuses circonstances, en le faisant arriver vers les sphères supérieures de la société, l'eussent envoyé dans les congrès où se traitaient les affaires des nations, et qu'il s'y fût servi du genie dont l'avait doté son intérêt personnel, nul doute qu'il n'y eût été glorieusement utile à la France". [33] This admission is just as characteristic as the indication that Balzac, like Gogol, is concerned about the monstrous waste of human talent, crushed or perverted by a lust for material gain. Both old Séchard and Félix Grandet are extraordinarily meaningful *social* archetypes. But the fatal consequences of the greed which possesses them, described by Balzac in *Les Illusions perdues* and *Eugénie Grandet,* are primarily revealed through the prism of private, family relations. Terrible torments are suffered by poor Eugénie and her mother, when her father learns about the gold which they have trustingly given to her cousin, but still worse is the fact that Eugénie, having survived her moral duel with her father, outlives him and gradually, imperceptibly, even against her own will, assumes his way of life and behaviour. She, as Balzac tells us, did not taint herself "au contact du monde" but she has all the "roideur de la vieille fille et les habitudes mesquines que donne l'existence étroite de la province".

Gogol is much less concerned with this side of the lives of his "strange heroes". He gives only two or three sentences to his account of Plyushkin's rejection of his officer son and the untimely death of his younger daughter. The fate of the older daughter, the luckless Alexandra Stepanovna, who eloped from her father's house with a visiting officer, and then came to see her father first with one, then with two children, in the vain hope of obtaining at least a little assistance from him, is touched on in a little more detail but still only in passing. Individual destinies are of little interest to the author of *Dead Souls.* Plyushkin's transformation from a "most intelligent, wealthy man" (VI, 145) into a wretched old miser, devoid of any trace of humanity, is regarded by Gogol as something tragic. But this tragedy, if we can judge from the entire context of chapter six, consists above all in the fate of the people (observe the way the ruined peasant huts recall skeletons —on some of them only a single ridge remains on "the rib-like framework of the roof"—VI, 111), in the horrifying futility of serf labour, which yearly increases the wealth that is condemned to rot, while people die of hunger next to cellars full of petrified flour, storerooms and stacks of rotting grain and hay... The moral decline of Plyushkin, who himself finally became "a kind of gaping hole on the face of mankind" (VI, 119), is presented at the same generalizing, "transforming" level which characterizes the realism of *Dead Souls* as a whole, and it reads as an ominous warning of the unnaturalness of the life portrayed in the book, of the glaring incongruity between the nature and dignity of man. It is noteworthy that, by resorting to animal metaphors, like Balzac, Gogol is able to construct the portrait of his characters not so much with horrifying as with humiliating comparisons. Plyushkin's "little eyes ... darted about beneath the bushy eyebrows like mice" (VI, 116). His activities in the past, when they had not yet lost all meaning, are likened to the busy bustle of an industrious spider, "scurrying from end to end of his web" (VI, 118).

A comparison of Plyushkin and Gobseck, two giants of nineteenth century realism, particularly clearly demonstrates where Gogol's and Balzac's creative paths converge and where they part. The final part of Balzac's novella brings forward the theme of the hostility of egoistic cupidity towards the productive forces of mankind, a theme that concurs with the basic message of the Plyushkin episode in *Dead Souls*. After Gobseck's death his executor Derville discovers in his house, amongst all his belongings and gold, enormous masses of stores, stinking and covered with mould. The end of Gobseck, who has pointlessly and greedily amassed what can no longer be of use either to himself or to anyone else, demonstrates to Derville "les effets d'une avarice à laquelle il n'était plus resté que cet instinct illogique". Like Gogol, Balzac finds for this maniac, this "automaton" as he calls him, comparisons which show how human nature has been abased in him. His eyes are like the eyes of a weasel. His movements recall those of a wood-louse. Like Plyushkin, whom Chichikov first takes for a man, then for a woman, Gobseck sometimes makes Derville wonder what sex he is. But in contrast to the stultifying effect of Plyushkin's avarice, the same vice burns in Gobseck with the flame of volupté. There is something unmistakably Romantic in his image. He still cherishes memories of pirate raids, of the twenty years he spent in India, of the American war of independence, in which he had a hand... This is no Plyushkin, but a hero of a different, superhuman scale, who is more reminiscent of Maturin's *Melmoth the Wanderer* and such figures.

Although like Gogol Balzac frequently portrays people who have long before been hopelessly crippled by some all-consuming passion, he does however keep to his primarily analytical approach to reality and often allows the reader to witness all the peripeteia of the *choice* made by his hero. There is no place for this in *Dead Souls,* with the possible exception of certain faintly sketched situations in the fragments of Volume 2. Chichikov, Plyushkin, Manilov, Sobakevich and Nozdryov have long been covered with that "earthy crust", and Gogol does not allow the reader to suspect for a moment that any of them in their distant past struggled against the temptations of egoism, rapacity, avarice, futile dreaming, etc. Balzac's Rastignac and Chardon are initially still at the crossroads, and it would seem that the path of honest labour (admittedly combined with severe ascetic self-denial) is not proscribed to them; they still do not succumb at once to the brandishment of luxury, ambition and pleasure. The content of the novel forms a dramatically closed process of the spiritual degradation of its heroes. They impress with their undeniable ardour, talents and still unspent spiritual energy. At the same time the "earthy crust" is already restraining them from their impetuousness; Balzac uses direct parallels to this image of Gogol's: he writes of the "armour of egoism" which Rastignac forges around him, the "armour of a lobster".

In Thackeray's novels we find no place for the hyperbolic, Romantic passions which certain of Balzac's characters embody. Vanity and egoism are the two predominant principles which, in all their various manifestations, determine the characters and actions of his characters, in particular, those of *Vanity Fair.* The author insists that even the naïve Amelia and honest Dobbin are not free of these vices—after all, they worship false idols and persist in their self-inflicted blindness... Thackeray is a master of satire and the contrast between what his heroes think of themselves and of each other, and what the omniscient author actually knows about them, enables him, as it does Gogol in *Dead Souls,* to show that the corruption eating into human relations and characters is all the more terrible for the fact that it is regarded as the norm.

In this sense there is much in common between the conception and interpretation of Thackeray's high society schemer Rebecca Sharp and Gogol's "acquirer" Chichikov. Genetically both characters are not so distantly related to the heroes and heroines of the picaresque novel. Rebecca's maiden name points up this association: she is indeed sharp, a true descendant of all "sharpers". But neither

172

Thackeray nor Gogol regard the schemes and traditions of the picaresque novel as of significance in themselves. In accordance with the spirit of the nineteenth century critical realism they are concerned not so much with the exploits of an individual malefactor as with their typical social features. "Acquisition is to blame for everything," writes Gogol in Volume 1 chapter 11, explaining the character of his hero, "through it deals have been made which the world would describe as none too honest" (VI, 242).

But Chichikov's "none too honest" deals can be effected only in a "none too honest" social sphere. However brilliant and enterprising his scheme to buy dead souls may be, it basically serves as an indication of the general moral degradation of the world of property, to which Chichikov belongs. In the very first pages of the work, in the episode of the governor's reception, the ironic description of "fat and thin" men proclaims "acquisition" as the universally accepted basis for prosperous living, and even a good name. And surely it is precisely to this that all Chichikov's ambitions are directed. And it is to that same class of "fat" men, so mercilessly satirized by the author, that all the "respected officials of the town" belong. It is not surprising, therefore, that our enterprising Pavel Ivanovich should feel so at home in their midst: he is of the same species and is governed by the same rules. Manilov, Korobochka, Sobakevich and Plyushkin are all people of different ways of life and character, yet they all agree to sell their customer his strange wares with equal nonchalance. The only thing that disturbs the last three is that they may be selling too cheap.

The satirical symbolism of the general buying and selling in *Vanity Fair* is just as significant as that in *Dead Souls*. Like Gogol with his Chichikov, Thackeray, when describing his heroine, gives the reader to understand that she essentially acts in accordance with the laws of the society to which she belongs. Chichikov buys up dead souls. Rebecca Sharp deals in live wares—namely, herself, for at the Vanity Fair an advantageous marriage or liaison with a rich and noble "patron" is the best possible way of investing her "capital". She does the same as others. Her misfortune is merely that "poor dear Rebecca had all this work to do for herself", [34] which normally would have been done by a mother, seeking out a rich husband for her daughter. Thackeray frequently has recourse to the language of commerce, when he discusses the way live souls are traded in England. The old rake, Lord Steyne, is convinced that Colonel Rawdon Crawley, Rebecca's husband, is deliberately, calculatingly conniving at the former's intrigue with his wife. He is mistaken, but, as Thackeray ironically remarks, "My lord had bought so many men during his life that he was surely to be pardoned for supposing that he had found the price of this one". [35]

Thackeray's charming, green-eyed "siren" with her brilliant wit and refined manners would hardly seem comparable to Pavel Ivanovich Chichikov, with his rainbow coloured woollen neckerchief, loud nose-blowing and ponderous, although highly decorous, manners. But they both embody one and the same spirit of bourgeois enterprise, the spirit of cupidity, which has merely taken on different guises depending on the situation and circumstances. Each of them, to borrow Thackeray's expression, "do their dirty work" within their different circumstances. Rebecca plays on the aristocratic pretensions of English snobs, assuring them that she is descended from the noble line of Montmorency... Chichikov composes a quite different, but equally fictitious biography for himself, claiming that he "suffered in the cause of justice".

The shared principle of creating realistic, typical characters, followed both by Gogol and Thackeray, can also be seen at work in the attitude of the two writers to the "amorality" of their characters. Without in the least adorning or idealizing these characters, both Thackeray and Gogol persuade the reader, each in their own way, that their heartlessness, insensibility, hypocrisy and all-consuming pursuit of material gain are the consequence not of their *personal* moral degradation, but of unfavourable, *typical* circumstances—a false upbringing, poverty and the temptations that arise daily out of social inequality. Neither Becky Sharp nor Chichikov, as their creators stress, are actually bad by nature.

But Thackeray frequently admires the enterprise, perspicacity and wit of his heroine, who in her performances on the stage of the Vanity Fair frequently uses against her antagonists their very own weapons. In what way is she worse than the cowardly, self-interested and greedy Joseph Sedley, the "nabob" who has grown fat on the taxes he has collected from the natives of India? How is she worse than the respected Crawley family, all the members of

174

which, from the tippling parson to his sanctimonious nephew, can think only about how to get their own hands on to the inheritance of Miss Crawley? How is she worse than all those aristocratic snobs, to whom Thackeray gives sarcastically disrespectful names, indicative of their kinship with horses or sheep, or possessing other, equally expressive, associations? And finally, Rebecca's high-born "patron", the cruel and degenerate old cynic Lord Steyne, is so hardened by sin that he has no moral right, however much this charming schemer dupes him, to consider himself a victim.

Throughout their portrayal of all their leading characters both Gogol and Thackeray irresistibly draw the reader to an important conclusion: in those social circumstances in which they are placed their indecorous actions are somehow quite "normal"—this is their only defensive weapon. In his conversation with the reader in chapter 11 Gogol ironically refuses to call Chichikov an outright "rogue"—"it would be more just to call him a 'business man, an acquirer'" (VI, 241), he remarks. Becky Sharp proves to be just such an "acquirer" acting, like Chichikov, in accordance with the unwritten laws of society. They both have a secret box, in which, naturally, there is a secret compartment. Disaster overtakes them when things finally reach this focal point of all their efforts, plans and hopes. Cast into jail, Chichikov is upset most of all at being deprived of his precious box. Without this box he loses the ground beneath his feet; and no sooner is the box returned to him, with "the papers, the money—everything in perfect order" than the old "temptations" start to appear before his eyes again (VII, 116-117).

Becky, caught in flagrante delicto by her husband, still tries to extricate herself with lies; but when her little box is found with the bills of credit inside—some of them new, others ten years old—it is all over.

Both Gogol and Thackeray are concerned, even disturbed, by their awareness of how *relative* is the distinction between the offenders against public order and its guardians. "What is hard to bear is not that the people might be discontent with my hero," writes Gogol. "Nay, what does matter is the insuppressible certainty that they could be quite content with this very same hero, with this same Chichikov, if the author had not pried so deeply into his hero's soul, had he not stirred on its bedrock that which shunned and lay hidden from the light, had he not revealed those innermost thoughts which no man will confide in any other: Had he exhibited him exactly as he exhibited himself to the entire town, to Manilov and the rest, they would all have been quite delighted and would have voted him a most interesting man" (VI, 242-243).

Thackeray expresses a similar view in somewhat different terms. He makes Rebecca herself reflect how easily she could follow the path of virtue (in the generally accepted meaning of the word!) if she had "five thousand pounds a year".

For indeed would not Chichikov, had he been destined to become the owner of properly acquired village with three hundred or so peasants, alive and not dead, and to bury his past misdeeds, would he not have been as good in administering it as Sobakevich or Korobochka, and have enjoyed the good favour of all the surrounding landowners?

Other characters from Thackeray's writings have similar affinities with members of Gogol's gallery. Thus, the Soviet critic D.S. Yakhontova makes an interesting comparison between the figures of Sir Pitt Crawley and Plyushkin. Their affinity consists in the fact that both writers have depicted the same "petty-tyrant type of a landowner, coarse and miserly, widespread not only in England, but throughout the countries of Western Europe and Russia", and in the similarity of the very method of portrayal, since both writers have sought satirical portraits of equally universal stature.

"Sir Pitt Crawley," writes Yakhontova, "is related to Gogol's Plyushkin ... Certain particular details even coincide. Just as Chichikov takes the tattered, dirty and degenerate Plyushkin for his servant woman, so does Becky Sharp, when she sees Sir Pitt Crawley, decide that he is Sir Pitt's unwashed and dishevelled groom. The description of their appearance and clothing is also similar."

Comparing two parallel episodes—the portraits of Plyushkin and of Sir Pitt, Yakhontova continues: "On Plyushkin's table we see a dried-up lemon and a glass over which crawl three flies; on Sir Pitt's a piece of sugar, a scrap of bread and a mug with the remains of some black porter.

"Plyushkin does not hide his relief when he hears that his guest has already eaten, and at once returns his liquor to its cupboard; Sir Pitt, learning that his guest has already dined, proceeds to enjoy a plate of tripe and onions on his own.

"There can be no question of one writer influencing the other here, but the similarity between these two images is striking and not coincidental." [36]

We should also note another important aspect of this question. Sir Pitt Crawley and others like him only provoke Thackeray's derision and scorn. He sees right through them and knows their true worth, but for him they remain a constant in the algebra of human society. Gogol similarly shows Plyushkin to be both repellent and comic. But he also presents, albeit briefly, the development of this character. He recalls Plyushkin's past, when his parsimony had not yet grown into maniac avarice. At the same time we cannot but feel in the subtext of this episode the intense horror with which Gogol surveys this *former* person, who has lost any human semblance. For all the similarity between the portraits of their heroes, between the detailed descriptions of their lives and circumstances, of the dialogues, etc., Gogol sustains his account of Chichikov's visit to Plyushkin in quite a different emotional key, than that adopted by Thackeray for his description of Sir Pitt Crawley.

5

Gogol, Balzac, Thackeray and Dickens all find new methods of character portrayal which were not attested in the realistic writings of the Enlightenment. The portrait itself retains its importance, but with fundamental innovations, such as fine nuances and shades which are rarely found in eighteenth century novels, and sometimes (particularly with Dickens), achieved by contrasting a coarse or even comic exterior and a profoundly humane personality.

But alongside the portrait we find details of the character's environment playing an important role, complementing the portrait itself: the architecture of his home, the interior, right down to details about the furnishings. This side of domestic life with its concrete, individual detail rarely attracted the attention of the Enlightenment writers. One rich home was much like another, one furnished room like another, while the hovels of the poor did not even have any "special features". Only on rare occasions are we given details of the furnishings: thus the reader of *Joseph Andrews* and *Roderick Random* cannot fail to remember the pigsty in which Adams sprawls after being knocked over by parson Trulliber's fat boar, or the stinking hold of the ship in which the forcibly recruited young surgeon Roderick Random is hurled, as if into prison. But here, as we can see from the context, the description of the surroundings serves not so much to reveal the characters as to point up, in the first case, the comedy, and in the second, the tragedy of their *situations*.

In general we should note that the role of situations in the development of the narrative, on the one hand, and the portrayal of the characters, on the other, are quite different in the case of Gogol and of the West European critical realists of his day from those employed by Fielding in his "comic epic-poems" or Smollett in his satire. In the case of the latter writers comic situation is frequently seen as an end in itself, and also extends to characters regarded as entirely "positive", whom the author would have no desire to ridicule or compromise. In the critical realism of Gogol and his contemporaries in Western Europe all this moves into the background, and if it is preserved at all, it is not as an end in itself, but as a source for the portrayal of mores and characters.

Yet detail of all kinds and in every possible combination acquires an unprecedented importance. The first author to accord it such prominence as an important element in character portrayal was Sir Walter Scott.

Subsequent critics frequently noted the mass of inaccuracies committed by Scott in his description of architecture, interiors, clothing and tools, all of which play a vital part in his narrative. However, he did not himself lay claim to any pedantic faithfulness to the age, and blithely admitted inaccuracies here, as well as in the dialects of his characters. But what was important was that Scott established a correspondence between the setting and the people. This new principle of the unity of character and environment was eagerly seized upon and developed by the nineteenth century critical realists.

The image of the snail and its shell are found in almost identical form in the writings of Balzac and Gogol, when they discuss the way man manifests his relation to his habitat, and how, vice versa, the environment influences those it surrounds. With Balzac the action is, as a rule, preceded by a most detailed analysis not only of the interior of the houses in which his heroes live, but also of their exteriors, or of the quarter and even town in which the house is situated. Balzac frequently accompanies these descriptions with detailed excursi into the economics and technology of the production or trade he is concerned with. In order to understand the drama taking place in the Séchard family we have to know all about the improvements in printing technology that have been made before the beginning of the novel, and about the increased demand for cheap printed matter, occasioned by the growth of the reading public. The story of César Birotteau requires that the reader be initiated into the production, advertizing and marketing of perfumes. To say nothing of the world of journalism, of literature, or of the theatre! Balzac shows in the most elaborate detail the behind-the-scenes workings of this "production" of ideas, describes the minutiae of all the various newspapers, publishers, the secret passages, theatre stages and fleshpots where "public" opinion is created and where his heroes and heroines sell their souls.

With both Dickens and Thackeray such detailed economic and technological excurses are rare. Even in *Hard Times*, where we know that industrial Coketown maims people morally and physically, we do not know what exactly it produces, apart from profits for Mr. Bounderby. And this is not important to Dickens.

The author of *Dead Souls* carefully scrutinizes not only the way of life and mores of his country, but also its economic situation. Together with Chichikov, but from a different standpoint, he underlines the disturbing signs of decline and ruin of the land: the wretched huts of Plyushkin's peasants, the neglected farm and house of Khlobuyev are deeply eloquent. A note of satire can even be felt in the description of the town N, of its public buildings and the inn in which Chichikov puts up. Here the writer does not individualize, so much as generalize: "the room was of a familiar type, for the inn was also of a familiar type, namely the type of inns that are to be found in provincial towns..." (VI, 8). This already informs the reader about the lamentable sight in the Russian countryside of mud, vulgarity and misery, in an atmosphere of which the action begins. Subsequently, however, he describes the appearance of the dwellings, inside and outside, right down to such trivia as the clothing, behaviour and speech of their owners, as a means of revealing their characters.

In this sense Balzac, Dickens, Thackeray and Gogol, for all the differences between their artistic manners, follow one and the same course.

"I am only able to achieve this full embodiment in the flesh, this full circumscription of character, when I take into my mind the whole of this prosaic debris of life, when I contain in my head all the salient features of a character and at the same time assemble around it all that rubbish, right down to the smallest pin, which daily surrounds man—in other words, when I assemble everything, from the small to the large, and omit nothing" (VIII, 453), writes Gogol in his *Author's Confession*. In the foreword to the second edition of *Dead Souls*, in which he asks his readers to share with him their "experience and knowledge of life", he requests in particular that when recounting any incidents they "should not omit either the people and their mores, inclinations and customs, or the inanimate things which surround them, from their clothes to the furniture and walls of the houses in which they live" (VIII, 589).

Just as Manilov, Nozdryov, Sobakevich, Korobochka and Plyushkin are all inseparable from their "shells" and their characters are fully revealed only in the light of their surroundings, so does Dickens illustrate the spiritual coldness of the arrogant merchant Dombey by portraying his equally cold, severe, gloomy house. Thus too skinflint Scrooge cannot be understood until the reader has visited his unheated, dismal office and his neglected home, which is so ill-equipped for habitation that even the staircase somehow makes the visitor think how easily a funeral catafalque could ascend it and enter the rooms within.

Details of the interior also perform an ironic function in the works of these authors. Birotteau's naïve and costly idea of rebuilding and refurnishing his house is to be one of the main reasons for his financial ruin. Even the very pretentiousness of this garish, philistine luxury characterizes the vulgarity and limited vision of this confirmed bourgeois citizen.

Sometimes the irony is revealed through contrast: a detail of the surroundings somehow insinuates itself into the action, explaining or evaluating what is happening. We see this, for example, in the episode of the visit to Sobakevich, while Chichikov is bargaining with the master of the house for the "real price" of dead souls that "Bagration with his aquiline nose observed this purchase from the wall with the most rapt attention" (VI, 105). This detail brilliantly expresses the ironic contrast between the recent heroic past of Russia, instantly evoked by the mere mention of Bagration's name, and the shady deal being struck, as it were, beneath his very nose.

Dickens's famous illustrator "Phiz" (Hablot Browne) makes a slightly different use of this same device in one of his engravings to *Martin Chuzzlewit* in which he depicts the contretemps between Pecksniff and Martin junior. While Pecksniff lies sprawling on the ground, squinting in stunned and angry amazement at his opponent, the marble bust in the corner of the room surveys the scene with an ironic sneer.

We might also recall, as another example of ironic detail being used with a dramatic "transforming" effect, the description in *Vanity Fair* of the clock which stands in the rich despot Osborne's drawing room, adorned with bas-reliefs depicting the sacrifice of Iphigenia. This is, of course, more than a mere satirical brush stroke, designed to illustrate the tastelessness of the extravagant and ponderous furnishings of this gloomy residence, it is also an expressive hint of the real, and not mythological sacrifices which are destined to take place within these same walls. For it is here that the happiness of Osborne's elder daughter, Maria, will be broken, here too that he will sunder Amelia Sedley's engagement to his son George after the bankruptcy of her father, and finally here that he will disown his son when this disobedient youngster defies his father by marrying Amelia after all.

All the shifts of fortune suffered by the portrait of Amelia's elder brother Joseph Sedley, a conceited and dimwitted official of the East India Company, are described in ironic tones. This portrait, in which the clumsy and cowardly Joseph is depicted proudly mounted on an elephant in the middle of a tropical jungle, adorns his parents' drawing room, and after the bankruptcy of old Sedley is sold together with all their property at an auction. The auctioneer gives full rein to his eloquence in lauding the virtues of this work of art. However, the "masterpiece" is sold for a trifling sum, being bought, but of sheer mischief, by none other than Rebecca Sharp, now Mrs. Crawley, who has once tried to ensnare fat Joseph in her matrimonial nets beneath this very same portrait. Then, many years later, rejected by her husband and the world, at the very end of her luck, Rebecca makes skilful use of this portrait to revive her attack against the feeble defences of Joseph Sedley, and this time catches him hook, line and sinker.

In Thackeray's *The Newcomes* there is an abundance of satirically charged detail, which characterizes the transient happiness, so fraught with disaster, of old Colonel Newcome, a trusting soul, latterday Don Quixote, duped by crafty entrepreneurs into joining the managing board of the nonexistent Bundelkund colonial bank. He is presented with a silver vase in the form of a coconut palm, which stands on the colonel's dining-room table as an emblem of the business with its many branches. At its foot, symbolizing the flourishing of India under British rule, stand the figures of a rajah, holding out his hand to a British officer, a Brahmin, Britain herself and Commerce with the horn of plenty, a howitzer and a bale of cotton... This vulgar extravaganza jars in the reader's mind and at once awakens his mistrust in the commercial undertakings of the poor colonel, who is heading for inglorious bankruptcy and a poverty-stricken old age.

With Gogol, as with Balzac, Thackeray and Dickens, people are frequently likened to inanimate objects, a comparison which underlines their moral and spiritual aridity. In *Dead Souls* the faces of Sobakevich and his wife remind Chichikov of a Moldavian pumpkin and a long cucumber. Balzac describes an obtuse bourgeois family who come to the studio of an untalented artist to commission him to paint their portraits, and compares them to an entire procession of vegetables: the father is like a pumpkin, the mother like a coconut, the scrawny, anemic daughter like a stick of pale green asparagus ("Pierre Grassou"). In *Vanity Fair* Thackeray describes a sisterly kiss as cold as an oyster; fingers held out to shake someone's hand are like sausages.

Objects for these writers do not merely characterize people by indirect association. They even enslave these same people. Plyushkin is slave to his heap of rubbish, just as Gobseck is slave to his piles of rotting and mouldy goods and valuables. Thus do Chichikov and Rebecca Sharp cling on to their respective boxes as if to life itself. Korobochka cannot be imagined without her cheap "cotton bags" in which she saves her money. Old Grandet is so enslaved by his passion for gold that the last gesture of this human automaton on his very death bed is to try and seize hold of the gold cross held out to him by the priest.

Sometimes this fetishism is embodied in a symbolic, fantastic image. Thus, in Dickens's *A Christmas Carol in Prose* the ghost of Marley, which appears to his companion Scrooge, is entangled in a heavy chain consisting of safes, steel purses, ledgers, keys, locks, etc. In Thackeray's fable "The Rose and the Ring" an evil doorkeeper is himself turned for many years into a hideous door knocker.

Dickens is particularly generous with his expressive material detail. Referring apparently only to the outward situation, or to the costume and appearance of the characters, these details are in fact, as with Gogol, pregnant with psychological and social meaning. Like Gogol again, Dickens is able to discern what is most *characteristic* in the prosaic debris of life.

We are sometimes struck by the exact correspondence of Gogol's and Dickens's comic "genre" scenes. Thus, for example, we recall from *Dead Souls* the "shopkeeper with his brass samovar and face just as red as the samovar, so that from a distance one might have thought that there were two samovars in the window, had not one of them been adorned with a coal-black beard" (VI, 8). In *Martin Chuzzlewit* Dickens describes a hotel room in which "a graphic representation in oil of a remarkably fat ox hung over the fireplace, and the portrait of some former landlord (who might have been the ox's brother, he was so like him) stared roundly in, at the foot of the bed". [37]

There are other affinities between Gogol and Dickens, where the latter author employs a detail of the interior (in particular, a picture) to convey the inhumanity and soullessness of his characters. A good example is the scene from *Little Dorrit* in which three pillars of society—the banker Merdle, the official Tite Barnacle and the minister Lord Decimus, in the course of a profound conversation by the fire, are disrespectfully compared to the group of cows chewing the cud depicted in the picture by Cape which hangs over their heads. Characters are revealed in details of costume, in facial features and in settings, just as they are in Gogol's world.

Miss Jane Murdstone, sister of David Copperfield's cruel step-father, does not have time to utter a single word before

the author is able, through a brief description of her costume and appearance, to convey to us the cold which eman-
ates from this sombre, desiccated, and hypocritically strait-
laced "metallic lady".

A little further on David Copperfield, who narrates the
story himself, recalls the room set aside for Miss Murdstone, which was to become for him "a place of awe and
dread"; in it "numerous little steel fetters and rivets, with
which Miss Murdstone embellished herself when she was
dressed, generally hung upon the looking-glass in formidable array". [38] Thus we arrive at a most repellent image, all
the more expressive for its contrast with the warmth of the
young boy's perception, and we are alerted in advance to
the despotic cruelty of the Murdstones, to which David's
gentle and fragile mother is to fall victim and which is to
plague his own childhood.

Dickens employs a great variety of exterior detail, which
on occasion serves to provide a benign façade concealing
hypocrisy and baseness. The respected "patriarch" Casby,
proprietor of "Bleeding Heart Yard", enjoys universal es-
teem, although through the agencies of his manager Pancks
he extorts every last farthing out of his lodgers. The reputation of this elderly gentleman, as Dickens so ironically
shows, is inseparable from old-fashioned, wide-brimmed hat
and silvery hair. And when the enraged Pancks seizes hold
of a pair of scissors and dares to raise his hand against his
master and hack off his silver locks, and at the same time
the brim of his hat, a catastrophic metamorphosis takes
place before the very eyes of the Yard's inmates: instead
of their stately "patriarch" they behold a bald, bulbous-
eyed, big-headed scarecrow, which does not fill them with
the slightest respect, and which, it seems, has risen out of
the ground in order to ask what has become of the former
Casby! (*Little Dorrit*).

With Gogol a character's moral unmasking is also accompanied by the sudden loss of his decorous exterior: thus
there is good reason for the author's decision, in the final
chapter of *Dead Souls*, Volume 2, to have his hero arrested and brought before the governor-general in all the magnificence of his new tail-coat and smoke-grey trousers shot
with flame, a velvet waistcoat, blue silk cravat and coiffure
"wafting the sweet breath of the very best eau de Cologne"
(VII, 108). It is in this same splendour that he crawls
along the floor, grovelling at the great man's boots, and

then, in his cell, tears both his fashionable tail-coat from him, and his hair, about the arrangement of which he had previously so exerted himself.

The similarity of the entire artistic structure of Dickens's satirically portrayed characters and the characters of *Dead Souls* could be most effectively demonstrated by a comparison of Pecksniff and Chichikov. Both are masters of a type of business "which the world prefers to term not very honest" (VI, 242), both are so well-versed in the science of life that they can inspire others to trust in their good intentions.

"His very throat was moral," writes Dickens of Pecksniff. "You saw a good deal of it. You looked over a very low fence of white cravat (whereof no man had ever beheld the tie, for he fastened it behind), and there it lay, a valley between two jutting heights of collar, serene and whiskerless before you. It seemed to say, on the part of Mr. Pecksniff, 'There is no deception, ladies and gentlemen; all is peace; a holy calm pervades me.' So did his hair, just grizzled with an iron grey, which was all brushed off his forehead, and stood bolt upright, or slightly drooped in kindred action with his heavy eyelids... So did his manner, which was soft and oily. In a word, even his plain black suit, and state of widower, and dangling double eye-glass, all tended to the same purpose, and cried aloud, 'Behold the moral Pecksniff!'" [39]

Gogol depicts the decorous looks, manners and attire of Chichikov with the same ironic scrupulousness, feigning rapture over his neatness and other virtues. Like Pecksniff Chichikov knows how to win the approval of those around him. Just as Pecksniff impresses his beholders with his most moral appearance, so does Chichikov appear the very embodiment of benignity. Vasily Platonov is on the point of doubting his brother's travelling companion: "And eyeing Chichikov as narrowly as civility permitted he saw that his appearance was that of a perfectly respectable individual." Once again doubts arise in him, "full of uncertainty, he squinted sideways at Chichikov and saw a vision of the most remarkable decorum" (VII, 90-91). After this there can be no more room for doubt.

Both Pecksniff and Chichikov are able to strike the right key with their interlocutors. Pecksniff is regarded throughout the area as a most respected man; people look upon him with great admiration and seek his advice in difficult moments... Both Dickens and Gogol satirically indicate to the reader, between the lines, as it were, how little logic there is in the reputation of their heroes.

The two heroes are equally courteous and distinguished by their inexhaustible oratory. Chichikov was "somehow able in all things to find his feet and showed himself to be a man with great experience of the world. Whatever the subject of conversation he was able to contribute." (VI, 17). Amongst the ensuing list of subjects in which Chichikov showed himself to be a connoisseur, we should single out one for special mention: "and should they talk of virtue he would acquit himself most excellently, even with tears in his eyes" (VI, 17). This too is the hobby horse of his English confrère, Pecksniff, who holds forth on the subject of virtue with a passion that is all the more exalted the viler and more repulsive his own activities become.

The very structure of Pecksniff's and Chichikov's speech patterns has much in common. They both have a proclivity for bombast and complex metaphors which do not always cohabit happily. Talking of themselves they lapse into abject self-abasement. Chichikov talks of himself "with a marked modesty, and his discourse at such times would take on certain bookish phrases: that he was but a wretched worm of this world, and was deserving of no consideration from the part of his fellows" (VI, 13). Thus Pecksniff, too, is prepared to describe himself as a worm.

Pecksniff's unctuous rhetoric, with its inimitable manner of mixing metaphors and soaring upwards on flights of figurative language, from which the speaker is afterwards hard put to descend, in fact conceals a parody of the rhetorical bombast of the political and church "orators" of Victorian England. "Mr. Pecksniff," writes Dickens, "was in the frequent habit of using any word that occurred to him as having a good sound, and rounding a sentence well, without much care for its meaning. And he did this so boldly, and in such an imposing manner, that he would sometimes stagger the wisest people with his eloquence, and make them gasp again." [40]

As for Chichikov, Gogol does not even stop short of submitting his most sacred themes to this scoundrel's vulgar and complacent rhetoric. Gogol's courage and remarkable depth of observation is manifested in the way he allows his petty-minded hero to pave the way to his shady deals with deliberations on these exalted matters, on which the author himself only ventures to speak when borne aloft on a flight of true inspiration. Let us listen for a moment to Gogol's account of how Chichikov broaches his deal with Sobakevich: "Chichikov started off from a great distance, touching on the subject of the great Russian state in general and expressing the most lavish praise of its expanses, remarking that not even the most ancient monarchy of Rome had been so great, and that foreign visitors are justly amazed..." (VI, 100). Do we not hear parodistic echoes of the author's own impassioned digressions, in which Gogol himself—but in quite a different, prophetic key—recalls "the vastness of spaces" (VI, 221) of Russia, and observes how "other nations and states step aside to make way for her" (VI, 247)?

Thus too does Dickens show to what nadir of vulgarity his most cherished ideals of brotherly love and justice could be abased in the hypocritical raptures of Pecksniff.

But, in contrast to Chichikov whose character takes shape in Volume 1, chapter 11, Pecksniff is presented to the reader in *Martin Chuzzlewit* as already completely formed and unchangeable character. We know nothing about his childhood and youth—but we are fully able to account for his destructive influence on the people around him. Pecksniff's daughters, to whom with characteristic hypocrisy he gave the symbolic names Charity and Mercy, are just as far removed as their father from these Christian virtues, and are able, no worse than him, to adopt special roles for the sake of vulgar selfish goals. The younger, Mercy, the victim of an unhappy marriage, becomes softer in heart under the influence of the cruel blows of fate. Charity, like her father, remains unrepentant even when her schemes end in total failure.

Chichikov's "pre-history" is to some extent comparable with that of another Dickens's hero, the careerist and swindler Uriah Heep. Since an early age Heep has employed as a protective mask a skilfully feigned humility. "I'm much too umble," he whines, repeating it at every possible opportunity. Behind this humility (which has been so assiduously inculcated into Heep, and before him into his parents, by their masters and teachers in various refuges, Sunday schools and charitable establishments) is concealed a predatory malice, a greedy desire to snatch his own share of the spoils. Like Pecksniff he is a rogue unrepentant and incorrigible; he remains a hypocrite and succeeds in his own aims, earning through his unctuous speeches the favour of his superiors, even in prison.

For all the obvious similarity between these Dickensian figures, both Pecksniff and Heep are still different from Chichikov, and not only in the scale of their shady enterprise, but also in terms of their social significance. Chichikov, the "businessman and acquirer", as Gogol ironically dubs him, is a disturbing symbol of the times for his own creator. At the same time Chichikov, such as Gogol wishes to show him, with all his vulgar interests and narrow-mindedness, is far from being a nonentity; he is a man of rare patience, of iron determination, indefatigable and skilled in the pursuit of his goals... Even in Volume 1 Gogol hints at the secret significance of this character, who is to be more fully revealed in the parts that follow; while in Volume 2 Murazov bitterly reproaches Chichikov for being guilty "before the rich powers and gifts, which have been bestowed upon him" (VII, 112). In the surviving notebooks for Volume 2 the author, by way of farewell, shows the reader his hero in a state of spiritual ferment and bewilderment: "This was but a ruin of the old Chichikov. The inner state of his soul could have been compared to a dismantled building, which has been pulled down with the aim of erecting a new one in its place; but the new building has not yet begun, because the final plan has not yet been received from the architect and the workers were puzzled" (VII, 124). To some extent this image also shows the indecision of the author himself, who had experienced a profound creative crisis. But this volte-face by Chichikov had been partially prepared, "programmed" for the author by the character of his hero, as outlined earlier. It was impossible for him to dispense so easily with Pavel Ivanovich—a typical significant phenomenon in Russia at the time—as Dickens was able to with Pecksniff or Heep. With Dickens these final "tribunals" are reminiscent, with their air of comedy, of the religious pantomimes so popular in England at that time, or the Punch and Judy show, in which Punch generously dispenses and receives all manner of physical punishment.

Chichikov is also destined to get his punishment. But when he grovels at the feet of the governor-general, pushed aside by the latter's princely boot, Chichikov is more pathetic and sickening than comic; Gogol even calls him "poor", "unhappy" (VII, 109, 111), although he is still far from convinced, as becomes apparent from Volume 2, of the staunchness of his hero's repentance.

The characters from Dickens's later work stand up best to comparison with those of *Dead Souls*. It would be very difficult to sustain any thoroughgoing comparison between *Pickwick Papers* and *Dead Souls* (in particular, of Jingle and Chichikov): the tonality of the two works is so different, as are the objectives of their authors. The "villains" of Dickens's subsequent novels—Monks, Fagin, Ralph Nickleby, Quilp—are all too *exceptional* in their moral and physical deformity; they are possessed by hate and malice as by a mania, and although Dickens does at times attempt to motivate their destructive passions by egoistic interest, these feebly defined "rational motives" are markedly out of proportion with the frenzied behaviour they are called upon to explain.

Certain acquisitive and selfish characters from Dickens's later novels have closer affinities with the characters of *Dead Souls,* those, for example, in *Martin Chuzzlewit, Dombey and Son, David Copperfield, Little Dorrit, Great Expectations,* and *Our Mutual Friend.*

At times, Dickens, in contrast to Gogol, has recourse to "false moves", in order by a subsequent unexpected twist of the plot to lighten a too sombre impression of the fateful power of money that would otherwise remain with the reader. Thus, the initial exposition of *Martin Chuzzlewit* is based on the fact that all the members of the many-branched Chuzzlewit family (to whom Pecksniff is also related) are all extreme egoists. The novel thus begins as a sort of analysis of this lethal passion, which holds the entire Chuzzlewit clan in its grasp. The reader is thus prepared for the most terrible revelations. He sees suspicions gathering over Jonas Chuzzlewit that he is his father's murderer; while the dead man's brother, the decrepit Martin Chuzzlewit, blinded by his selfish, naturally suspicious nature, disowns his grandson and allows himself to be manipulated by the revolting Pecksniff. But the fog of suspicion lifts and the reader learns that while Jonas has considered poisoning his father, the old man died a natural death, having guessed his son's intentions in time. As for Martin Chuzzlewit senior, the author prepares a most remarkable metamorphosis for him at the end of the novel: it turns out that this hero, having reformed his own views long before, was only acting out a particular role he had adopted in order to reveal all of Pecksniff's roguery and to teach him a lesson. The former egoist casts off, together with his feigned frailty, all his former prejudices and throws open his arms wide in an embrace of all the novel's worthy heroes and heroines, as their generous and good-hearted patron.

Dickens employs a similar "false move" in *Our Mutual Friend*, in which the reader is led, during the course of several chapters, to share the belief of the novel's young heroine Bella Wilfer that the Golden Dustman Boffin has fallen prey to the perverting influence of money; his natural goodness and ingenuousness appear to have been crushed by his maniacal avarice, greed and contempt for all the toiling poor. But this too proves to be no more than a cunning trap set to cure Bella from her vanity and test the depth of feelings for Boffin's secretary Rokesmith, who has fallen in love with her. (Rokesmith in his turn also plays a role, that of a poor man, when in fact he is the heir of the Harmon fortune).

There are not and cannot be any such "false moves" in Gogol's work. Aspiring in *Dead Souls* to achieve a feat of artistic endeavour, he could not play tricks on his readers, although this might have facilitated their entertainment. If he does talk of "mystery" which is yet to be revealed in the course of the narrative, we may almost invariably assume that it is not the contrived mystery of an intricate pot-boiler but the mystery of life itself, divined but not yet revealed by the artist's thought and imagination.

But Dickens the realist did not of course limit himself to such a simplified, conventional treatment of the "spiritual death and resurrection" of the human soul in the property world, as in the case of Martin Chuzzlewit senior or Boffin.

Amongst his characters we may think of many who are entirely comparable with the "strange heroes" of *Dead Souls* (as Gogol himself calls them), insofar as their real human souls have been numbed or choked by an "earthy crust". Paul Dombey senior, Mrs. Clennam in *Little Dorrit*, Miss Havisham in *Great Expectations*, these are all figures in whose portrayal Dickens's grotesque borders on tragedy.

Podsnap and the phenomenon of Podsnappery are described in a rather different, consistently comic and satirical key. Podsnap does not play an active role in the development of the plot of *Our Mutual Friend*. But he is essential to Dickens as an important part of that social "background", against which the action unfolds: a background which sets the sphere of genuinely human responses, feelings and relations, inhabited by the author's best-loved heroes. Podsnaps and their Podsnappery stand as a sort of symbol of Victorian England, preserved in the brine of property (to borrow Galsworthy's expressive metaphor). Dickens intentionally passes over all the personal idiosyncrasies, which might help mollify Podsnap's image. In his portrayal he identifies what he regards as Podsnap's primary and intransient trait: an automatism of habit and thought, which is based on purely "businesslike" principles, for Podsnap is a businessman from the City and remains such in all aspects of his existence.

"Mr. Podsnap's world," writes Dickens, "was not a very large world, morally; no, nor even geographically: seeing that although his business was sustained upon commerce with other countries, he considered other countries, with that important reservation, a mistake, and of their manners and customs would conclusively observe, 'Not English!' when, PRESTO! with a flourish of the arm, and a flush of the face, they were swept away. Elsewise, the world got up at eight, shaved close at a quarter-past, breakfasted at nine, went to the City at ten, came home at half-past five, and dined at seven". [41] Seen as a private person Podsnap can only be comic; but the Podsnaps claim to represent public opinion, just as the Barnacles (in *Little Dorrit*) claim to control the British ship of state to which they have too firmly attached themselves. It is for this reason that their collective satirical image is pervaded by such biting sarcasm on the part of the author.

Dombey senior, Mrs. Clennam, and Miss Havisham have affinities with Gogol's characters (particularly Plyushkin) in terms of the terrible power which their all-consuming egoistic passions have come to exercise over them. As with Gogol's characters, their domestic surroundings reflect and intensify the maniacal state of their souls. In Dombey's opulent house everything is pervaded by a deathly cold, and displays the same abhorrent pedantry as the owner's manners and his very clothes, whose most salient feature is the stiffly starched cravat squeezed round Mr. Dombey's neck. The ill-starred past and joyless present of Mrs. Clennam's life can be ascertained not only from the few allusions scattered about the novel *Little Dorrit,* but from the very appearance of the "shell" in which this "snail" lives.

The sombre widow's weeds, an invalid chair to which this woman is confined, still tormented by jealousy, a longing for revenge and hatred for people no longer living—these add to our vision of a life pressed for ever into the tight, almost prison-like confines of a severe Calvinist piety, which does however admit some worldly blandishments. Hardened by her ascetic sanctimony Mrs. Clennam, who has three lives on her conscience, does not however forget at certain strictly ordained hours to partake of her oysters and white wine or roast venison. Miss Havisham, consumed by the vanity of grief, which has possessed her like a mania, shuts herself away in a little world of fantasy, utterly divorced from reality. The clocks in her house are stopped at the minute when she received the fateful letter from her fiancé cancelling their wedding. As a grey-haired, feeble old woman she remains attired in her decaying wedding dress, while on the table, opened out as for a banquet, stand the by now unrecognizable wedding delicacies, long since the haunt of cockroaches and spiders.

For all these "dead souls" in Dickens's works there is a moment of awakening: but it is connected with the total and tragic collapse of the egoistic fantasy "myth" which they have created around their entire lives. This destruction of their imaginary moral bastions (Dombey's pride, the imagined "virtue" of Mrs. Clennam, the egoism of Miss Havisham, who has destroyed the life of her ward Estelle by feeding her since early childhood the poison of cruelty and egoism) is symbolically accompanied by the collapse of the entire outer fabric of their lives. The firm Dombey and Son is ruined, Dombey's house is dishonoured, his property sold by auction. Mrs. Clennam's decrepit house, whose decaying rafters and walls have long been creaking and cracking ominously, at last crumbles to the ground. An inextinguishable flame finally consumes Miss Havisham's rotten wedding dress and the fire scares the vermin away from the remains of the wedding feast-that-never-was.

Moral enlightenment is only achieved in pain and at a great cost, and the past is irretrievable. Admittedly, old Dombey can still look forward to the caresses of his grandchildren, but Mrs. Clennam lives out the last years of her life speechless and paralyzed, and Miss Havisham dies, succumbing to her qualms of conscience.

The moral issues with which Dickens is concerned in his portrayal of the development of these characters have much in common with those tackled by Gogol. But the Russian author was alien to those exceptional, Romantic circumstances which bring about the spiritual "catastrophes" suffered by Dickens's heroes, and he set himself the task of finding the means of restoring the man within man in the most commonplace conditions of everyday life.

NOTES

[1] K. Marx, F. Engels, "The Holy Family", *Collected Works*, Vol. 4, Progress Publishers, Moscow, 1975, pp. 130-131.

[2] J.W.v. Goethe, *Faust*, Leipzig, 1958, pp. 137-138.

[3] V. V. Rozanov, *Legenda o Velikom Inkvizitore F. M. Dostoyevskogo. Opyt kriticheskogo kommentariya s prisoedineniem dvukh etyudov o Gogole* ("Dostoyevsky's Legend of the Grand Inquisitor". Attempt at a critical commentary with an appendix of two studies on Gogol), 2nd edition, St. Petersburg, 1902, pp. 10-11.

[4] Ibid., p. 12.

[5] Ibid., p. 133.

[6] Victor Erlich, *Gogol*, New-Haven-London, 1969, p. 133.

[7] Ibid., p. 177.

[8] Ibid., p. 221.

[9] Ibid., p. 158.

[10] Ibid., p. 222.

[11] Vladimir Nabokov, *Nikolai Gogol*, New Direction Books, Norfolk, Connecticut, 1941, p. 160.

[12] Ibid., p. 133.

[13] Ibid., p. 133.

[14] Ibid., p. 138.

[15] Y. V. Mann, *O groteske v literature* (The Grotesque in Literature), Moscow, 1966, p. 49.

[16] H. Fielding, *The Adventures of Joseph Andrews and His Friend Mr. Abraham Adams,* London, 1931, p. 199.

[17] Ibid., p. 200.

[18] T. Smollett, *The Adventures of Roderick Random,* London, 1890, p. 61.

[19] Walter Scott, *The Miscellaneous Prose Works,* Vol. III, Paris, 1837, p. 94.

[20] *Athenaeum,* 1854, December 2, No. 1414.

[21] Tobias Smollet, *The Expedition of Humphry Clinker,* London, 1943, p. 162.

[22] E. A. Smirnova, "Gogol i ideya 'yestestvennogo' cheloveka v literature XVIII v." (Gogol and the idea of "natural" man in 18th century literature). In: *Russkaya Literatura XVIII veka. Epokha klassitsizma* (18th Century Russian Literature. The Age of Classicism), Moscow-Leningrad, 1964, p. 292.

[23] Charles de Coster, *La Légende d'Ulenspiegel,* Zurich, 1962, p. 457.

[24] F. M. Dostoyevsky, *Collected Works,* Vol. XIII, Leningrad-Moscow, 1930, p. 526 (in Russian).

[25] Victor Hugo, *Les Misérables,* tome premier, Paris, p. 163.

[26] I. M. Katarsky, *Dickens v Rossii* (Dickens in Russia), Moscow, 1966, p. 157.

[27] Honoré de Balzac, *Œuvres complètes,* Scènes de la vie parisienne, Paris, 1895, p. 195-196.

[28] Ibid., p. 228-229.

[29] Honoré de Balzac, *Œuvres complètes,* t. 8, Paris, 1958, p. 569.

[30] Op. cit., t. 11, Paris, 1959, p. 207.

[31] Op. cit., t. 8, p. 99.

[32] Ibid., p. 50.

[33] Op. cit., t. 5, p. 342.

[34] W. M. Thackeray, *Vanity Fair.* A Novel Without a Hero, London, 1963, p. 34.

[35] Ibid., p. 506.

[36] D. S. Yakhontova, *Novatorstvo tvorcheskogo metoda Tekkereya v romane "Yarmarka Tshcheslaviya"* (Innovations in Thackeray's Method in "Vanity Fair"), Lvov, 1965, pp. 134-136.

[37] Charles Dickens, *Martin Chuzzlewit,* London and Glasgow, 1966, p. 503.

[38] Charles Dickens, *The Personal History and Experience of David Copperfield the Younger,* 1952, London, p. 43.

[39] Charles Dickens, *Martin Chuzzlewit,* p. 30.

[40] Ibid., p. 32.

[41] Charles Dickens, *Our Mutual Friend,* London, 1906, p. 110.

CHAPTER THREE

DEAD SOULS AND THE UTOPIAN NOVEL

1

"While a writer is young he writes much and fast. He is constantly spurred on by his imagination. He creates, he constructs delightful castles in the air, and it is just as well known that his writing, like such castles, knows no bounds. But when the truth has become his exclusive object and he endeavours *translucently to reflect life in its supreme glory, such as it must and can be on earth* and such as it is, for the moment, only lived by a chosen, outstanding few, now the writer will be somewhat stirred by his imagination; *for he must fight for every feature*" (XIV, 216; my italics.—*A.Y.*). Thus Gogol from Odessa wrote to Zhukovsky on the 16th December 1850, when he felt he "was nearing completion" (XIV, 215) of his third—and last—version of *Dead Souls*, Volume 2.

This is a most noteworthy statement. It expresses with unmistakable clarity the *utopian* task Gogol set himself in *Dead Souls*, as well as the task of portraying life as it really is. At the same time we are made aware of the difficulties which confronted the writer who attempted to build his utopia not in accordance with the whim of his imagination, but on the secure foundations of real life.

The problem we have isolated in the heading of this chapter has not altogether escaped the notice of Soviet scholars working on Gogol, but neither has it been exhaustively studied. On the whole it has been accorded scant attention.

The fullest analysis of the utopian element in Gogol's work was made by G. A. Gukovsky in his monograph on Gogol. [1] But Gukovsky ignores the question of the transformation, or "resurrection", of the heroes of *Dead Souls*, with which Gogol was so concerned, and concentrates instead on an extreme contrast of the two volumes of the book, * thus eliminating the possibility of considering the development of the utopian theme, so vital to Gogol's design.

In his article "On Gogol", N. L. Stepanov includes a summary of the documentary evidence of the continuation of *Dead Souls*, which has only survived in fragments, furthermore belonging to different editions. After studying all this evidence the author concludes that "the question of the continuation of *Dead Souls* has not yet been adequately studied, nor finally resolved". [2]

E. A. Smirnova-Chikina is bolder in her hypotheses. In her article "*Dead Souls*, Volume 2", which is based on a thorough analysis of the surviving fragments of Gogol's letters and the memoirs of his contemporaries, she makes a fascinating attempt to reconstruct the final edition of this work. In Smirnova-Chikina's opinion, this edition was fundamentally different in its philosophical and artistic merits from the chapters of the 1844-1845 edition which have fortuitously survived. In particular, she argues that Kostanzhoglo did not figure in the final edition as a positive character ("The last time Gogol read the chapters about Kostanzhoglo to A. O. Smirnova was in 1849, and in the winter he revised them ... in 1850-1851 his listeners heard nothing about Kostanzhoglo" [3]). But Tentetnikov, it seems, was now portrayed in a different, more positive light. "It is difficult to ascertain the direction taken by Tentetnikov's views," writes Smirnova-Chikina, with reference to the lost final edition of Volume 2. "He is friendly with a character who reflects the noble image of Belinsky, and on his arrest, as he leaves his village and takes his leave of the peasants, he makes a farewell speech to them, which, according to an account by Shevyryov, was in itself a remarkable work of art. To judge from this reaction, the content of his speech was acceptable for a guardian of the bastions of serf-

---

* "Volume 1 of *Dead Souls* is a *poema*. Volume 2 is, it would seem, a not entirely successful novel." *Realizm Gogolya*, p. 476.

dom; but then why did Shevyryov write nothing about either this remarkable 'speech' or Volume 2 of *Dead Souls* in general?.. It is possible," concludes the author of the article, "that in his last years Gogol found some solution of his own to the question of Tentetnikov's social views, one of the social utopias of that time". [4] She also suggests that Belinsky's indignant letter about *Selected Passages* might have provided Gogol with a way out of the creative impasse in which he had been caught since the late 1840s. "An analysis of the content of Volume 2, which we know from the memoirs of D. A. Obolensky, L. I. Arnoldi, A. O. Smirnova, N. V. Berg and others, as well as allusions in Gogol's own letters, lead us to suppose that in Volume 2 Gogol returned to the ideas and moods of Volume 1," concludes Smirnova-Chikina in a later article on the same theme. [5]

Unfortunately these hypotheses remain pure speculation. When considering what direction was taken by Gogol in his passionate and agonized quest for Russia's future, we can only proceed from the facts, namely, the surviving fragments of the early edition of Volume 2, the fragments of other versions, letters and Gogol's *Author's Confession*, as well in part on the memoirs of his contemporaries, who heard the author himself read the chapters of this later edition. Thus we can only make very tentative hypotheses as to the embodiment in Volume 2 of Gogol's utopian design, which he had already proclaimed in Volume 1.

Nevertheless, hypotheses are still worth making. To quote the Soviet poet Pavel Antokolsky's expressive image, "shifts and cracks"—cracks in the very consciousness of man— "also await the reader in *Dead Souls,* Volume 2. Here they are particularly noticeable—for the very reason that the work remained incomplete and exists in the eyes of successive generations of Russian readers as a mysterious ruin, inhabited, like some Romantic creation, by ghosts. Sometimes this ruin is deaf and dumb, but for the most part it is passionately eloquent—even in its incoherence, even in its silences". [6]

In order to understand the direction of Gogol's utopian thought in *Dead Souls* we must first look back at the road he had already travelled, at what he himself felt he had already exhausted, overcome, and at what he still wished to preserve and maintain—not only in his work, but also in life itself.

197

The era of *Village Evenings Near Dikanka,* in which life is presented in the naïve images of folklore, and when poetic fantasy was able, as the author willed, to restore the harmony destroyed by the interference of evil forces, belonged, by the time Gogol wrote *Dead Souls*, to the irretrievable past.

It is indicative that when working on *Dead Souls*, Volume 1 Gogol was re-reading Hoffmann,* and at the same time poking fun at his Romantic extravaganzas. In the autumn of 1838 he chided jokingly his young correspondent M. P. Balabina for her passion for Germany, moreover, as we can see from the context, he had in mind precisely a Hoffmannesque, Romantic Germany. "Of course, I do not argue that there is the occasional moment when one would like to soar out of the midst of the tobacco smoke and the German kitchen and fly to the moon, seated on the magical cloak of a German student, as I think you put it. But I doubt if Germany is still such as we imagine it. Is it not only like that in the tales of Hoffmann?" (XI, 180).

But this humorous polemic with the Romanticism of Hoffmann is followed by the remarkable admission: "I know there is such a world, where everything is marvellous and not like here; but not everyone knows the road to this world... But I feel, I know, that it is powerful and genuine truth. It is difficult, most difficult to take the middle way, to expel imagination and one's splendid favourite dreams when these are so alive in our minds; it is difficult suddenly to turn altogether to the prose of reality; but *it is most difficult of all to harmonize these two heterogeneous objects—to live at the same time in both one and the other world*" (XI, 180-181; my italics.—*A.Y.*).

May we not suppose that this was precisely the most difficult task that Gogol had set himself in the creation of *Dead Souls*?

Gogol was unable to resort to Romanticism of Hoffmann, the procedure whereby, after returning to earth from its tragic flights of fancy, the author harmonizes its poetic vision with the "prose of reality". The utopian outcome of such works as *Der Goldene Topf* or *Klein Zaches*, which is

---

* Falling ill in the summer of 1838 in Castellamare, Gogol requested V. N. Repnina to lend him "some volume or other of Hoffmann", explaining: "It seems that at present tales of fantasy are just what I need" (XIV, 289).

ironic by simple virtue of its fanciful nature, does not, however, change anything in the prosaic misery of the vulgar reality in which the works are set. The radiant colours of this utopia have clearly only been created by the artist's imagination. Thus, the narrator of the *Goldener Topf* is able to take consolation in the knowledge that he too possesses—in his dreams!—a glorious country mansion in the magical Atlantis of the archivarius Lindhorst. While Balthazar and his betrothed come into possession, after the inglorious death of the monstrous Zaches, of an estate, bequeathed to them by the magician Alpanus, an estate where the finest cabbages grow, where the crockery never breaks and the sun always shines on washing day.... This philistine idyll, to which Hoffmann adds a fair dose of ironic venom, could not have satisfied Gogol. Even in his Petersburg tales he does not close his eyes to the inevitable and tragic incongruity between the subjective Romantic dream and harsh reality. While the reality of Russia itself was portrayed as a veritable kingdom of base vulgarity, of false values, universal disharmony, the eroding of personalities and the alienation of man from society and himself.

In order to preserve the right "to live at the same time in both one and the other world", not to despair in the face of universal egoism and vanity, Gogol was forced to seek a more reliable foundation for his utopian vision than the whim of poetic fancy.

The uncontrolled flight of his artistic imagination, which ventured in its fancy and dreams to oppose a magical utopia to the real world, eventually spells ruin to the unhappy Piskaryov, hero of *Nevsky Prospekt*. As for the joys of plain comfort and family love, are not these what Gogol portrays in his *Old-World Landowners*—but in quite a different, anti-Hoffmannesque light—not as the radiant ideal of true humanity, but as a sad, and in its own way also vulgar tale of everyday life?

Gogol sought a different basis for the dream which had already inspired him in the creation of *Dead Souls*, Volume 1. He looked to the national character and the historical destiny of the people; in the past and present of his country, in its nature and in the vastness of its spaces he discerned the hidden potential of the future and the forces which would enable this potential to find embodiment in life. The utopian element which is present in the very idea behind the creation of *Dead Souls*, should, in the author's opinion, be born not only from "a fearful tempest of fresh inspiration", in "a majestic chorus of other voices" (VI, 135), but also *from study*, from a precise and profound analysis of the properties of the Russian man and Russian nature. Balzac described himself as a historian and "secretary" of French society. Gogol also talks of the "mystic bond" that exists between his *poema* and Russian life but in different, impassioned images, such as are not encountered in this context in the works of any West European realist of that time. He regards the task facing him in *Dead Souls* as an exalted civic mission, as a great feat, which he pursues in subjection to his country. Let us recall again the remarkable lyrical digression from Volume 1, chapter 11, in which the description of Chichikov's ignominious departure from the town is suddenly interrupted by the author's impassioned appeal from the "beautiful afar" to his country: "Russia! What is your demand on me? What is that mystic bond that exists between us? Why do you look at me like that, and why everything there is in you turn eyes full of expectation on me?.. And I stand motionless, in utter perplexity, with a storm cloud, heavy with rain, gathering above my head, and my mind is benumbed by the vastness of your spaces... What is the promise held out by the immensity of your expanses? Is it not the place for a legendary giant, here where there is the room for him to launch out and stride about?.. Fearful forces encompass me to find reflection in all my inner being and light up my eyes with a supernatural power. O Russia! What breath-taking marvellous unexplored vistas you unfold to the view!" (XI, 221).

The theme of the infinite expanses of Russia, calling out for action, for the application of a similarly infinite effort of concerted labour, and the theme of heroism, as exemplified by the Russian legendary hero *bogatyr* *, with which it is connected, run throughout both parts of *Dead Souls*. Russian nature itself, so often represented in its depressing monotony, where everything is "poor, scattered about and uncomfortable" (VI, 220), at times seems to acquire a voice of its own and stands before the people as a living reproach.

We find such an emotionally charged description of the landscape in the passage where the reader is shown the

---

* *Bogatyr*—a figure from Russian legend, who combines historical and mythical properties, often of fabulous strength and stature and embodying such virtues as bravery, nobility.—*Tr.*

luscious greenery of Plyushkin's garden and the wretched village, decaying estate and pointlessly hoarded, rotting mounds of stores. Another is that of the loafer Tentetnikov's holdings, the forests, meadows and slopes from which immense expanses open out to the onlooker's entranced gaze. Or the picture of the Volga expanses, where the boatmen are whooping it up before returning to their "toil and sweat, hauling the tow-rope to the accompaniment of their one song, as endless as Russia herself" (VI, 139).

But there is no harmony between the "heroes" of his *poema*, and this "vastness of spaces". It is not only the census souls, purchased by Chichikov, that are dead. The book's "heroes" are also dead, dead within, and only seemingly alive—Chichikov, his new landowner friends and the "jug-snouts" from the municipal offices, and even Petrushka and Selifan.

Gogol sticks fast to this point of departure of his narrative. He sarcastically rejects the role of the "happy" writer, who walks past all "tedious and repugnant characters, who appal us with their sad lives", the writer who "from the great maelstrom of images that revolve about him daily selects only the rare exceptions, who has never once changed the exalted tone of his lyre, has never descended from his heights to his poor, insignificant fellow creatures, and who has lost himself body and soul, without ever touching the ground, in exalted images far removed from it" (VI, 133). Gogol is anxious to remain faithful to this "sad reality", he does not want to spare his readers. Romanticism with its unrestrained hyperbole, idealization, sharp and conventional contrasts between light and dark, good and evil, so vividly manifested in the works of such West European writers as Victor Hugo, Dumas, Sue and others, was decisively rejected by Gogol in *Dead Souls*.

Yet at this time he was able to accord great significance to the heroic element of *Taras Bulba*, in which earth and people cohabit in a remarkable poetic life and the mighty sensation of comradeship forms the stimulus for great feats of heroism and self-sacrifice. "And no bonds are more holier than those of comradeship!" (II, 133) exclaims Taras Bulba in his address to his army. Comradeship contains a guarantee of possible spiritual resurrection even for those who would appear to have fallen hopelessly and lost their dignity: "But even the most miserable scoundrel, however loathsome, however sullied by grovelling in the muck—even he, kinsmen, hath a grain of Russian feeling. And that feeling will awaken one day, and the wretched wight will beat with his fists on the floor, and will tear his hair and curse his vile life, ready to atone for his shame with suffering. Let them all know what comradeship means in Russia!" [7]

It would seem that Gogol wishes to bring his own contemporaries, the dramatis personae of *Dead Souls*, to just such an awakening. To judge from his last letters and other documents, his intentions went even further than this: he wished to resurrect to a new life not only Chichikov, Tentetnikov and Plyushkin, but to reawaken the whole of Russia...

But what is artistically—and, indeed, historically—justified in the heroic, Romantic context of *Taras Bulba*, was too incongruous with the "sad reality" of pre-reform Russia, this "country of slaves, country of masters", as Lermontov describes it. The realism of Gogol the satirist opposes Gogol the utopian dreamer, preventing him from violating the logical development of the heroes he has taken from real life and who have acquired their own existence. In Volume 1 Gogol only makes occasional passing reference to the fact that Chichikov is also a "Russian person", and even entrusts Chichikov, against all the laws of psychological probability, with his own profound reflections. In his ecstatic review of Volume 1 of *Dead Souls* Belinsky does, however, note these "slips against the spontaneity of his creation, and most important slips, although they are few in number". Thus, in Belinsky's opinion, "the poet quite unjustifiably makes Chichikov give rein to his fancy and reflect on the life of the simple people while studying the register of dead souls he has bought. It is true that this 'flight of imagination' is one of the best passages in the book: it has a profundity of thought and power of feeling, an infinite poetry and at the same time a remarkable vraisemblance; nevertheless it comes from Chichikov, a man of genius as a rogue and acquirer, but utterly empty and nondescript in every other respect. Here the poet has clearly given his own noblest and purest tears, unseen and unknown by the world, to his hero, as well as his deep humour, filled with a sad love, and he has made him express thoughts which should have come from himself. Similarly inappropriate to Chichikov are his reflections on Sobakevich ... these reflections are too intelligent, noble and humane; the author should have uttered them in his own voice". [8]

But were these really unintentional errors on Gogol's part? There is another view, well substantiated, that in Volume 1 the author is as it were preparing the reader for the eventual transformation of his hero, and hinting at his soul's revival and resurrection.

The theme of the folk hero, *bogatyr*, remains fairly abstract in *Dead Souls*, Volume 1, although it is persistent, and appears to have some portentous significance. Initially it arises in a satirical form, in connection with Sobakevich's gigantic boot, "for which it would be well nigh impossible to find a suitable foot, particularly in the present time, when people of *bogatyr* stature are beginning to disappear even in Russia" (VI, 17). Later on, near the end, it appears as lyrical prophecy, although in the guise of a question "Is this not the place for legendary giant, here where there is room for him to launch out and stride about?" (VI, 221).

However, in Volume 2, in the notebooks for the final chapter, Gogol attempts—albeit indirectly, in the subjunctive mood—to indicate that Chichikov might be just one such hero. The reader is appalled and sickened when he recalls the gripping, poetic passages in Volume 1 which describe the heroic qualities of the Russian people. Here, in Volume 2, these words are uttered by one of Gogol's most improbable "positive" heroes—Afanasy Vasilievich Murazov, a millionaire government contractor who began his career with a single kopeck and has amassed his fortune in the "most irreproachable way" (VII, 75). It seems that Murazov was intended by Gogol to play the role of one of the beneficiaries of mankind in his utopia, who endeavour both through precept and through active involvement in people's lives to correct their ways and save their fellow-men, leading them back to the true path. It is thus that he deals with Khlobuyev; thus too does he wish to reform Chichikov. When, like Gogol himself, he analyses Chichikov's character, he tries to identify those passions, those properties which, if directed towards an honest purpose, might wreak miracles: "Heavens, Pavel Ivanovich, you have a strength which others lack, an iron patience—and yet you cannot master it? For you, I do believe, would be a true *bogatyr*" (VII, 114).

As he comes across these and similar passages in Volume 2 the reader is loath to accept that Belinsky's fears were justified, when he noted with concern the promise solemnly given by Gogol himself in *Dead Souls*. "Perhaps hidden in this very story there are other, hitherto unplucked strings, an immense richness of the Russian soul will be revealed, a man possessed of divine valour, or an enchanting Russian maiden, such as you will not find anywhere in the world, with all the wondrous beauty of the female soul, the very embodiment of magnanimous striving and self-sacrifice. And virtuous people of other races will seem as dead men before them, as a book is dead before the living word. Russian feelings will rise up ... and all will see how deeply implanted in the Slav soul are those qualities which only touched the surface of other peoples' nature..." (VI, 223). There is no mistaking the sincerity of these words by Gogol.

After quoting practically the whole of this programmatic author's digression and placing certain passages in italics, Belinsky admits: "Yes, these words by the creator of *Dead Souls* have caused us time and time again to repeat in our anxiety: 'Who knows, indeed, how the content of *Dead Souls* will unfold?' Truly, *who knows?*.. Much, far too much has been promised ... because there is as yet none of all this in this world; it somehow alarms us that the first part, in which everything is comic, should not remain a true tragedy, and that the remaining two parts, in which tragic elements are to become prominent, should not become comic—at least in its more impassioned passages... All the same, who knows?..." [9]

Belinsky's anxiety was increased by the fact that he could not but see how the Slavophiles were delighted at precisely those conservative, "grass-roots-Russian" features of the Utopia sketched out by Gogol. The above quoted reservations were expressed by Belinsky in a debate with K. S. Aksakov, just such a Slavophile. At the same time Belinsky himself admires many of the lyrical digressions of Volume 1, with their ardent faith in the future of Russia and its people, and he concludes his first article on this book by transcribing in full the two of these that strike him as the finest and most significant, viz., the impassioned address to Russia and the celebrated final passage of Volume 1, in which the rapid flight of a Russian *troika* is taken as a symbol of the nation's great historical destiny. In this article Belinsky is most distressed by the thought that not everyone will properly appreciate these aspects of Gogol's work. "It is sad to think," he writes, "that this lyrical exaltation, these resounding, singing dithyrambs of an exultant national self-awareness, lines worthy of the greatest Russian poet, should be far from accessible to all, the simple and ignorant will laugh heartily at the things which with others cause their hair to stand on end in holy terror... Yet this is how it is, and it cannot be otherwise. This elevated, spiritual poema will pass for the majority as a 'killingly funny joke'...." [10]

Thus the utopian principle contained in Volume 1 of *Dead Souls* was accepted by Belinsky, but in precisely its universal, lyrical expression. As for Gogol's intention to embody his positive ideal in real characters and situations of an epic narrative, this aroused the revolutionary-democratic minded critic's most serious misgivings.

The surviving fragments of Volume 2 of *Dead Souls* do indeed seem to indicate that Belinsky's misgivings were well-founded.

In order to surround the efficient landowner Kostanzhoglo with an almost "regal" aura, Gogol resorts to a number of devices which ring false, for Kostanzhoglo is essentially really just another kulak-landowner, like Sobakevich, only with more enterprise and scope in his farming methods, in accordance with the spirit of his time. As for Murazov, he is entirely false, in his own way no less improbable, both in character and in his allotted role in the novel, than such a figure as the omnipotent and mysterious prince Rodolphe in Eugène Sue's *Les Mystères de Paris*. Murazov is a virtuous government contractor, who performs the role of a universal benefactor, active not only in private life, where he attempts to reform Khlobuyev, a good man who has gone to seed, and Chichikov, a thoroughgoing scoundrel, but also in public life. In a time of need he is even prepared to take on himself the onus of governing the Russian empire—he gives advice to the governor-general, shares his own wheat with the starving people, intends to "have a talk" with the insurgent sectarians and even—through the agency of Khlobuyev, who is sent to "collect for the church"!—to avert popular uprisings, for there is trouble brewing in the province and "reprisals should not begin from below" (VII, 244).

Nevertheless it would be a mistake to regard Volume 2 of *Dead Souls*, insofar as we can judge from the remaining fragments and testimony of Gogol's contemporaries, who read or heard other, lost chapters, as a mere fictionalization of *Selected Passages from Correspondence with My Friends*, an act of capitulation by Gogol to the status quo of Orthodox, pre-reform, Tsarist Russia.

It was not for *reconciliation* with this Russia that Gogol longed. He rejected this ambition in no uncertain terms, for example in his letter to Shevyryov: "Believe me, you will not get the Russian to say his word, not unless you provoke him. He will continue to lie on his back and demand that the author provide him with something to *reconcile him with life* (as they say). What rubbish! As if one could *imagine* something that would reconcile him with life. Believe me, whatever you write it will have no effect now if it doesn't touch on precisely those questions which so engage the attention of modern society, and if it does not depict those people whom we need at the present time. If it lacks this it will be destroyed by the very next novel from the Dumas factory" (XIII, 293, letter of April 27, 1847).

Gogol wishes to construct his utopia against a backcloth of universal suffering and injustice: the Russia of Volume 2 is no less terrible than that of Volume 1. There is some mention of this injustice and suffering in *Selected Passages*, too. For it was there that Gogol wrote that in Russia "such forms of corruption have developed that mankind lacks the means to destroy them ... that a new, illegal code of conduct has emerged alongside the state laws and has almost become legal, so that the laws only remain for appearance's sake; and the cleverest man needs only to take a close look at the things which other people only see superficially, without suspecting anything, for his head to start spinning" (VIII, 350). In *Dead Souls*, Volume 2 this illegal code of conduct was given graphic representation in the criminal antics that arise in connection with the will of Khlobuyev's aunt, fabricated with Chichikov's collaboration. Here he is concerned not merely with some fraudulent scheme, devised at his own risk by an enterprising crook: this business involves the provincial top brass, right up to the governor himself.

Meanwhile, in the background, beyond the limits of the provincial town, we can make out the vague but ominous spectres of widespread poverty and insurrection. Whereas in Volume 1 the "Story of Captain Kopeikin" (in its first edition)—for the inclusion of which Gogol fought with the censors as for a most vital part of his work—upsets the sleepy stupefaction of the overfed provincial officials and landowners, reminding them of those people who are rebelling against the "legal" authorities, now we are concerned with not just one Captain Kopeikin leading a band of robbers. The governor-general is "concerned about a large number of matters, each more unpleasant than the last". There is famine and theft of state wheat in one part of the province; "disturbances" amongst the sectarians, who "under the guise of hunting out the Antichrist, have bumped off a number of non-Antichrists". Finally, he is faced by an entire rebellion of peasants "against the landowners and rural police": "an entire *volost* has refused to pay any tax" (VII, 118).

But then it turns out that all the governor-general can do in the final chapter of Volume 2 is to assemble the officials, and make a speech in a voice of thunder, threatening them all with court martial and special penalties which will be requested for them from the Tsar himself. But through all these threats one can sense an awareness of the weakness of bureaucratic power, and can hear a distinct note of panic. It is no longer a matter of disturbances in some provincial office. "The point is that we have had to save our land, that this our land is perishing not from the invasion of the twenty heathen tribes, but from us ourselves; that *alongside the legal administration a new administration has been formed,* far more powerful than any legal one. Its conditions have been universally known. And no ruler, though he may be wiser than all other lawmakers and rulers, is capable of correcting the evil..." (VII, 126; my italics.—*A.Y.*). A mere two or three years after Gogol's death the monstrous catastrophe of the Crimean War demonstrated the accuracy of his vision of the decay of the entire bureaucratic apparatus of Tsarist Russia.

But in what does the governor-general place his hopes? He appeals to the patriotic feelings, the "nobility of thought", of his officials—those same blatant bribe-takers, embezzlers and thieves that previously had been ruthlessly exposed. Before it is too late they are "to rise up against injustice" (VII, 126). In another version of this same speech the governor-general's aspirations are even more pitiful: he publicly expresses the hope that it would be good "if the *police themselves, without further ado, limit their extortion,* because I now appeal to them as Russians in heart, to whom, I trust, Russia is dear" (VII, 227; my italics.—*A.Y.*).

What could be more preposterous, even in the most uncontrolled flight of administrative fantasy, than a Gogolian policeman—say, Derzhimorda from *The Government Inspector*—setting a heroic example to the people of probity and self-restraint?

Nikolai Chernyshevsky, in his circumstantial study of *Dead Souls*, Volume 2 in *Ocherki gogolevskogo perioda russkoi literatury* (An Outline of the Gogolian Period in Russian Literature), chapter 1, cites as one of the finest remaining fragments, "which will delight the reader with their artistic merit and, more important, with the righteousness and power of their noble indignation", precisely that "marvellous final passage of one fragment—the governor-general's speech, which has no parallel anywhere in Russian literature, not even in the works of Gogol. These passages will convince even the most hostile critic of the author of *Selected Passages from Correspondence with My Friends* that the writer who created *The Government Inspector* and *Dead Souls*, Volume 2 remained true to his artistic principles to the very end of his life, despite the fact he sometimes erred as a thinker". [11]

It is precisely here, right next to the picture of the bankrupt tsarist bureaucracy, that the question of the landowner's responsibility for his peasants is realized far more insistently than anywhere in Volume 1. "Just look to what poverty he has reduced the peasant. He has neither cart nor horse" (VII, 81), observes Kostanzhoglo indignantly when he sees Khlobuyev's ruined estate. "I am sorriest of all for the wretched peasants," grieves Khlobuyev himself. But where are they, these peasants of his? "Of every hundred souls listed in the census only fifty are still alive; such has been the toll of cholera here. The rest have fled without passports. So you might consider them dead too" (VI, 83, 85).

In the surviving fragments of Volume 2 of *Dead Souls* we find no examples of the blindly oblivious justification of the serf system that so enraged Belinsky in *Selected Passages* (it appears that Gogol's artistic sensibility as a realist writer would not permit him to include in his *poema* the false pictures he paints in some of his letters). It is noteworthy that even Kostanzhoglo, when destitute peasants from another estate ask to be taken on by him, replies: "But you'll still be in bondage after all" (VII, 60).

Amongst the fragments which do not form part of the main edition of the surviving first chapters of Volume 2 we even find the outright accusation levelled at the landowners—and not at isolated examples like Plyushkin or Khlobyuev, but at the entire landowning class, that they are the source of "the unhappiness of the entire land, of its ultimate destitution and collapse. Droughts and premature ruin".

"In what way have the landowners ruined their estates?" asks Gogol, and replies: "By abandoning these estates. They have surrendered their lands into the hands of managers and hired men, who are concerned only with their own benefits, with the attainment of short-term profits, and pay no heed to the future, reaping everything and planting nothing, as has already come to pass in Russia, with the destruction of many forests. This has caused rivers to silt up and to give off less of the badly needed moisture. The land has become drier and more barren. The rains, formerly attracted by forested areas, have now ceased" (VII, 272).

It thus appears that the serf-owning system of farming hinders the development of the country's productive forces, destroys the land and destroys those who toil on it. The isolated exceptions—Kostanzhoglo, and to some extent Vasily Platonov—do not alter the general gloomy picture of the devastation of Russia.

And it is precisely here, in this merciless accurate picture of Russia, that Gogol wishes to embody his own ideal, and, furthermore, to embody it in such a way that this ideal will not depend on any isolated exceptions, but will be of universal validity, pointing the way to the rebirth of the entire land and all the people. This is an absurdly bold undertaking, which would be impossible to effect through the metier of realistic narrative.

As we review the utopian tendencies of Gogol's work we should, of course, make the reservation that *Dead Souls* cannot be compared with such epitomes of the genre as More's *Utopia*, Bacon's unfinished *New Atlantis* or Cabet's social utopia, chronologically closer to *Dead Souls*, *Voyage en Icarie* (1840). In these works the authors set themselves the task of presenting a systematic, consistent picture of nonexistent, but desirable social and private relations between people, and of showing their advantages over the existing forms of cohabitation. This ideal utopian picture extends beyond the bounds of reality; its geographical coordinates—even if these are sometimes specified—are entirely imaginary, even mythical. More often than not the utopian world is lost somewhere on an unknown island or land beyond the oceans...

a faraway
ideal land

Gogol did not set himself the task of constructing such an ideal and, inevitably, schematic utopian *system*. He wished to seek out and divine the possibilities of moral resurrection within the Russia of his day, and in Russian society itself, taking guidance from his artistic observation, imagination and awareness. The utopian tendencies of *Dead Souls* are in this sense cognate with the moral utopia revealed in Tolstoy's *Resurrection*: in his portrayal of the social "disorder" and social ills of Russia Gogol, like Tolstoy after him, pinned his hopes in the moral, spiritual rebirth and renewal of his fellow Russians. For all the differences between them, Tolstoy's and Gogol's various utopian visions have one important feature in common: they go hand-in-hand with realistic satire.

Gogol's utopian quest pervades the whole of *Dead Souls*, and has a variety of manifestations, which are by no means restricted to the description of the crises de conscience suffered by Chichikov and Khlobuyev. The utopian theme is felt most prominently in the theme of Russian *bogatyrs* and the pictures of popular life which relate to this theme, the lyrical landscapes, the impassioned author's digressions, in which he speaks to Russia as her prophet and herald... We cannot therefore accept Erlich's preconceived opinion, when he argues that in *Dead Souls* Gogol's utopia "was bound to shrink to the size of a conservative idyll". [12] Gogol's tragedy was precisely that he strove after greater dimensions.

Many distinguished contemporaries of Gogol, in particular Goethe and Balzac, dreamt of the re-education of their fellow-men and of the reformation of society. But their utopian experiments in the genre of the novel were all to some extent independent of the life of their entire country.

The social utopias which Balzac describes in *Le Médecin de campagne* and *Le Curé de village* have an exact geographical location, but each of them embraced only a fragment of one of the departments of France.

In Goethe's *Wilhelm Meisters Lehrjahre* and *Wilhelm Meisters Wanderjahre* we can detect shifts from north to south in the landscapes and certain details of everyday life... But it would be futile to try and guess from the Italianized names of the nobles and princes where exactly the Gesellschaft was sited and what actual forces composed the Verbündeten.

Dickens, like Gogol, was concerned with the utopian

210

problem of the resurrection of "dead souls", destroyed by "legal" profiteering or criminal cupidity. He found a positive solution to this problem only in special, exceptional cases, which frequently introduce fabulous motifs into the development of what is otherwise an entirely realistic, socio-typical situation. Such, for example, is the quite fantastic metamorphosis of the old miser Scrooge, after the intervention in his fate of the omnipotent spirits of Christmas. Where there are no such fantastic interventions the moral volte-face takes place too late to bring about any substantial change in the *social* aspect of the hero, or it is portrayed as unreliable. Thus, for example, Paul Dombey senior becomes softer in heart and repents of his early pride only when his life, which has been one long succession of fateful mistakes, is more or less over, and before him lies a helpless old age. Under the influence of the goodhearted Mr. Pickwick the inveterate shyster Jingle shows signs of a possible reformation, as he is left alone with his sorrows in prison. But this is also an isolated case, which is still "problematic" in many respects—it is with good reason that Pickwick's worldly-wise advocate Perker thus describes it.

Both Balzac and Goethe subject many characters to a beneficial moral re-education, but these characters are nothing like Chichikov and his colleagues! The members of the Society ("Die Gesellschaft") and the Union ("Die Verbündeten") teach the apathetic to be thoughtful, the dreamers and indolent to be useful and return the flighty and the wayward to the path of virtue. But they do not sink so far as to extend their philanthropy to rogues and thieves.

In Balzac's utopian novels moral transformation is usually achieved by those who have suffered a profound spiritual drama, like Dr. Bénassis or Véronique Graslin; they in their turn draw others into this benign probationary experience of spiritual cleansing. But however bad the crimes and misdemeanours weighing on their consciences —even murder!—they are at any rate never vulgar or selfish. As we have already noted, for all their geographical and chronological credibility, they are separated by an insurmountable barrier from the other parts of *La Comédie humaine*. Vautrin, along with the lesser scoundrels from these books, is not threatened by the danger of repentance.

It is already apparent from this cursory comparison that the utopian task Gogol set himself in *Dead Souls* was vastly more complex and unrealisable than those undertaken by his contemporaries in their utopian works.

Gogol remained a "social poet", as Belinsky termed him, even in the utopian themes of *Dead Souls*. His objective was not to entertain his readers, but to find answers to the most crucial questions facing Russian society, to discover precisely what Russia needed and why did she turn her eyes, full of expectation, on him. He was charged with arrogance, even delusions of grandeur, but when we reread the letters he wrote at the time of *Dead Souls* and the memoirs of his contemporaries, we cannot but sense that his work on the *poema* was so much more than mere literary endeavour for this experienced writer, it was nothing less than a great civic feat.

But the higher the artistic duty Gogol placed upon himself before his country, the heavier the burden he had to carry.

Less than ten years after the death of Gogol another Russian novel was published which was memorable for its "words that unite people". One of the characters, a young scientist, recites the following words in a conversation with a friend: "Art... homeland, science, freedom, justice..." As things turn out in the course of the novel the most powerful of these "words that unite people" proves to be struggle for the freedom of one's country. However, the heroes of Turgenev's *On the Eve* are not destined to carry out this struggle in Russia, instead they go beyond its frontiers, to distant Bulgaria. Lev Tolstoy was also to search for "words that unite". One such word he finds in *War and Peace*: the national patriotism of the 1812 war. (It is interesting that this motif had already appeared, as we shall see, in *Dead Souls,* Volume 2, in chapters which have not survived, but about which we know from the memoirs of Gogol's contemporaries). In *Resurrection* Tolstoy attempts to find such a "word of unity" in fraternal Christian love.

Gogol also searches for "words of unity". At times in his utopian constructs he seems to come very close to those groundswells which were only able at that time to feed the "living soul" of Russia.

D. Yofanov, S. Mashinsky and other scholars, in their close study of the so-called "free-thinking movement" in the Nezhin Lycée, at the time when Gogol was a student there, believe that it strongly influenced the worldview of the future writer. These critics argue that Gogol's teacher Belousov * might have served as the prototype for the idealized preceptor Alexander Petrovich, whose premature death plays such a tragic role in the formation of Tentetnikov's character.

Ulenka, and to some extent Tentetnikov himself, may be taken as an analogous example, if we can judge from the memoirs left by Gogol's contemporaries about the content of lost chapters of the book. The heroism of the Decembrist wives, who remained loyal to their husbands and followed them to Siberia, cannot have failed to impress Gogol, as it did all educated Russia at that time (the young Maria Volkonskaya, née Rayevskaya, was, like Gogol's Ulenka, the daughter of a general, one of the heroes of the Patriotic War of 1812). In the final chapters of *Dead Souls*, Volume 2, Ulenka, by this time affianced to Tentetnikov, who has been arrested and exiled for belonging to a secret society, sets off after him to Siberia where they are eventually to be wedded.

But Gogol attempts, so to speak, to "postulate" the great nobility of spirit of such characters as Alexander Petrovich or Ulenka, without giving it any inner social content. No trace remains of their "free thinking" ideals—yet it is only this that could have determined the pedagogic activity of Tentetnikov's wise teacher and the resolution and righteousness of Ulenka. As for Tentetnikov's participation in the secret society, this society itself and Tentetnikov's role in it are only sketched out in caricature. The name of one of the leaders of the society—Voronoy-Dryannov, "Rubbishy-Jet-Black", is itself sufficient to show how Gogol debases Tentetnikov's colleagues. The description of the "philanthropic union", which Tentetnikov almost joins in his youthful ignorance, is permeated with deliberate irony: "The society was formed with a wide-ranging aim: to provide stable happiness for all mankind, from the banks of the Thames to Kamchatka. Enormous funds of money were required; fabulous donations were collected from generous

---

* N. G. Belousov, who taught the students at the Lycée "natural law" in the spirit of enlightened democratism, was dismissed together with a number of other teachers. Some of them were even sent into exile.

members. Whither all this money went was known only to one man, the head of the society," whom Gogol describes as "an old rogue and freemason, and also a gambler, but with the gift of the gab" (VII, 26).

At the same time, for all Gogol's "disassociation" from the Decembrist movement (as in other passages he disassociates himself from West European philanthropic schemes, in which we can detect socialist utopianism) he himself nevertheless dreams of a radical *revolution* in the manner of thought, life and activity of his fellow citizens, but hopes that this revolution will take place on a spiritual basis, without affecting the existing political, economic and social relations.

He is deeply grieved not only about the destruction of natural resources—the land, forests and rivers. He is even more dismayed by the vain squandering of the talents and abilities of the people.

Paradoxically, one of the main ideas in Belinsky's celebrated letter about *Selected Passages from Correspondence with My Friends* has a direct echo in many entirely unconnected letters of Gogol's, relating to the period when he was writing *Dead Souls,* Volume 2. Furthermore, it is precisely this thought, but—a most important distinction! —interpreted not in the spirit of social struggle, but in that of a Slavophil national abstraction, which determines the general design of Gogol's utopia.

"The character of the Russian public," Belinsky writes to Gogol, "is determined by the situation of Russian society, in which fresh forces seethe and seek their way to the surface, but, under the weight of oppression, are unable to find an outlet, and lead only to dejection, distress and apathy". [13]

And Gogol writes to the poet Yazykov: "Today's young man feels involuntary agitation, because he has a force within him that thirsts for action, but it does not know where, how, or in what place" (XIII, 52, letter of April 21, 1846). Earlier, in a letter to Y. F. Samarin Gogol advises his correspondent to endeavour in his contacts with people "to notice and reveal in each of them that main talent with which he has been endowed and which has lain dormant". "Appeal to his sense of his own worth," continues Gogol, "and reproach him for having neglected and despised it; try to direct him to that form of activity and work for which he possesses secret talents, and he

214

will be saved..." (XIII, 26, letter of January 3, 1846).

This dream of awakening the "dormant" talents and strength of human nature, which have been suppressed, in Gogol's own image, "by an outer layer of egoism", or, as he writes elsewhere, "by an earthy crust", owes much to the Enlightenment view of human nature *in general* and of the possibilities of its perfection. But in some respects Gogol, probably unsuspectingly, is objectively close to the socialist utopian thinkers, in particular Fourier with his theory of the dialectics of dominant passions, which in the prevailing social order are directed towards evil, but might in different conditions be beneficial to society, and perform the directly opposite function.

In this sense Gogol's utopia, despite his attempts in *Dead Souls,* Volume 2 to base it on religion and the church, was essentially humanistic. He proceeds not from the original sin of man, but from the unlimited possibilities for his perfection.

The wonderful, inspired flights of lyricism of both volumes are as vivid today as they were when Gogol wrote them. Gogol's faith in the future of his country has thus justified itself—a faith which has survived both the end of serfdom, monarchy and "legal" profiteering.

It was only natural that the great Russian poet Alexander Blok should have understood so profoundly and been so inspired by the *poetic* utopia of *Dead Souls.*

In his article "The Child of Gogol" (1909), written during the oppressive period of reaction after the 1905 revolution, Blok creates a remarkable image of Gogol as a writer misunderstood by the majority of his contemporaries and utterly possessed by his "creative torment". "Having renounced worldly delights and the love of women this man did himself, like a woman, bear a fruit beneath his heart: he was a being rapt in sombre concentration and indifferent of all things but one; not really a being at all, but rather a personified sense of hearing, alert only to the sound of its child's slow movements, its shifting in the womb... Only a man capable of perceiving new things with the keenest awareness could have discerned in them a new, unborn world, the world that Gogol was destined to reveal to his people". [14]

Describing how Gogol is "irresistibly drawn by his new land, by the hazy distance, by a Russia of his dreams, born in ferment", Blok strikes a clear distinction between

215

Gogol and the Slavophiles, and quotes Gogol's address to Russia in the celebrated pasage from Volume 1.

"That same Russia, about which the Slavophiles shrieked and sang like the Corybants endeavouring to drown the cries of the Mother of God, this Russia flashes before Gogol in the blinding image of a short creative dream...

"What has Gogol's dazzling vision changed in real life? Nothing. *Here* the old Russia, reviled by Khomyakov as 'unworthy to be chosen', has remained:

> *Judged with the black stain of injustice*
> *and sealed with yoke of bondage.*

"A wondrous vision flashed past. Just as in the days before spring the heavy clouds disperse to reveal huge, seemingly newborn and freshly washed stars, so did the impenetrable screen of the tormented days of Gogol's life suddenly dropped before him, and with it the screen of Russia's centuries of toil to reveal the Russia of the future, infinite breath-taking vistas unknown to the world, washed by the rains of spring". [15] Only another poet could have understood so well the agonies suffered by Gogol in the quest of his poetic utopia.

2

There are certain fragments of Volume 2, reflecting Gogol's social ideals, in which one hears distinct echoes of those "micro-utopias" which, like small islands harbouring true human values, rational and "natural" toil, featured in the eighteenth century Enlightenment novel amidst the chaos of despotic and selfish social forces.

The estate of Fielding's "gentleman-farmer" Wilson, who turns his back on the futile and vain life of the city for the humble joys of honest labour surrounded by his family on his small piece of lovingly tended land *(The Adventures of Joseph Andrews)* is one of the earliest examples of such a "micro-utopia". Alongside it we might place the estate of the philanthropic squire Allworthy (particularly after the expulsion from this estate, at the end of *Tom Jones,* of the insidious hypocrite Blifil and the heartless pedants Thwackum and Square). Goldsmith's utopian idyll in *The Vicar of Wakefield* is on the point of collapsing under the onslaught of hostile forces of the real world, but thanks to the timely intervention of the all-powerful philanthropist Sir James Thornhill the author is able to secure the release from prison of his ingenuous heroes, led by vicar Primrose, and to save them from poverty and ignominy, as well as to restore and strengthen their happy little world, in which love, trust and selfless toil reign supreme. In Smollett's novel *The Journey of Humphrey Clinker* Brambleton Hall, the Welsh home of Matthew Bramble, a hot-tempered and sharp-tongued man, but with the kindest of hearts, remains throughout all the peripeteia of the novel's plot as a glorious haven from the petty, vulgar cares and worries of the world outside. The Horatian apostrophe "O rus!" runs as a leitmotif throughout the narrative. Here, surrounded by picturesque landscapes, so dear to his heart, amongst his neighbours and other farmers, over whose welfare he presides like a good father, Matthew Bramble is to find the spiritual peace which eludes him in London resembling "an overgrown monster".

The English Enlightenment novelists did not even feel the need to ask the question: how just are the social bases of these "micro-utopias" where the natural order prevails, such as the homes of Wilson, Allworthy, Bramble and others? The philanthropy of their owners was attested and accepted with complete willingness, and without any critical scrutiny, while the symbolic dénouements, in which the sacked manservant Joseph proves to be Wilson's son, the foundling Tom Jones—Allworthy's nephew, and Clinker—Bramble's son, have a mollifying, conciliatory effect, restoring the "natural" ties which have briefly been violated, and with them the social contradictions of the upper and lower classes, which had not gained the significance in the eighteenth century novel that they were to have a century later.

The theme of social and ethical utopia was to receive a far more thorough psychological treatment by the French Enlightenment writer Jean-Jacques Rousseau. In the three last parts of *Julie, ou la Nouvelle Héloïse* (1760), a book which Belinsky described as "prophecy", the estate of the Wolmars in Clarens is portrayed as an embodiment of all that is rational and natural in human coexistence. Here social conflicts and seething passions are resolved and soothed—insofar as this is possible in our world. Rational labour—the unwritten moral law for all the inhabitants of the Wolmar estate—unites masters and servants, leaving no place for sloth, boredom or vain desires. Always a sensitive writer, Rousseau is not shy of prosaic detail, but for him such detail is pregnant with spiritual significance. The hiring of servants and conduct towards them, the division of duties between the master and mistress of the house— to all this he devotes as much attention as Gogol was to devote to his portrayal of the lives of Kostanzhoglo and the Platonovs. The insistence with which Rousseau praises the rational self-denial and untiring labour that distinguishes all the inhabitants of the Wolmar estate has a direct analogue in the enthusiastic descriptions of *Dead Souls*, Volume 2. With Rousseau the reader learns about this remarkable organization mainly from the letters of Saint-Preux, who resolves after a long and agonizing spiritual ordeal to settle under one roof with his beloved Julie and her husband, and studies the life and labour of the Wolmars and their servants with the scrutiny of a philosopher and ardour of one in love.

Rousseau emphatically states that the place of action is Switzerland: the Wolmars live amongst free peasants and not the bondsmen of France. But in their dealings with these free peasants Julie and her husband both display not only friendship and solicitude, but also studied caution with regard to anything that might upset the existing conditions of the villagers' lives.

A certain harsh stoicism can be felt to underlie the Clarens idyll of the Wolmars, despite the poetic colours with which Rousseau paints it. The problem of "self-denial", which, as we shall see, is to play such an important role in the utopian works of Goethe and the social utopias of Balzac, is already present here in the novel's subtext, just as it can be felt in Gogol's search for a positive ideal in *Dead Souls*, Volume 2. The psychological situation which Rousseau creates in the three last parts of *La Nouvelle Héloïse* is based on the following foundation: three people live in constant friendship and open sincerity under one roof—an elderly husband, his wife and her former lover. Passions are held in check by duty and reason. Nevertheless, for all that Rousseau cherished this triumph of the supreme moral duty, he was unable to give it a firm basis and sustain it to the end of his novel. An accident results in the sudden death of Julie; in the last lines of the letter written shortly before she dies, which Wolmar so conscientiously forwards to Saint-Preux, she is unable to restrain herself from the fateful admission: "I love you".

Here we are leaving the area of direct typological analogy with Gogol's *Dead Souls*. But it is important to note that the artist in Rousseau was so strong that, whilst elaborating his utopia with great detail and thorough substantiation, aiming thereby to prove to the world the possibility of the rational and efficient community of a group of people united by a stoic awareness of duty and "natural" virtue, he had in the end to bow his head before the omnipotence of passion, which holds in its grip even such ennobled natures. We can imagine, therefore, how much harder the task faced by Gogol and his contemporaries, the realists of the nineteenth century, confronted by the egoistic, predatory and vain passions of this new, bourgeois age!

Certain aspects of the utopian project which Gogol endeavoured with such agony to embody in the second and third volumes of *Dead Souls,* could be better understood from a comparison with the social utopias of two of his older contemporaries, Goethe and Balzac.

A comparison of *Dead Souls* with the Wilhelm Meister novels, or with *Le Médecin de campagne* and *Le Curé de village*, might seem at first glance to be forced and arbitrary, so strikingly different are they in genre and style. However, a closer analysis will reveal certain common tendencies.

At the same time features of similarity or community of aim will be most clearly manifested here not in the completed artistic achievements of the writers, but in the *direction* followed by their thoughts, in their *struggle* to surmount the logic of reality and even in those *compromises* and *defeats* which occur in all their quests. We may justifiably argue that there is a typological regularity in these apparently coincidental similarities.

The *Wilhelm Meister* novels are not amongst Goethe's more popular and highly regarded works. They do, however, occupy a vital position in the history of his artistic quests. With the exception of *Faust* no other literary project demanded so much time or so engaged the attention of the author, at the most varied stages of his career. In a letter to Professor Göttling Goethe describes the agonies with which the creation of *Wilhelm Meister*—finally published in 1829—was fraught. He compares this novel to the stone of Sisyphus, which time and again rolled back onto him. The publication of *Wilhelm Meister* marked the end of more than fifty years of titanic labours—and still the objective, as Goethe understood it, had not been attained.

From at least the beginning of the twenties we can see Goethe working in his mind on the plan for a *Wilhelm Meister* trilogy; the *Lehrjahre* and *Wanderjahre* were to have been followed by a concluding novel: the *Meisterjahre*, the hardest novel in the cycle, as Goethe himself realized. But it was never in fact written, and the trilogy was destined to remain incomplete.

As we read of this great disproportion between the exertion of creative endeavour and a constantly elusive objective, we involuntarily recall the creative torment and "Sisyphean labours" of another, Russian artist, who also dreamt of three-part composition which would culminate in an inspired, life-affirming finale, having begun with satirical pictures of the "poverty and imperfection" of Russian life.

While satirical motifs can sometimes distinctly be heard in the *Wilhelm Meister* novels, these do not provide sufficient grounds for a comparison with *Dead Souls*, as Goethe was far less concerned with satire than Gogol.

These two works, so different in many respects, are however related by their concern, inherited from the Enlightenment but reinterpreted in accordance with the historical conditions of the nineteenth century, with the *designation* of man and the activity that is truly worthy of him.

It is hard to judge how well-acquainted Gogol was with Goethe's work and in particular *Wilhelm Meister*. His first direct reference to Goethe in the epilogue to his youthful poem *Hans Küchelgarten* (1828) is as romantically vague as it is ecstatic.

Goethe features in a quite different light in the ironic context of the episode in *Dead Souls* where Chichikov, mellowed by a good meal, endeavours to entertain Sobakevich (!) with readings from the emotional correspondence between Werther and Charlotte (VI, 152).

In *Selected Passages from Correspondence with My Friends* Gogol pays due respect to Goethe, but treats him rather from above, with a morose irritation: he blames the German writer for his own universality. "Goethe himself, this Proteus of poets, both in the world of nature and in the world of science, showed his own personality in this essentially scientific striving, a personality filled with a sort of Germanic decorum and a theoretical German tendency to accommodate himself to all times and ages" (VIII, 382).

However well he knew Goethe's actual writings Gogol could not fail to have been well-informed about the debates that raged around Goethe in Russian literary circles in the thirties and forties. This is all the more indisputable since, as we can see from the materials assembled by V. M. Zhirmunsky in his outstanding monograph: *Goethe in Russian Literature,* it was precisely the *Moskovsky vestnik* (Moscow Herald) circle, and after it the *Moskvityanin* (The Muscovite), who did most for the popularization of Goethe amongst Russian readers, and prominent in these circles were men like Pogodin, Shevyryov and Yazykov, to whom Gogol was particularly close.

Marking one of the final stages in the development of the Enlightenment "Bildungsroman" Goethe's *Wilhelm Meister* at the same time possesses features not hitherto attested in that genre. Himself a dedicated opponent of Romanticism, Goethe does, however (particularly in the *Lehrjahre*), pay tribute to the poetry of the mysterious and unusual: in the stream of strange events, as he describes the plot of his novel, particular prominence is accorded to the poetic figures of Mignon and the indigent harpist, whose appeal goes hand-in-hand with their mystery.

But however significant these incursions by *Wilhelm Meister* into the field of Romantic art, the main direction followed by the genre in this work leads it away from the Enlightenment "Bildungsroman" to the social novel of the nineteenth century. The *Lehrjahre* already includes not only the story of Wilhelm Meister's moral and aesthetic education, but also the formation of his social awareness. Besides the pageant of the life and mores of the German provinces that unfolds before us in the *Wanderjahre* we also confront an entirely new problem: the destiny of the nation as a whole.

Lothario, one of the pillars of the Gesellschaft, "was acquainted with history," and "kept his eye trained on the fertile, promising youth of his fatherland, on the quiet labours of industrious and efficient people, engaged in so

221

many different professions". As Aurelia recalls, relating all this to Wilhelm Meister, Lothario gave her "a general survey of Germany, *what she is* and *what she could be...*" [16] (my italics.—*A.Y.*).

We should note in particular the way in which Lothario's imagination endeavours to discern through the present and as yet unattained, but longed for, and, so it seems to the speaker, possible future. This temporal shift, this anxiety to see in the present day the embryo of the future, so characteristic of Goethe in *Wilhelm Meister* and *Faust,* points up the kinship between his realism and that of Gogol.

"We need only look more closely into the present and the future will appear before us. He who thinks of the future with disregard for the present is a fool: he will either lie, or make vague guesses," writes Gogol to Alexandra Smirnova on June 6, 1846, and at once adds: "We have all forgotten that the paths and roads to this radiant *future* are hidden in precisely this dark and tangled *present* which no one wishes to recognize, and which each of us regards as too lowly to merit our attention!" (XIII, 79).

In another letter to the same correspondent he compares this "idea of *possibility*" to a "lantern"—with which "we will in the end find something to do, but without which we will remain utterly in the dark" (XIII, 223-224. letter of February 22, 1847; my italics.—*A.Y.*).

At the time when he was continually returning to his work on Volume 2 of *Dead Souls* Gogol was constantly concerned with the idea that only the school of life itself can properly mature and strengthen the spirit.

Furthermore the idea of the development of special, individual talents, such as are latent in every person, grows in Gogol's mind into the remarkably profound notion of the harmonic cohesion of all these individual efforts in joint social endeavour and progress. This idea finds its fullest expression in a memorable letter to P.V. Annenkov of September 7, 1847, in which, demonstrating to his correspondent the necessity for each of us of, "in addition of being on the top of the developments of modern life", a certain "special labour", Gogol writes: "It cannot be that you, too, do not have one. Otherwise we would all be as like one another as peas in a pod, and the whole world would be nothing more than a factory. Without this special labour the character of the individual would never take shape, and it is of these characters that a *forward moving* society is composed. There can be no universal progress without these units, each working in his own way" (XIII, 384-385).

There is an obvious echo in these remarks by Gogol of Goethe's proclamation of the supreme wisdom of the Gesellschaft, which is conveyed to the hero when he reaches the end of his Lehrjahre. We recall this magnificent picture of the cohesion of individual forces and talents, revealed to Wilhelm Meister by Jarno.

" 'Mankind can only be composed of all men, and the world only of all their forces in their totality. These are often in conflict with one another, and while they seek to destroy themselves Nature controls and restores them. From the slightest animal attraction to a craft to the highest exercise of intellectual art, from the babbling and cries of joy of a babe to the choicest utterance of an orator and singer, from the first squabble of boys to the monstrous institutions through which countries are defended and conquered, from the slightest benevolence and the most fleeting love to the most vehement passion and the most sacred union, from the purest feeling of sensory existence to the most subtle notions and hopes of the remote spiritual future, all this and far more lies within men and must be developed—developed not in one man alone, but in many men. Every talent is important and must be encouraged' ".[17]

What with Gogol applies to the progressive movement of society is also expressed here by Goethe, albeit in a more abstract and starry-eyed form. It is indicative that the author himself, engaging in a form of self-criticism, has Wilhelm Meister interrupt this protracted admonition ("...Thus let us always endeavour to see with proper clarity and to hold fast to that which is in us and which we can develop within us") with the impatient and irritated exclamation: " 'For God's sake! Enough of these maxims!' "

The logical development of the *Wilhelm Meister* cycle is in fact determined by the author's search for a bridge from such general "maxims" about the beneficience of the development of the individuality to its practical application and to the real forms of their embodiment in life.

This search was long and arduous. The special place occupied by the *Wilhelm Meister* cycle amongst the "Bildungsromane" of the eighteenth century Enlightenment is largely characterized by the particular difficulty experienced by the author in his desire to give a definitive answer to this problem of problems—an answer which could be realized in life and which at the same time would fully satisfy all the intellectual and spiritual demands made by Goethe himself and by his heroes. The two novels share a common leitmotif: the necessity for rational *action*.

However, the content of such action is not always easy to determine. Initially Wilhelm Meister believes that he has found his true vocation in the theatre. But this childhood dream "to embody everything good, noble and great in his acting", [18] for the sake of which he so quickly rejects the humble prose of his family business, itself collapses when confronted by real life.

But this setback does not prevent Wilhelm Meister from returning to the departure point of his life's journey. Wilhelm's brother-in-law and co-heir Werner appeals to him from the world of commerce, which he has previously rejected. In Werner's narrowly practical mind the future can easily be plotted out on a graph of income and expenditure. He advises Wilhelm to buy a profitable estate on credit which has fallen into disuse, restore it, increase its turnover, sell it at a profit and buy another estate, a little larger than the first: "You are the best man to do this," he urges. But Goethe's hero is horrified by the base cupidity of this pursuit of financial gain. How can a man bring an estate into order when he is disunited with himself? wonders Wilhelm.

Thus, as we can see from this response, the spiritual principle overcomes base business concerns, and the spiritual "disunity" which so torments him becomes the main object of Wilhelm Meister's activities. Goethe appears to be acting in full conformity with this twist in the plot when he ruptures the composition of the novel by inserting the "Bekenntnisse einer schönen Seele" (Confessions of a Fine Soul), which forms the whole of Book 6 of the *Lehrjahre*. These are the notes of a pious old maid (aunt to Lothario and Natalie), a zealous pietist, who has been influenced by the Herrngut sect. Wilhelm Meister reads this confession and is convinced that it will influence the whole of his own life; he is most impressed by the writer's "purity of existence" and the purity of "everything that surrounded her; the self-sufficiency of her nature and the impossibility that it should admit to itself anything which did not harmonize with its noble, loving mood". But what could be more depressingly egocentric than this "nobility and love", directed exclusively to the benefit of the subject's own spiritual state?

But even the "Olympian heathen" Goethe could not dispense with pietism, with religious "sanction", when laying the moral foundations for his humanistic utopia, and neither in his turn can Gogol. For this reason it is not only the "Confessions of a Fine Soul", but also the programme of the Gesellschaft and its ritual—which historically seems to derive from the actual rites of eighteenth century Masonic lodges—that are full of mystical echoes and allusions.

Yet it is here, amongst these wise and powerful patrons, who finally emerge from their dark secrecy and bring Wilhelm into their circle, that he is at last destined, so it seems, to discover the road to that rational activity that is truly worthy of his talents, and to which he has been called throughout the novel both by his own imagination and by the voices of his advisers. But here too there is so much that remains dark and elusive, so many steps, each of which appears for a moment to be the last, only then to slip away beneath his feet! But what is important is that Goethe is endeavouring here to transcend the bounds of *individual* self-education.

His Lothario reflects on the possible future of Germany. Previously, to realize his utopian ideals he wished to emigrate to America, but in the *Wanderjahre* he declares: "Here—or nowhere—is my America!"

This enlightened aristocrat and landowner, who bows to the revolutionary spirit of his time, wishes through peaceful reforms to establish in Germany a system of free civilian land-use, for the attainment of which such an immense, historical, world-shattering revolution has just been effected in France with the spilling of so much blood. Is this, we might wonder, the central nerve of the utopia proclaimed by *Wilhelm Meisters Wanderjahre*?

The detailed description of Lothario's estate, such as it had earlier been perceived by Wilhelm Meister, cannot but reinforce this hypothesis. Just as with Gogol, the dwellings of Goethe's heroes are bound to give an idea of the habits and mores of their inhabitants. Lothario's home impresses the visitor with its obvious and deliberate disregard for beauty, decoration, or tradition. Pride of place goes to utility, comfort and efficiency.

But no sooner has the reader decided that he has at last divined the essence of Goethe's utopia and can take a closer look into it, than its outlines become hazy, melt away and change before his eyes; the utopia turns a new, unexpected side to the astounded observer. We were already inclined to think Lothario an enlightened zealot of bourgeois innovations, prepared to sacrifice to these the traditions of his aristocratic heritage. But as we approach the end of the *Lehrjahre* completely new, *conservative* motifs predominate in determining the future activities of the Gesellschaft (in which Lothario has one of the leading roles): this union of energetic people, who invite their new friend Wilhelm Meister to join their number, has been formed, it turns out, to secure the property and wealth of its members against any future upheavals! A detailed and substantial account of precisely this is given at the end of the novel by Jarno.

These truly Protean transformations, these shifts in emphasis in all aspects of the realization of Goethe's utopian vision, do not of course proceed from any subjective inconsistency or eclecticism on the part of the writer. Their main cause is that real life had not provided the author of *Wilhelm Meisters Lehrjahre* with the necessary concrete images, situations or motives that would have made his ideas plausible and tangible in the context of realist narrative.

Goethe here permitted himself something that Gogol did not want, or did not dare permit himself in a very similar situation. He revealed to the reader his own doubts and inquiries, presenting to them the entire course of his thought, with all its paradox and conflicts. We know that he rejected much of what he wrote, crossing it out or leaving it buried (as he did, in particular, with the first version of the novel—*Wilhelm Meisters theatralische Sendung*). But subsequently he often merely substitutes one episode for another, swapping one move of the plot for the next; the two parts of the cycle can in this sense be treated as two variations on a single theme. Gogol wrote Volume 2 of *Dead Souls,* burnt the manuscript, rewrote it and burnt it again, until at his third attempt the author himself died after destroying his book.

Goethe did not burn the rough notes which he then

rejected in favour of other inquiries after the truth, which seemed to him to come closer to his objective. He left it up to the reader to find his own way through the chaotic mass of observations, exhortations, prognoses and speculations of which the humanistic utopia of *Wilhelm Meister* is composed—the end result of his Sisyphean labour.

The aesthetics of the cycle are profoundly affected by this feature. The composition of the *Wanderjahre* lacks even the relative unity which can still be found in that of the *Lehrjahre*. The interpolated novellas (or material for novellas) interrupt the plot in the most capricious way. One of these is the Romantic story "Die Heilige Familie" about the pious carpenter Joseph, a transposition into a nineteenth century German provincial setting of the naïve poetry of a mediaeval German fresco devoted to the life of St. Joseph. Another: the frivolous Lenardo's search of Nachodine before whom, against his own wishes, he has committed an offence. Or the psychological novel in miniature, which describes the amorous errors of two ill-matched couples ("Der Mann von fünfzig Jahren"—"The Fifty-Year-Old Man"), and his free version of a French novella, "Die pilgernde Törin" ("The Mad Pilgrim") and another, "Wer ist der Verräter?" ("Who Is the Traitor?"), devoted to the "simple loyalty and honesty of German life". Finally, we have "Die neue Melusine", a fairy tale about a miniature fairy, the princess of a tribe of dwarfs, written from the motifs of old German folk tales... Alongside all these Goethe includes a mass of "raw", artistically unworked information about how and whence Germany obtains its cotton, about the production of cotton cloth, or the equally detailed didactic descriptions of educational methods practised in the "pedagogical province".

In the first edition, at the end of books two and three, Goethe supplements this rag-bag of rich but totally heterogeneous material with two selections of the most uncoordinated aphorisms, observations and sketches, edited at the author's request by Eckermann. One of these was entitled "Im Sinne der Wanderer" ("Reflections in the spirit of the pilgrims. Art, ethics, nature"); the other: "Aus Makariens Archiv" ("From the archives of Makaria"). Each of these selections ends with a poem ("Auf Schillers Schädel"— "On beholding Schiller's skull", and "Kein wesen kann zu nichts zerfallen"—"No being can crumble into nothing").

Thus, the first edition of the novel was even more chaotic in its composition than the later edition.

As Eckermann recalls, "when the *Wanderjahre* was published it had the strangest effect on everyone. The course of the novel is interrupted by a mass of puzzling utterances, the meaning of which was only apparent to experts ... while all other readers, particularly those of the fair sex, felt quite discomforted in this labyrinth. The two poems were also poorly understood, and the readers were puzzled by their inclusion in the novel at all".

At the same time there was something in the novel which let it, if not a formal compositional unity, at least a philosophical cohesion. It is this single-minded, almost frenetic quest by the author that constitutes the true driving force behind the *Wanderjahre*. The novel, in Goethe's own words, was made "not of a single piece, but still of a single meaning". This generalizing single "meaning" of the *Wanderjahre* consists in the author's striving after the ideal not of *individual* harmony (which was the primary concern of the *Lehrjahre*), but of *social relations* between people, which would remove the conflict between labour and property, between philanthropy and profit...

But what, we might wonder, is the price that the people must pay for the attainment of this utopia? What are Goethe's feelings about industrial development?

The Soviet critic N. N. Vilmont adduces an interesting fact in his study of Goethe: in the notebooks for *Wilhelm Meister* there was a passage, subsequently rejected by the author, in which an abbot describes his attitude to mechanical industry. He would like Lothario "to lose, bit by bit, his negative attitude towards machines. After all," the abbot argues, "to assist the development of technology is to assist everyone to be able to do everything. The development of technology frees us from many cares and gradually raises mankind above itself, training the necessary organs for higher reason and purest will". [19]

After quoting this interesting remark Vilmont suggests that Goethe crossed it out of the manuscript of his novel because he had decided to save it for the unwritten third part of *Wilhelm Meister*. This, however, is pure conjecture. We might equally suggest the opposite: the *human price* which the people would have to pay for the destruction of the old, patriarchal order with their traditional handicrafts, might have appeared excessive to the author of the *Wander-*

jahre and he might—within the context of this novel—have deliberately withheld such an apologia of the machine.

There are many such volte-faces in literary history. Gogol himself affords an interesting example of the same phenomenon. In his article "On the Teaching of World History" (*Arabesques*, 1835), he accepts the rise of industry with buoyant optimism. "Enlightenment, which cannot be hindered by any thing, is beginning to develop even amongst the lower classes; steam engines are raising manufacture to remarkable perfection; it is as if invisible spirits were helping man everywhere and rendering his powers still more awesome and still more beneficial..." (VIII, 35).

Later this optimism deserts him. In *Selected Passages* technical progress is treated with irritation: "What has mankind gained from these railways and such like, what has it profited from all the varieties of its development and what benefit is there that now one town is impoverished and another has become a thriving market?" (VIII, 352-353).

But alongside such general statements of moral criticism of industrial progress Gogol does express one original and genuinely humanistic idea on this matter. "I swear," he exclaims, *"man deserves to be regarded with greater interest than a factory and a ruin"* (VIII, 303; my italics. —*A.Y.*).

This remark is most significant. Man is promoted here as the one true value and measure of all things. Neither the feudal past ("the ruin") nor capitalist industrialism (the "factory") has the right to enslave and oppress mankind.

The position occupied by Goethe in the *Wanderjahre* has many affinities with this belief of Gogol's. The novel ends by revealing to the author the prospect of a grand *departure* from the world of ruins and factories by all those who wish to remain people and to develop the best aspects of their human nature. Yesterday's aristocratic landowners abandon their family castles and the traditional craftsmen their ancestral shops, where they have plied their trade from generation to generation.

But with Goethe this view of a future of fraternal unity of all classes and estates (something that Gogol also dreamt of, but in the context of tsarist pre-reform Russia) requires for its realization the total rejection—not only of the old world, but also of the old class society. We recall Lothario's earlier declaration, "Here—or nowhere—is my America!" as he turned his gaze away from the New World to his native Germany. Now he and the others set off across the ocean—but not in order to become part of the new society of the United States! In the novel the vagueness of the social conditions in which the new colony is to live not only corresponds to the hazy contours of the future: it is even programmatic in a way. The colonists will be brought back to nature. They will be able to "start everything all over again".

But the ending of the novel, which describes with prosaic precision how each of the heroes and heroines is given his individual professional "load"—Wilhelm will be a surgeon, Philine a cutter, Lydia a seamstress, Friedrich a stenographer while Lothario will instruct the colonists in military matters—leaves the reader with the sudden impression of routine. It is as though the artist's imagination has suddenly grown dim, and that which should have been stirring and heroic in the magic rays of his imagination has become dull and grey in the light of commonplace reality.

Had he elected to write in another genre and with different artistic means Goethe might have been able to express many of the ideas which so occupied his mind during the time of writing *Wilhelm Meisters Wanderjahre* with far greater effect and poetic force. *Faust,* on which, as on *Wilhelm Meister,* he worked for most of his life, also has as its main theme that of spiritual growth in constant search, struggle and striving after the new. But in *Faust* this theme is presented in universal poetic images of colossal stature and significance. Here the artist is least of all concerned with ordinary verisimilitude, and if there is such verisimilitude it usually acquires an ironic nuance (e.g. the scenes where Mephistopheles talks to Martha about her late husband or astounds the philistine patrons in Auerbachs Keller). On the other hand, the lyrical element, which practically disappears from *Wilhelm Meister* with the departure of Mignon and the old harpist, is most pronounced and effective in Goethe's dramatic poem. It enables the artist to express in the most succinct way, through a perfect marriage of thought and feeling, the very quintessence of his social utopian vision, which in *Wil-*

helm Meisters Wanderjahre requires dozens of pages of turgid didactic prose, unrelieved by any poetic inspiration.

In *Faust,* particularly in Part 2, there is as much obscurity and paradox as in the *Wilhelm Meister* cycle. But what in a "Bildungsroman" or novel of manners might appear illogical or absurd from the point of view of common sense is elevated here to the status of poetic necessity.

The celebrated lyrical monologue of Faust, which at the end of Part 2 proclaims the "final conclusion of all wisdom", possesses, thanks precisely to its laconic and highly generalized poetic form, a force of conviction that cannot be found anywhere in all the description of the preparations, projects and plans of the colonists departing to the New World in *Wilhelm Meisters Wanderjahre.* Yet Goethe is essentially writing about the same thing: about free constructive activity, that alone can give meaning and justification to a person's existence. But what remains schematic in the narrative genre of a realist novel, in which the reader expects a vivid and consistent portrayal of mores, behaviour and characters, only acquires artistic authenticity in the dramatic lyricism of *Faust,* which suffers under no constraints of real-life motivation, nor is set about with commonplace detail...

Faust talks of his people, of his free land. And we see no throng of collaborators around him—Faust is alone. Beside him stands the scornful Mephistopheles and the loathsome lemurs, who are digging his grave... Yet the great lines of Faust's lyrical monologue inspire the reader, enabling him to rise above the *transient* irony of the situation in which a lonely, blind old man is standing on the edge of his own grave and dreaming of the victories of the free labour of free people.

> *Ja! diesem Sinne bin ich ganz ergeben,*
> *Das ist der Weisheit letzter Schluß;*
> *Nur der verdient sich Freiheit wie das Leben,*
> *Der täglich sie erobern muß!*
> *Und so verbringt, umrungen von Gefahr,*
> *Hier Kindheit, Mann und Greis sein tüchtig Jahr.*
> *Solch ein Gewimmel möcht ich sehn,*
> *Auf freiem Grund mit freiem Volke stehen!*
> *Zum Augenblicke dürft ich sagen:*
> *"Verweile doch, du bist so schön!*

*Es kann die Spur von meinen Erdetagen
Nicht in Äonen untergehn."
Im Vorgefühl von solchem hohen Glück
Genieß ich jetzt den höchsten Augenblick.* *

Lothario, Odoard, the abbot and other members of the Gesellschaft in the *Wanderjahre* are unable, in the context of the real, commonplace circumstances of backward, disunited feudal Germany, to give such expression to their ideals and hopes. And the author of the novel does not attempt to make their case for them.

In contrast to Goethe Gogol was deeply aware of the lyrical element in his narrative, and it was thus that he declared it a *poema,* rather than novel. The authorial lyrical digressions, as well as the lyrically inspired descriptions of nature, which metaphorically suggest the possible destinies of people, convey to the reader not in didactic admonition, but with all the power of artistic conviction the humanistic message of Gogol's utopia.

In his letters referring to his work on *Dead Souls* Gogol constantly stresses what he calls the "lyrical allusions" in its text. "You must not be alarmed even at your first impression that the exultation in many passages seemed to be excessive to the point of comedy," he writes, for example, to Sergei Aksakov after the publication of *Dead Souls,* Volume 1. "This is quite true, because the full meaning of the lyrical allusions will only be apparent after the last part has come out" (XII, 93; letter of August 6, 1842).

The poetry of the unbounded expanses of Russia in the "lyrical allusions" of *Dead Souls* goes hand in hand with the author's poetic adulation of the mighty powers latent

---

* Yes, to this thought I hold with firm persistence;
The last result of wisdom stamps it true:
He only earns his freedom and existence,
Who daily conquers them anew.
Thus here, by dangers girt, shall glide away
Of childhood, manhood, age, the vigorous day:
And such a throng I fain would see,—
Stand on free soil among a people free!
Then dared I hail the Moment fleeing:
"Ah, still delay—thou art so fair!"
The traces cannot, of mine earthly being,
In aeons perish,—they are there!—
In proud fore-feeling of such lofty bliss,
I now enjoy the highest Moment—this!

in the Russian national character. Thus, when indicating to the reader in Volume 1 how the horizons of the work are to be extended in its subsequent parts, Gogol deliberately isolates even in this as yet unrealised project its *lyrical* element. "The reader has already seen how the first purchases have been made; he has yet to see what successes and failures will befall the hero, how he is to resolve and overcome the most difficult hurdles on his path, what immense images will appear before him, how the secret levers of the expansive tale will move, how its horizon will recede further into the distance, and how it will all acquire a *magnificent lyrical flow*" (VI, 241; my italics.— A.Y.).

In this sense, paradoxical though it may seem, *Dead Souls* is closer with its lyrical pathos to *Faust* than to the *Wilhelm Meister* cycle, in that it is a poetic utopia, devoted to the quest for man's true designation and his worthy role in life.

A comparison of *Dead Souls* and *Wilhelm Meisters Lehrjahre* and *Wanderjahre* shows that for all the difference between the particular historical circumstances around the creation of these works and between the creative manner of their respective authors, they do still have something in common in the problems they treat and in the difficulties experienced by their authors in their endeavour to carry out their designs.

Goethe's utopia and Gogol's utopia are both ultimately derived from Enlightenment humanism with its view of the fundamentally noble character of "unspoilt" human nature, of the immense value of learning in the "school of life" and of the great potential of human passions and talents, which can, depending on circumstances, be directed towards either good or evil.

This common heritage of Enlightenment humanism was enriched and rendered more sophisticated in the work of both writers through, on the one hand, the experience of world history, and, on the other, the special national, social and individual features of their respective talents.

Both Goethe and Gogol extend the problem of the education or re-education of individuals as the problem of popular destinies.

With Goethe this process of "extension" is quite manifest, and can be traced from the *Lehrjahre,* which initially focuses on the gradual formation of the social awareness of a young citizen (a sort of "anti-Werther"), through to the *Wanderjahre*, which culminates with grandiose plans for a world "Gesellschaft" of free and active people, each of whom is to seek out that which is purposeful "not in the outward circumstances, but in himself". [20]

With Gogol the utopian dream of the "illumination" or moral transformation of social relations in Russia, which first appears in *Dead Souls*, Volume 1, informs all the lyrical digressions in the book, and the poetic force and conviction of these digressions are largely due to the just and patriotic ideals of its creator. Belinsky, who so mercilessly condemned *Selected Passages from Correspondence with My Friends* for its author's capitulation to tyranny, Orthodoxy and serfdom, correctly apprehended the utopian theme in the form of lyrical allusions to a possible future of the country and the people, as it is expressed in *Dead Souls*, Volume 1. "The pathos of the work," writes Belinsky, "consists in the contradiction of the social forms of Russian life with its profound substantial element, hitherto mysterious and unrevealed to our awareness and thus eluding any attempt at definition." [21]

We may note these characteristic epithets—"mysterious" and "elusive"! They provide still further evidence of the problems faced by Gogol when he undertook in the continuation of *Dead Souls* to grasp the "elusive", to divine the "mysterious" and to express it in the language of living images.

We already know how frequently and radically Goethe altered both the course of his narrative and the concrete embodiments of his utopian ideal in the *Wilhelm Meister* novels, casting aside one situation after another, before they had had time to find artistic form, changing his heroes' designs and plans... We have also seen how he filled in the gaps in the development of his narrative with extensive didactic passages (particularly in the *Wanderjahre*) or simply left the reader to fill the gaps himself. A far more balanced artist than Gogol, and afflicted with none of the latter's agonizing doubts about his own responsibility to society, Goethe quite calmly admitted that his *Wilhelm Meister* novels are difficult to understand, and even confessed to Eckermann that he was himself unable to identify their "central point". He was well aware of the incongruity between the philosophical content and artistic embodiment of the Wilhelm Meister cycle, and was calmly, even amusedly, reconciled to this.

For Gogol such incongruity would have been the source of an insuperable artistic tragedy.

He was quite unable to resort to the sort of pure didactic transitions and summaries that Goethe so blithely employs in the *Wanderjahre*. This would have run counter to his nature as an artist; while the profound disaster of *Selected Passages* only served to strengthen his conviction that he must speak to the people in the living language of images and feelings and not in didactic homilies. However agonizing the creative crisis suffered by Gogol in the last years of his life, the artist within him lived to the very end.

"My images will not live if I do not create them from our own material, from our land, so that every one of us can feel that they are drawn from his own body" (XIII, 224). This idea, expressed in a variety of forms, constantly appears in his letters. In a letter to Sergei Aksakov, discussing Konstantin Aksakov's patriotic play set in the most troubled times of Russian history, Gogol admits that it "grasps the *supreme property* of our people—and this is its greatest merit!" But he at once adds: "Its shortcoming is that the people are not shown in any other aspect than this supreme property, they do not have our sinful body, they are disembodied." He goes on to explain his views: a dramatist (and any artist in general, we may add) "needs a *palpable, plastic* creation and nothing less. This cannot be replaced by anything" (XIV, 79).

It is remarkable that Gogol, who was so intolerant of criticism towards the end of his life, still heeded the comments of his listeners when reading Volume 2 of *Dead Souls*, concerning the flat and schematic nature of the book's positive figures (such as Tentetnikov's idealized preceptor, Alexander Petrovich, or Ulenka). "...I will breathe life into him later", [22] "...She will appear in stronger relief in the later chapters", [23] Gogol promised. "I am not at all content myself; much needs to be added for the characters to acquire more stature." [24]

Goethe's utopian creation also lacked this "*palpable, plastic*" body, as we have already seen. But he was able to reconcile himself with this lack because his *Wilhelm Meister* novels, although not fitting entirely within the aesthetic framework of "Weimar classicism", still stood in a direct line of descendance from this movement. The slightly archaic, classical abstraction of his images could therefore have seemed natural to Goethe.

Dead Souls was created within an altogether different tradition. Gogol, to quote Gukovsky, was one of those writers who "derive their realistic conceptions of art from their own Romantic experience". [25] The utopian motifs of Gogol's realist *poema* were preceded by the fairy-tale utopia of *Village Evenings Near Dikanka* and the more severe, but equally poetic utopia of the Cossack *volnitsa* in *Taras Bulba.* The folkloric imagery which Gogol employs so extensively in these early works can also be felt in *Dead Souls,* in the lyrical digressions of Volume 1, and does not contradict the realism of the work, but serves rather to raise it to an epic grandeur. Admittedly it was impossible by this method to attain the artistic objective which Gogol set himself in *Dead Souls,* Volume 2: the métier of folk poetry could not provide a key to the moral transformation of the vulgar "acquirers" and "loafers", like Chichikov, Khlobuyev, Tentetnikov or Platonov... Here Gogol's utopian design proved to be artistically quite unrealizable. But the "lyrical allusions"—the digressions, in which, counter to the surrounding vulgarity which the author has just been describing, the reader is shown the fine and heroic world of the author's own consciousness, the national spirit of the Russian people, and the magnificence of the immense expanses of the Russian land— these lyrical digressions convey in their own way Gogol's humanistic utopia with true artistic conviction.

Alexander Herzen made an apt observation to this effect in his diary. "Gogol's *Dead Souls,*" he wrote, "is a remarkable book, a bitter reproach to modern Russia, but not a hopeless one. Wherever the eye can penetrate the fog of impure dung-fumes it will see a spirited and powerful nationality. His portraits are remarkably fine, life has been preserved in all its fullness, his characters are not abstract types, but good people, the like of whom each of us has seen a hundred times. It is as sad in Chichikov's world as it is in our own reality, and in both worlds the only comfort is in faith and hope in the future. But this faith cannot be denied, and it is no mere Romantic aspiration *ins Blaue,* but has a realistic basis: the blood somehow circulates well in the Russian breast." [26]

Balzac's social utopian novels *Le Médecin de campagne*
and *Le Curé de village* are not amongst his more popular
works. Balzac the historian, critic and judge of French society, the author of realistic studies of manners and characters, the master of fine and penetrating socio-psychological
analysis, far outshadowed, in the mind of his contemporaries and successors, Balzac the utopian dreamer.

Although certain French critics have made special studies of these novels such analysis is of a primarily textolog-
ical character. [27] Soviet scholars have accorded them comparatively scant attention, noting with some chagrin that
in his utopian works Balzac did not transcend the bounds
of bourgeois society. An exception is the view of Anatoly
Lunacharsky, who expressed the highest opinion of Balzac's
Médecin de campagne, hailing it as a "work of genius".

Analysis of Balzac's realism above all as *critical* realism all too often ignored or simply took for granted the
profound and remarkable tender love of this great satirist
and sceptic for his native land. Throughout *La Comédie
humaine* this love can be sensed between the lines, and with
it the remarkably intimate knowledge, which it inspired, of
all the details of the soil, climate, relief, village and urban
landscapes—in short, of everything which together makes
up the changeable and beautiful face of France, from Bre-
tagne to Languedoc. But nowhere is this love expressed so
intensely and with such fervour as in *Le Médecin de campagne* and *Le Curé de village*, where it forms the powerful
lyrical leitmotif of the narrative and at the same time almost its main motivating force.

"La douce"—the term of endearment for France he takes
from *La Chanson de Roland*—determines the emotional tone
of both novels. Perhaps in no other book did the French
landscape occupy so much space or play such an important
role as it does here. The appearance of the craggy ravines
and valleys of Le Dauphiné in *Le Médecin de campagne*,
the massive, desolate valleys of Limousin in *Le Curé de
village* are described with scrupulous care, with the hand
of an artist who was keenly aware of both the poetic and,
we might say, the hidden philosophical import of each picturesque detail.

Gogol, as we may recall, dreamt of writing, at the same
time as the last volumes of *Dead Souls* or after their com-

pletion, a living geography of Russia—a geography which would at the same time be inseparable from the history of its people, "with all the variety of detail which distinguishes its branches and clans" (XIV, 280).* "What we need," he wrote in the same official note, "is a living, not a dead portrayal of Russia ... a vivid, speaking geography of the country, drawn in a strong and living style... Such a book (so it always seemed to me) could only be composed by a writer who was able correctly to apprehend and to project powerfully and in true relief the features and properties of the people, and to be able to portray any *locality* with all its colour so vividly that it would remain for ever in our mind's eye ... that the entire country from edge to edge, with all the variety of its regions, the various features of its mountain ranges and soils would imprint itself as something living on even the memory of a little child..." (XIV, 280).

It is just such a living "speaking geography" that we find in these two novels by Balzac. The life of the land and the destiny of the people who work it are presented in an inviolable unity and, which is of great importance to an understanding of Balzac's utopian vision, in all their movement, transformation and development.

In *Le Curé de village* the reader, through the eyes of Captain Génestas, the eccentric new-arrival, for the first time sees before him the *results* of this movement and transformation.

The very first pages of the novel are imbued with a radiant, joyous lyricism. Génestas here approaches the goal of his journey, a village lost in the mountains, where Dr. Bénassis has been working with great self-sacrifice for many years. The mountain landscape breathes the fresh fragrance of flowering shrubs and young deciduous shoots, and is enlivened by the noise of waterfalls. "Quelques nuages courraient parmi les rochers en en voilant, en en découvrant tour à tour les cimes grisâtres, souvent aussi vapoureuses que les nuées dont les moelleux flocons s'y déchiraient. À tout moment le pays changeait d'aspect et le ciel de lumière; les montagnes changeaient de couleur, les versants de nuances, les vallons de forme; images multipliées que des

* An official note, dating from July 10-18, 1850, which Gogol sent to A. O. Smirnova to be passed on to L. A. Petrovsky, P. A. Shirinsky-Shikhmatov or A. F. Orlov.

oppositions inattendues, soit un rayon de soleil à travers les troncs d'arbres, soit une clairière naturelle ou quelques éboulis, rendaient délicieuses à voir au milieu de silence, dans la maison où tout est jeune, où le soleil enflamme un ciel pur. Enfin c'était un beau pays, c'était la France!" *

But this is still just a lyrical introduction, setting the predominantly major key of the novel. The essence of the action is indicated a few pages later through the dramatic contrast of two villages, an old and a new, as perceived by Captain Génestas.

Of the old village, situated on low ground, in the shade of a mountain slope, there remain only a few abandoned huts, without windows or doors and with dilapidated roofs. The last inhabitant of this doomed spot lies dying in one of the huts—and he is a monstrous old man and cretin, "cette masse de chair," with a flattened head and eyes "semblables à ceux d'un poisson cuit". When he enters this hut in search of Dr. Bénassis Génestas is struck by the scene of appalling poverty.

This is the village community's past. The death of the old cretin as it were symbolizes the final leave taking with the last relics of this gloomy, wretched and utterly futile life. Earlier in his search for Bénassis the captain had travelled through the new village, down a broad street, past solidly-built houses. Here all the signs are of a life of plenty, and cheerful, purposeful toil.

Later on Bénassis himself recounts to the visitor the story of the transformations which so strikingly altered the face of this quiet corner of France. As a doctor he had started his work by attending to the health of the inhabitants of his region, but he soon realized that medicine was powerless unless the conditions in which they lived were to be changed first. The unfortunate situation of the village and the slothful existence of its inhabitants had resulted in widespread cretinism. The village lies in a hollow "sans courant d'air, pres du torrent dont l'eau provient des neiges fondues, privé des bienfaits du soleil, ... tout y favorise la

* Bernard Guyon casually dismisses this final sentence as "l'exclamation banale, mais naïvement enthousiaste" (Bernard Guyon, *La création littéraire chez Balzac. La génèse du 'Médecin de campagne'*, p. 67). This comment is unjust—it is due to an underestimation of Balzac's profound love for his native land and its people.

propagation de cette affreuse maladie". Taking decisive steps Bénassis first secures his appointment as mayor of the canton and saves the village community from the degeneration and eventual extinction with which it is threatened. He has the majority of the cretins moved, finds a new, healthier site for the village and persuades the villagers to move into the new houses that have been built for them. Further triumphs follow on the heels of this first one: Bénassis digs irrigational canals, creating excellent pastures, lays roads which facilitate trade with Grenoble, encourages local industry, which had been unheard of before... During the ten years that he has been patiently working to "améliorer ce coin de terre encore inculte et de civiliser ses habitants jusqu'alors depourvus d'intelligence", the village has started to grow wheat in the virgin fields and the wheat loaf has taken its place on every table. On the hilly slopes, unsuitable for ploughing, vineyards have been planted. Excellent, pedigree herds of cows and flocks of sheep have been reared in the new farm buildings, with proper drainage and feeding apparatus.

The methods applied by Bénassis would of course have been condemned by Gogol. The village doctor is delighted to have brought this corner of France into civilization, to have created "des nécessités nouvelles, inconnues jusqu'alors à ces pauvres gens. Le besoin engendrait l'industrie, l'industrie le commerce, le commerce un gain, le gain un bien-être, el la bien-être des idées utiles". [28]

The author of *Dead Souls*, Volume 2 would have regarded this formula for progress as devil-inspired: "O Creator! How fair is Thy world, where in remote, rural seclusion, it lies apart from the towns and nasty highways" (VII, 21). If he does admit any incipient industry it is only in the form of Kostanzhoglo's "legitimate factories" ("every year another factory would appear, depending on what remains and refuse had been accumulated"), "and none of these needs that have so debilitated modern people" (VII, 68-69).

From a sober economic point of view both Gogol's patriarchal, serf-exploiting utopia and Balzac's patriarchal, bourgeois utopia are equally inconsistent, fraught with compromise and implausible. But from the point of view of literary history the artist's dream reflected in these utopias of an unprecedented awakening and transformation of the land, of the souls of the people, should not on any account be dismissed with scorn, as it is worthy of admiration and merits closer study.

We are told by Génestas about the joy Bénassis was to experience as he saw nature answering to his attention and labours. With Gogol Kostanzhoglo himself, a jaundiced, prosaic and taciturn man of action, makes repeated use of the "gratification" he receives from his enterprise. "And that, not because his wealth is increasing—money is only money—but because he feels that everything is the work of his own hands, and he has been the cause of everything, its creator, and that from him, as from a magician, there has flowed bounty and goodness for all. In what other calling will you find such gratification?.. In all the world you will find no such gratification as this, for herein man emulates God, the God who took upon himself the task of creation, as the highest form of gratification, and he requires of man that he too should act as the creator of prosperity around him" (VII, 73).

The poetry of creative, "Godlike" endeavour, transforming the land for the good of people—this is what both these utopian writers seek to express through their various images. But it is precisely here, in their hymn to toil, that we find the most vulnerable place of their utopian visions—vulnerable not only from the speculative, theoretical point of view, but also from that of artistic merit.

However great Bénassis's zeal and energy, or Kostanzhoglo's businesslike efficiency, their triumphs are sustained by the toil of the people, an unfree and muted toil. By the people we mean those French peasants who sweated together on Sundays to build the road to Grenoble and planted poplars down either side of it, and those Russian muzhiks who raised protective forest strips on Kostanzhoglo's fields—and in both Balzac's and Gogol's versions of utopia it is these people who have no words for themselves. We do, admittedly, read that in Kostanzhoglo's village one might meet peasants with "intelligent look on their faces" (VII, 58). And that is all. All that we hear is the voice of a serf from a neighbouring, poverty-stricken village, who is dispatched by the village to ask Kostanzhoglo to buy them.

The more talkative peasants of Balzac's *Le Médecin de campagne* heap praises on their "good M. Bénassis", but merely carry out his projects with greater or lesser resistance. And Bénassis himself, recalling that "je crois avoir assez prouvé mon attachement à la classe pauvre et souffrante, ... tout en l'admirant dans la voie laborieuse où elle chemine, sublime de patience et de résignation," nevertheless insists that these people are "les mineurs d'une nation, et doivent toujours rester en tutelle". [29]

But how are all these others who are still mute, but no less important—how are they to be brought together with those who hold them "en tutelle" and exploit them, by right of their wealth and power? How to overcome this egoistic fragmentation of society and inspire all with a common goal? These questions disturbed Balzac as deeply as they did Gogol, and in their search the writers follow two distinct paths. One of these is that of egoism, or individualism, as a powerful factor, but turned to serve the common good. This is the reason for the detailed calculations of profits and income given both by Bénassis and Kostanzhoglo (whose peasants, in Gogol's words, "as it says in the song, 'pick up silver by the shovelful'"—VII, 58). It also gives rise to the utopian idea—which by remarkable coincidence is expressed by both writers—that to attain "honest" wealth is really no more difficult than to grow rich through roguery. The work is the same, insists Bénassis, "si les coquins voulaient se bien conduire, ils seraient millionaires au lieu d'être pendus, voilà tout." "You will be amazed to find how many ways we have for an enterprising mind to grow rich, and benefiting both himself and others," Gogol admonishes his friend Prokopovich (XII, 189). In *Dead Souls,* Volume 2 he creates the image of the philanthropic government contractor millionaire Murazov, whose entire fortune has been acquired "in the most irreproachable fashion and by the most just means" (VII, 75).

But even when Gogol is scaling the heights of rhetoric in the defence of this notion, so vital to his utopia, of the possibility of honest enrichment, he cannot resist introducing a note of satire and thereby exposes more graphically than any critic could the falsity of the impassioned bombast in praise of his imagined ideal. Pavel Ivanovich Chichikov is affixed to the exemplary Kostanzhoglo as his most deferential, but at the same time debunking, buffooning alter ego, and the ironic effect of this contrast becomes quite devastating. Kostanzhoglo grows heated, as he exposes the "Don Quixotes of enlightenment", who fail to understand the true needs of the people; but "Chichikov's mind is not on enlightenment. He wanted to question Kostanzhoglo closely on how any old rubbish could be turned to profit; but the latter would not let him get a word in edgeways" (VII, 68). In a flight of uncharacteristic lyrical rapture Kostanzhoglo becomes quite transformed as he lauds his own industry; Gogol selects a bold and uplifting comparison to convey all the significance of this moment: "He positively radiated, like a king on the solemn day of his coronation, and rays of brilliance seems to shine from his very face". But we have only to follow the writer and turn our eyes to Chichikov, and the abrupt change from stilted dithyramb to commonplace, unfeigned vulgarity, returns us with a thump from utopia to reality: "Kostanzhoglo's mellifluous periods fell upon Chichikov's ear like the notes of a bird of paradise. His mouth ran with saliva. His eyes misted over and were themselves the very expression of sweetness, of the pleasure it gave him to listen" (VII, 73).

Objectively Chichikov is presented to us here as an evil parody of Kostanzhoglo. On the one hand Gogol deliberately tries to minimize the distance between these characters, to establish some sort of spiritual kinship between them (perhaps in the utopian hope of preparing the ground for Chichikov's "resurrection", which looms dimly in the distant future). Kostanzhoglo—an astute operator, who understands people—is pleased with his guest ("moderate in his words and no fool," he thinks, and becomes "all the jollier ... as if rejoicing at having found a man who knew how to listen to wise counsel"—VII, 73). He even lends him money to buy Khlobuyev's ruined estate. On the other hand, Gogol the satirist does not let slip the opportunity to initiate the readers to Chichikov's secret designs, which elude the complacent Kostanzhoglo: in the mind of his "moderate" guest, whose very face seems to be ennobled by the thought of "legitimate" acquisition, a "strange thought" is stirring, occurring to him suddenly as of itself: "What a roguish thought! The scamp!" Why not, he wonders, mortgage the estate together with his dead souls? "Perhaps he could even give Kostanzhoglo the slip, without paying him back?" (VII, 89).

Such is Gogol's method. But with Balzac's utopian community, led by the wisdom and will-power of Dr. Bénassis, there would seem to be no room for such "roguish" thoughts. Yet the soil is ready for them, and the inconspicuous usurer Taboureau has already quietly insinuated himself into the community, lending grain to all the needy farmers in the département. His story, which is briefly related with bitterness by Dr. Bénassis, leaves absolutely no hope for any moral reformation of this rascal, who "might well amass a million if nothing stops him".

Thus, for all the two writers' shared desire to find a bridge leading from unjust profiteering to the honest accumulation of wealth, their own sense of reality and knowledge of life prevents them bringing this fragile project to its conclusion. At the same time Gogol's consciously satirical rejection of the mooted "idyllic" volte-face in the movement of the plot is expressed with an abruptness that has no analogue in Balzac's social utopia.

But there still remains one possible path to the improvement of society—by endeavouring to identify in the recent and distant past those inspiring, unifying principles of life which might help suppress selfish egoism in the name of the common weal. This is where, in particular, the theme of Napoleon comes in, a theme that at first glance appears to occupy an unwarranted importance in *Le Médecin de campagne.*

This novel, written in the first years of the July monarchy, is full (as is the later *Curé de village*) of unconcealed hostility for the France of the "citizen king" Louis Philippe. But whilst contrasting the heroic epoch of the Napoleonic wars to the hegemony of tradesmen and bankers, Balzac employs the tact of a true artist by using not the official version of Bonapartism, but according prominence to the popular legend of a fictitious, but inspiring Napoleon—friend of the people, protector of France, lord of the world, shamefully betrayed by the Parisians, who "ont peur pour leur peau de deux liards et pour leurs boutiques de deux sous", and refused to follow his guiding star. In this legend, which in Balzac's book is recounted at a village gathering by the old retainer Hagla (who becomes a postman in Bénassis's community), Napoleon is immortal, and the news of his death is a malicious slander by the enemies of France.

The popular imagination forgives, forgets and smoothes over everything that might tarnish the image of "le père du peuple et du soldat"—i.e., his betrayal of the legacy of the French Revolution, his predatory, aggressive politics, for which France paid so dearly with her own blood, even his scandalous flight in panic from his army on their retreat from Russia.

Balzac also seeks support in time-hallowed, patriarchal

traditions, in the customs and rites of the people. He inserts in his novel a detailed scene of the funeral rites performed over the body of a wealthy peasant. All those present, the deceased's heirs and his hired labourers, form a sort of extended family, united by this wake. Bénassis prefaces this account with his own reflections. "J'avoue qu'après avoir passé par des jours d'incrédulité moqueuse, j'ai compris ici la valeur des cérémonies religieuses, celle des solennités de famille, l'importance des usages et des fêtes du foyer domestique." [30] He speaks with admiration of the patriarchal peasant families, in which "l'autorité du père est illimitée, sa parole est souveraine, il mange seul assis au haut bout de la table, sa femme et ses enfants le servent, ceux qui l'entourent ne lui parle point sans employer certaines formules respectueuses, devant lui chacun se tient debout et découvert... Ses usages constituent à mon sens une noble éducation". [31] It is but a small step from here to an appeal to religion, viewed as the one force capable of reinforcing these patriarchal foundations, and fusing together a society which threatens to fall apart.

If *Le Médecin de campagne* was still primarily a "secular" novel—the implementation of Dr. Bénassis's philanthropic designs initially even meets the opposition of the church and he has to instigate the replacement of the former curé, who thundered in his sermons against the godless innovations of the foreign reformer, in *Le Curé de village* the religious theme becomes dominant in realizing Balzac's social utopian dream.

In his search for the right substance which must be given to the sacred rallying call "Forward!" in order that it may at once rally and uplift all the people, Gogol follows Balzac in turning to patriotism. The idea of patriotism is predominantly expressed in *Dead Souls*, Volume 1, as we have noted above, in the lyrical rapture of his authorial digressions about the greatness of his country and the special destiny of its people. In Volume 2 this theme is joined by new motifs. Insofar as we can judge from the memoirs of Lev Arnoldi (A.O. Smirnova's brother), who heard Gogol read the non-extant chapters, Chichikov's apparent slip of the tongue, when in chapter 2 he confides to General Betrishchev that Tentetnikov is supposedly writing the "history of the generals" who took part in the 1812 campaign, was intended to have serious consequences later on. As Arnoldi recalls, the theme of popular patriotism in the 1812 war had a central role in the description of the dinner given by Betrishchev for Chichikov and Tentetnikov. Tentetnikov replies to a question from the general that, to his mind, what is important is not the history of the 1812 campaign, of the individual battles and personalities: "...This epoch should be viewed from a different aspect; it was important, in his opinion, that the entire nation stood up as one man in the defence of their country; all selfish thoughts, passions and intrigues were forgotten; the most important thing was that all classes of population were to unite in their feeling of love for their country; that every one of them hastened to surrender his very last possession in his willingness to sacrifice everything to the salvation of society... Tentetnikov was quite carried away, he became utterly absorbed at this moment by his love for Russia. Betrishchev listened to him in rapture... The general was a wonder to behold; but what about Ulenka? Her eyes beheld Tentetnikov with rapt attention, she appeared to hang eagerly on his every word, and became intoxicated by his speeches as if by music, she loved him, she was proud of him."

According to Arnoldi again, the description of this dinner "was the best passage in Volume 2". [32]

Gogol was here on firmer historical ground than Balzac with his legend about Le Napoléon du Peuple. His definition of the 1812 war as a war of the people was accurate and profound: here, as in many other respects, Gogol anticipated the thinking of Lev Tolstoy. But Gogol's sense of realism persuades him to introduce even into this scene, which appears so full of sincere patriotic feeling, uniting Tentetnikov and his listeners, a caustic satirical dissonance: Chichikov interrupts the anxious silence of his friends, wishing to "put in a word of his own... 'Yes,' he said, 'there were terrible frosts in 1812!' 'It's not the frosts we were thinking of,' observed the general, giving him a severe look. Chichikov was covered with confusion." Arnoldi published his memoirs some eleven years after he had heard Gogol reading this chapter (in the summer of 1849). Nevertheless, they do seem to convey Gogol's thoughts and intonation, and this final ironic stroke is particularly characteristic of Gogol's style. The complacent vulgarity of Chichikov's despicable acquisitive instincts here attempts to attach itself to the speaker's surge of patriotism, tarnishing and rendering it sordid. It had proved impossible in the real conditions of his Russia to implement the patriotic ideal of "comradeship", so vividly portrayed in the Romantic images of *Taras Bulba*, even with the support of the heroic memories of Russia's Patriotic War of 1812.

Gogol also attempts to introduce into *Dead Souls*, Volume 2 echoes of the Romantic world of carefree village life, which he had depicted with such spontaneous ease and audacity in the collection *Village Evenings Near Dikanka*. He draws on the ingenuous poetry of folk song and dance, as if wishing to recall to his heroes their true commonalty with the people, with the Russian soil, to which they all belong by their birth right, irrespective of their differences in class and wealth.

Thus we find, for example, a lyrical scene of festivity by the river "on this remarkable spring evening", which comes in striking emotional contrast to the grotesque description of Petukh's monstrous hospitality in chapter 3: "The oarsmen, plying their four and twenty oars in unison, suddenly raised them aloft and the boat glided like a swift bird over the glassy surface of the water. The chorus leader, a well-built young lad sitting third from the stern, raised the opening staves of a song in a clear, ringing voice, bringing forth the melody as if from the throat of a nightingale, the next five oarsmen took up the song, and the last six joined in descant until the song filled the air, as infinite as Russia herself. Even Petukh, visibly moved, lent his lusty voice where he thought the choir lacked strength, and Chichikov himself felt conscious that he was a Russian" (VII, 55).

But this lyrical exaltation, briefly inspired by folk song, is abruptly dampened by the inevitable note of irony. The author himself shatters his fragile illusion of spiritual union. On their way back Petukh can only think about "how he is to feed his guests". His offspring dream about the flesh-pots of the capital, where they will squander the remnants of their father's fortune. "Most lively of all was Chichikov. 'To be sure I shall have my own little village in time!' And before his mind's eye there arose a comely wife, and a brood of little Chichikovs" (VII, 55). While the eternally bored, totally indifferent Platonov only yawns: indeed from the very beginning he was thinking, "What is there so splendid in these doleful songs? They only increase one's depression of spirits" (VII, 55).

The writer Ivan Turgenev, a great admirer of Gogol's talent, was in raptures over this scene of evening festivities on the river, as he was over many passages from *Dead Souls*, Volume 2, which he had read in manuscript. But he was quite unable to accept another episode, similar in spirit and mood: the portrayal of the festivities at Tentetnikov's estate, where "when evening fell, they would sing and cavort merrily in spring round dances", and where Chichikov's coachman Selifan is presented in quite a different light from that in which we see him in Volume 1, no longer the permanently inebriated, cloddish servant who dully responds to his master's dire threats thus: "Beat me if you must. Why shouldn't you beat me..." (VI, 271), but as a poet and dreamer in spirit, whose very dreams are inspired by his stirring impressions of the festive side of country life. "When, taking maidens' white hands in his own, he moved slowly with them all in the round dance, or formed a line with the other lads opposite them, and the loud-voiced maidens chimed out with laughter: 'Boyars, show us the bridegroom!' while the evening was suddenly shrouded in darkness, and the faint plaintive echoes of the song floated back from far beyond the river—our Selifan scarcely knew if he was waking or dreaming" (VII, 32).

In vain did Annenkov assure Turgenev that, from the point of view of authenticity, there was nothing at fault with this episode: and why indeed should Selifan not lead round dances, why should he not dream about fair country maidens?.. Turgenev stood his ground regarding the whole of this episode as artistically spurious.

Gogol's intentions in this scene are quite understandable: he did not wish only to resurrect the "dead souls" of his landowners into a new life, but also to show the reformation of serfs, who must also, after all, embody the true Russian spirit and daring. But what was both harmonious and probable in the semi-fabulous world of *Village Evenings*—a world which, save a few isolated allusions, is almost completely abstracted from the real life of the enslaved Ukrainian peasantry—does not fit in with the satirical realism of *Dead Souls*. The joyous mood, intermingled with a pensive sadness, which is so natural at the end of *Sorochintsy Fair* or *May Night,* does not suit the prosaic and vulgar figure of Selifan, such as the reader already knows him; it is similarly impossible to imagine the bold and spirited lads from *Village Evenings*—say Levko or Gritsko—engaged in service to Chichikov. This is why Selifan's round dances and dreams seem so forced and stylized, although we can feel how hard Gogol was trying in this passage to elevate the existence of the Russian serf to the level of poetry. But even he was unable here to suppress his satirical instincts. If we are to believe Arnoldi, in one of the chapters of Volume 2 which have not survived, Chichikov's servant is described in the most prosaic way, entirely in the spirit of Volume 1: "In Tentetnikov's village Selifan became quite changed, he drank himself into a stupor and was not at all like a coachman." [33]

By comparison with the author of *Dead Souls* (insofar as we can judge about Volume 2 from the surviving fragments) Balzac the utopian dreamer appears far more assured both in *Le Médecin de campagne* and *Le Curé de village* in his utopian constructs and formulae. His zealous reformers—Bénassis, Véronique Graslin and her confessor, the village priest Bonnet, are consistently portrayed in a single, emotionally uplifted tone; Bénassis's conflicts with the people are shifted into the past. For this work Balzac did not make recourse to his close *knowledge* of the economic and social plight of the French peasantry and his profound and exact *analysis* of its inner class stratification and hostility to the upper, landed classes, preserving these in their entirety for his book *Les Paysans* (characteristically taking as the heading for the first part of this novel, the only part to be published in the author's lifetime, in 1844, the dictum: "Qui terre a, guerre a").

Gogol the utopian writer, however much he might at times deviate from satire in his words, nevertheless always remains a satirist even in *Dead Souls,* Volume 2. Testing through satire his "true-Russian" ideal the writer constantly undermines it. We have already observed this above in a number of examples, in which Chichikov's vulgarity, sometimes only conveyed by a single sentence, or by some "roguish" thought, at once shatters its uplifted context.

It would be apposite here to recall that, for all Gogol's close involvement in his last years with Slavophile circles, he never subscribed to the pretentious cult widespread amongst them of the superficial attributes of "ethnic" Russian life. We may judge from the biting irony with which Gogol comments on this subject in his letters and articles how little illusions he had on this score.

"True national quality consists not in the description of a *sarafan,* but in the very soul of the people. A poet can be national even when he is describing a completely foreign world, but viewing it with the eyes of his national element, the eyes of all the people" (VIII, 51). This remarkable definition, expressed by Gogol in his early article about Pushkin, which he himself dated to 1832 (included in the collection *Arabesques,* 1835), is repeated in some of his later pronouncements.

In a letter to S. P. Shevyryov from Rome, after hearing that Konstantin Aksakov had grown a beard, dressed peasant-fashion and so forth, Gogol dismisses all this quite simply as "idiocy" (XII, 537). In another letter to N. M. Yazykov about the activities of the Slavophiles participating in the journals *Moskvityanin* and *Moskovsky sbornik,* he ridicules those of them who imagine that "everything depends on a united strength and on some sort of pooling of resources. ... First develop your own resources... First educate yourself for the common cause, that you will really be able to talk about it coherently. As for them: they put on a kaftan and grow a beard, and imagine that they are thereby spreading the Russian spirit throughout Russia!" (XIII, 107, letter of October 5, 1846).

Even in *Selected Passages,* when he speaks of the as yet undiscovered, unrevealed secrets of the Russian people, sealed in the "inexplicable gay abandon" of their songs, in "the many-sided poetic fullness" of their imagination, in their very language with its remarkable variety, Gogol sharply opposes his ideal, which he would like to embody in art and in life—"our Russian Russia"—to that Russia, "which *we are coarsely shown* by some half-baked patriots..." (VIII, 408-409; my italics.—*A.Y.*).

This satirical sobriety, which stays with him in even the period of his most profound spiritual and creative crisis towards the end of his life, prevented him from concluding his work with an artificially optimistic construction, which would have been so easy to erect, had Gogol the realist wished to divorce himself from his own knowledge of people and life, and thus to renounce himself. His live characters refused to be accommodated within the frames set for them in the design he had mapped out. Chichikov, apparently already reformed by Kostanzhoglo's admonitions and having tasted the joys of "legitimate" acquisition, now embarks on new criminal adventures (forgery of Khlobuyev's "three-million-rouble aunt" Khanasarova's will) and encounters a disaster much worse than that which befalls him at the end of Volume 1. Locked up in a prison, under threat of the whip and Siberia, he listens in despair to the exhortations of the pious Murazov. But even in these moments of repentance the memory of his property, of his sacred box, will not leave his mind, and it is about these that he implores Murazov as he prostrates himself at the latter's feet. "*I will think about my soul,* only save me" (VII, 112; my italics.—*A.Y.*), he wails. "His entire person was shaken and softened" (VII, 115), we are assured by Gogol, who explains the transformation that has taken place in his hero with a bombastic and banal comparison with a sheet of platinum, the "hardest metal" of all. "In the unbearable heat of the furnace even the most stubborn metal glows white and turns to a liquid; thus too does the strongest man melt in the furnace of misfortune when intense and unbearable flame burns the hardened nature" (VII, 115).

But the logic of his own realistic image and the logic of the life this image embodies, militate against this forced rhetorical pathos. The most benevolent of rogues, Pavel Ivanovich Chichikov wastes no time in exploiting his "benefactor" Murazov. Even in his first repentant reflections after being put in solitary confinement Chichikov, who "seemed to have sensed something with a half-awakened effort of his soul", finds his mind turning relentlessly from thoughts about his duty, about honest labour, back to property and acquisition. "I could manage a household; I have the qualities of parsimony, mother wit and prudence, and even constancy." If only they would release him, he reflects, and give him back at least a part of his property... (VII, 115). But as soon as Chichikov's accomplice Samosvistov appears in his cell with the comforting news that everything is not yet lost, and Chichikov gets back his box, papers and money, this "strongest of men", to quote Gogol's comparison, begins to regret that he so quickly surrendered to contrition.

Here we can see with particular clarity how the conflict between Gogol the satirist and realist and Gogol the utopian idealist continues in Volume 2. He himself rejects the easy way out, the happy ending that would have been achieved with Chichikov's "conversion". Such a swift and convenient attainment of his utopian ideal would have run counter to reality and all its laws and would never have satisfied the demanding artist in Gogol.

In his social utopias Balzac adopts a different approach:

he as it were consciously demarcates from the rest of the world the area in which his experiment with people and nature will take place, and is careful not to admit any incursions into his narrative by irony, satire or critical scrutiny. All he asks of the reader is his faith. The writer in return refrains from including anything in his narrative that might upset this faith.

This is particularly true of *Le Curé de village,* in which the destinies of barren souls and arid lands are bound together, the two being miraculously resurrected to a new life.

Running through the entire novel is the analogy between Véronique Graslin—accomplice in a crime, who has kept concealed within her for many years, her terrible, shameful secret, which desiccated her inner nature—and the barren valleys of Limousin deprived of the water of the mountain springs by the chinks and cracks in the rock. When, after the death of her husband, she takes possession of an enormous, barren property around the Montégnac castle, Véronique travels round her new domain and seems to recognize herself in this harsh, desolate landscape. Struck by this image of desolation Véronique exclaims: "Il y a pourtant des âmes qui sont ainsi!"

All the same a miracle takes place: the Montégnac valley, irrigated by mountain waters which have been redirected along another course, is covered with "magnificent green meadows" and the wretched village, which has become a den of smugglers and thieves, is transformed into a thriving haven of peaceful toil. At the same time Véronique's own soul is reborn, after she has devoted her wealth, will-power and intelligence to the attainment of this grand objective.

In this respect the personal drama experienced by Véronique Graslin and from which she emerges victorious, is comparable with the regrettable past of Dr. Bénassis. Without being a criminal in the eyes of the law he is guilty of becoming so obsessed with his own glorification and vain concerns that he has destroyed the woman who sacrificed everything for him and only informed him on her death-bed about the existence of the infant son she has borne him. Resolving to devote himself to the upbringing of the child and withdrawing from the corrupt world Bénassis then meets, and falls in love with, a girl from a Jansenist family. Evelina becomes his fiancée. But, afraid of the strict moral code of her parents Bénassis lacks the courage to reveal to them his past. They themselves find out that he is the father of an illegitimate child and in their outrage break off the engagement. Bénassis's son dies soon after this. In his despair Bénassis hovers undecided between suicide and entering a monastery, but it is precisely within the walls of the Grand Chartreuse monastery that he realizes his true duty: to return to the world and put his mind and knowledge, his memories of the "agonizing joy of paternity" to the benefit of the entire region.

Religion, which Bénassis only appeals to as a useful ally, comes to play a dominant role in *Le Curé de village*. Véronique Graslin, her friends and helpers are mere instruments in the hands of the village priest Bonnet. Balzac introduces the curé into his novel as a modest, but, in the author's conception, extremely powerful figure. It is precisely Bonnet who is to perform the first of a series of moral "miracles"—the spiritual transformations documented in the book. Through the mighty power of religious conviction he is able to persuade the condemned double murderer Jean-François Tascheron to repent of his sins, something that the law-court, the jailers and the Bishop of Limoges together with his priests had all failed to do. Tascheron, who is Véronique Graslin's secret lover, had hoped to get his hands on the fortune of the old miser Pingret, and to use it to flee to America. But he is caught in the act and kills both the old man and his serving woman. In Balzac's imagination this young worker, who is consumed by despair and keeps his problems a secret, lest he compromise his beloved Véronique, emerges as a heroic figure, "a living sculpture of Prometheus". But this pagan pride succumbs to the admonitions of the village priest. Balzac chooses to pass over in silence the four-hour discussion during which Bonnet takes the condemned man's confession and gives him absolution. We only learn that Tascheron "died like a Christian".

He makes further "conversions" of this nature. Balzac, guided by his love for strong, energetic and sincere characters, singles Bonnet out from the general mass of the clergy. He even goes so far as to compare his village priest to "an artist who feels, and not an artist who passes judgement", or a poet.

Bonnet is to a certain extent the author's alter ego: Balzac imparts to this character his own talents as a reader of heart and a man of vision and bold endeavour; but he gives him also an additional, special power—the role of intercessor between God and his fallen, errant, but faithful flock. Bonnet it is who utters the proclamations which, taken by themselves, and out of their specifically *Catholic* context, seem very close to Gogol in his quest for the resurrection of "dead souls": "Nous sommes tous plus ou moins avancés vers notre entière régénération, personne n'est infaillible," he declares, *"tout est rachetable"* [34] (my italics.—*A.Y.*).

Indeed, this modest priest does succeed in re-fashioning the entire community. One of Bonnet's most striking victories is the "reformation" of Farrabesche. A former bandit, accomplice of a savage band, he is persuaded by Bonnet to give himself up to the police and into captivity; ten years later he returns from imprisonment to become an honest worker—a forester, taking as his abode the most forlorn corner of the forest on Véronique Graslin's Montégnac estate. The encounter with Farrabesche is one of the turning points in the story of Véronique's own moral resurrection. In the life of this recent criminal she as it were detects the prototype of her own existence and that of her condemned lover. Farrabesche's moral enlightenment awakens her own hope for redemption. But here too, as Balzac conceives of the story, the main role goes to Bonnet. It is he who appeals to Véronique to raise herself above the despair that is eating away her heart and to apply herself to philanthropic endeavours. Once he becomes her confessor and thus ascertains all her secrets he is able thenceforth to guide her in all things—but first and foremost in the implementation of his grand scheme to revitalize the desolate, arid wastes of the Montégnac region.

Yet another "wounded soul crying to be healed" comes to Véronique's aid. This is the young engineer Gérard, who after graduating from the École des Ponts et Chaussées moulders in the wretched job of "ingénieur ordinaire". A man of great talent and imagination Gérard is unable to express himself in his miserable job. Being one of those rare men who seek neither wealth, nor promotion, he yearns only to satisfy his noble desire to use his faculties for the benefit of his country. However, reduced to despair by the senseless bureaucracy of the state apparatus, he is on the point of embracing utopian socialism—"une des doctrines nouvelles qui paraissent devoir faire des changements importants à l'ordre social actuel, en dirigeant mieux les travailleurs. Que sommes—nous," (he refers to the young intelligentsia of France) "sinon des travailleurs sans ouvrage, des outils dans un magasin? Nous sommes organisés comme s'il s'agissait de remuer le globe, et nous n'avons rien à faire. Je sens en moi quelque chose de grand qui s'amoindrit, qui va périr." [35]

Gérard's confessional letter, which precedes his entry into the novel, is of crucial importance: it demonstrates how close Balzac comes at times to utopian socialism, to which he is drawn by his awareness that the political and social status quo is inimical to the development of productive forces, or at least inexcusably retards this development. The indifference of the July monarchy (which is the period in which the end of the novel is set) to the fate of young talented men like Gérard, is a particular example of the general disastrous state of affairs observed and condemned by Balzac. But the exigencies of the plot persuade him to bring about an abrupt volte-face in Gérard's career and to "disabuse" him of his socialist ideas. The church in the person of Bonnet and the church-inspired initiative of Véronique Graslin bring about, in conjunction with Gérard's knowledge and bold ideas, the transformation of the entire area, which has been so neglected by the administrators of bourgeois France.

Balzac the artist and humanist has to pay dearly for this appeal to religion, provoked by his idealist aim to construct the fundament of his utopia on it. The humanistic fervour of his design is in direct contradiction with that ascetic piety, so contrary to human nature, which imposes the heavy stamp of hagiography on the latter part of the novel. Even before this Bonnet had strictly restrained all these impulses of his spiritual daughter which strike him as being overworldly. When she finally traces Farrabesche's common-law wife and his illegitimate son in the slums of Paris, and reunites their family she is beside herself with joy, but her confessor spoils her happiness with his severe reproaches. Bonnet correctly surmises that Véronique has been secretly thinking of her own unrequited love while restoring the happiness of the ex-convict, and this angers Bonnet as inspiration from the Evil One. Bonnet succeeds in destroying every last trace of Véronique's erstwhile passionate and enchanting femininity before she dies. It is only through an incredible effort of will that she is able to retain the semblance of a living human being, moving, speaking, even sitting at table and entertaining guests—although she never joins in their feasts, but by now she is a mere "living corpse".

This apotheosis of religious self-chastisement can only repel the reader. The horrific details which are revealed in the hours before Véronique's death—the hair shirt, which has turned the whole of Véronique's body into one large sore, the clay pot, fit only to be used by a dog, in which she is secretly given her miserable food—all this is intended to impress us, but it rather evokes our indignation. Véronique's public confession and repentance, her last communion, which is administered to her by the archbishop himself, the supernatural transfiguration of the dying woman, and finally, yet another "miracle"—the sudden conversion to Catholicism of the atheistic doctor Roubaud, who is so moved by this scene—this is the conclusion of Véronique's biography, a suitable conclusion to the life of a saint. The novel ends with the victory of the Catholic Church; but, whilst glorifying the church Balzac inflicts such damage on his own utopia and casts a dark shadow over his humanistic ideal of the harmony and prosperity of people and nature.

In their portrayal of the mighty forces latent in the land and in the crippled souls of the people working this land, forces which are biding their time before emerging to a new flourishing, Balzac and Gogol follow paths that often converge. The appeal by both writers to religion as the only moral force capable of bringing their utopian ideal to life thus ceases to appear a mere individual aberration, but is rather an unfortunate but regular consequence of their respective beliefs. Both writers were loath to excite the revolutionary activity of the people, and hoped to accommodate their utopias within the existing status quo, and were thus drawn to religion as an ennobling source of illumination, a uniting, "bonding" force. There is something in common to both writers in the mystic elation, with which Gogol proclaims the exalted God-inspired mission of his *poema*, and which leads Balzac to declare *Le Médecin de campagne* "l'Evangelie en action", which is worth "plus que des lois et des batailles gagnées". [36]

We should also note here that the non-extant chapters of *Dead Souls*, Volume 2 should have featured an Orthodox priest, who was, however, portrayed *"with Catholic shades"*, according to the evidence of Gogol's confessor, M. Konstantinovsky, who read these chapters (VII, 422; my italics.—*A.Y.*). These "Catholic shades" in the image of the Russian priest indicate that this character, who was to be the mainstay of Gogol's utopia, was an entirely conventional and imaginary creation. They also enable us to surmise the role that had been assigned to this hero: he was probably destined, like Balzac's curé Bonnet, to be an untiring "catcher of souls", and to exercise a covert control over the ideas and actions of his parishioners...

Both Balzac and Gogol depart from realism in the portrayal of the ways and means of realizing their utopian ideals. In itself their dream of the resurrection of man and nature was vital and legitimate, but unrealizable in their time. "Nous sommes les nouveaux pontifs d'un avenir inconnu, dont nous préparons l'oeuvre," [37] exclaims Balzac in his "Lettre aux Écrivains Français du dix-neuvième siècle". The same could have been said by Gogol. Indeed, we may recall his own letter "On the Lyricism of Our Poets", in which he identifies as the distinguishing feature of Russian poetry the "vision of a splendid new edifice, which for the moment is apparently not being seen by all and which can only be perceived by the poet with his allhearing ear or by one who can discern its fruit *in the grain*" (VIII, 250-251).

But Balzac, following the extensive and flexible design of his *Comédie humaine*, was more easily able to give artistic form to the task of testing his utopian dream against the reality of his day than was Gogol in *Dead Souls*. The mercilessly accurate realism of *Les Paysans* left no place for the Romantic illusions of *Le Médecin de campagne* or *Le Curé de village*. At the same time Balzac includes both these novels together with *Les Paysans* in his *Scènes de la vie de campagne*. The reader is left to judge for himself what modern France is like, and what it could become.

The task which Gogol sets himself as an artist was far more arduous. He did not treat his subject matter in a series of isolated and independent works, but chose instead to portray in a single monumental *poema* both the deadly stagnation of pre-reform Russia and the awakening of its hidden forces, which are hinted at by the boundless expanses of the Russian land, by the sense of space in the Russian folk-song and by the mighty and formidable surge of inspiration that carries the author along... So long as

(in *Dead Souls,* Volume 1) these hints of the great rebirth
of his land and his heroes are presented in the guise of
prophetic lyrical digressions, the artistic harmony between
the utopian and realistic elements of his work could be retained. In Volume 2 this harmony is destroyed, seemingly
beyond all hope. This is not only because such figures as
Murazov and the rest seem dead and spurious, but also, and
mainly, because Gogol the satirist was unable to efface
himself here. As we have seen, occasionally by the slightest stroke, the merest hint of ridicule, he destroys the effect of his own rhetoric. Gogol's *poema* retains its satirical
features even in those passages where, it would appear, its
utopian ideals should have been accorded total dominance.

NOTES

[1] G. A. Gukovsky, *Realism Gogolya* (Realism of Gogol).
[2] *Moskva,* 1959, No. 4, p. 204.
[3] E. A. Smirnova-Chikina, "Vtoroi tom 'Mertvykh dush'". *Gogol v shkole* (Second Volume of *Dead Souls.* Gogol in the School. A Collection), Moscow, 1954, p. 430.
[4] Ibid., p. 461.
[5] E. A. Smirnova-Chikina, "Legenda o Gogole" (The Legend about Gogol); In: *Oktyabr,* 1959, No. 4, p. 180. The author argues that the final manuscript version of Vol. 2 was burnt by Gogol by mistake, while the rough versions were hidden and then destroyed by Count A. P. Tolstoy, who disapproved of their content.
[6] P. Antokolsky, "Dead Souls"; In: *N. V. Gogol. "Mertvye Dushi." Poema,* Moscow, 1969, p. 313.
[7] *Taras Bulba,* tr. by Angus Roxburgh. In: Nikolai Gogol, *A Selection,* Moscow, 1981, p. 320.
[8] V. G. Belinsky, *Collected Works,* Vol. 6, Moscow, 1955, p. 427 ("Further Remarks on the Explanation of Gogol's poema *Dead Souls)* (in Russian).
[9] Ibid., p. 418.
[10] Ibid., p. 222 (The Adventures of Chichikov, or *Dead Souls).*
[11] N. G. Chernyshevsky, *Collected Works,* Vol. 3, Moscow, 1947, p. 13 (in Russian).
[12] Victor Erlich, *Gogol,* New Haven and London, 1969, p. 178.
[13] V. G. Belinsky, Op. cit., Vol. 10, p. 217.
[14] Alexander Blok, *Collected Works,* Vol. 5, Moscow-Leningrad, 1962, p. 376 (in Russian).
[15] Ibid., p. 378.
[16] J. W. Goethe, *Wilhelm Meisters Lehrjahre,* Berlin-Weimar, 1970, p. 278.
[17] Ibid., pp. 584-585.
[18] Ibid., p. 108.
[19] N. N. Vilmont, *Goethe. Istoria ego zhizni i tvorchestva* (Goethe. His Life and Work), Moscow, n.d., p. 233.

[20] J. W. Goethe, *Wilhelm Meisters Wanderjahre*, Munich, 1961, p. 297.

[21] V. G. Belinsky, Op. cit., Vol. 6, pp. 430-431.

[22] D. A. Obolensky, "O pervom izdanii posmertnykh sochinenii Gogolya". *Gogol v vospominaniyakh sovremennikov* ("On the First Posthumous Edition of Gogol's Writings". In: *Gogol in the Memoirs of His Contemporaries*), Moscow, 1952. p. 552.

[23] L. I. Arnoldi, "Moyo znakomstvo s Gogolem" ("My Acquaintance with Gogol"), ibid., p. 488.

[24] Ibid.

[25] G. A. Gukovsky, Op. cit., p. 7.

[26] A. I. Herzen, *Collected Works* in 30 vols., Vol. 2, Moscow, 1954, p. 214 (in Russian).

[27] Cf., for example, the monograph: Bernard Guyon, *La création littéraire chez Balzac. La genèse du "Médecin de campagne"*, Paris, 1951.

[28] Honoré de Balzac, *Œuvres complètes*, Paris, 1960, Vol. 16, p. 66.

[29] Ibid., p. 156.

[30] Ibid., p. 96.

[31] Ibid., p. 97.

[32] L. I. Arnoldi, "Moyo znakomstvo s Gogolem" (My Acquaintance with Gogol), *Russki vestnik*, 1862, No. 1, p. 77.

[33] Ibid., p. 79.

[34] Honoré de Balzac, *Œuvres complètes*, Paris, 1960, Vol. 16, pp. 413-414.

[35] Ibid., p. 415.

[36] Bernard Guyon, Op. cit., p. 223.

[37] Honoré de Balzac, *Œuvres complètes*, Paris, 1962, Vol. 27, p. 239.

NAME INDEX

Request to Readers

Raduga Publishers would be glad to have your opinion of this book, its translation and design and any suggestions you may have for future publications.
Please send all your comments to 17, Zubovsky Boulevard, Moscow, USSR.